JEREMY BENTHAM
TEN CRITICAL ESSAYS

Jeremy Bentham
Ten Critical Essays

Edited by Bhikhu Parekh

Department of Political Studies
University of Hull

FRANK CASS : LONDON

First published 1974 in Great Britain by
FRANK CASS AND COMPANY LIMITED
67 Great Russell Street, London WC1B 3BT, England

and in United States of America by
FRANK CASS AND COMPANY LIMITED
c/o International Scholarly Book Services Inc.
P.O. Box 4347, Portland, Oregon 97208

ISBN 0 7146 2959 6

Library of Congress Catalog No. 72–92975

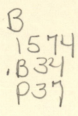

Made and printed in Great Britain by Williams Clowes & Sons, Limited
London, Beccles and Colchester

Contents

Acknowledgments

Thanks are due to the following for granting the permission to reprint the relevant articles: the editor of *Canadian Journal of Political Science* for Thomas Peardon's 'Bentham's Ideal Republic'; the Academy of Political Science, Columbia University, for Wesley Mitchell's 'Bentham's Felicific Calculus'; the editor of *The Irish Jurist* for H. L. A. Hart's 'Bentham on Sovereignty'; the British Academy for H. L. A. Hart's Master-Mind lecture on Bentham; and finally the editor of *Victorian Studies* for David Roberts's 'Jeremy Bentham and the Victorian Administrative State'. I had hoped to include Prof. A. J. Ayer's well-known article on 'The Principle of Utility', but the necessary permission could not be obtained from the publisher. As this appeared to leave a gap in the collection, I had to provide an inadequate substitute myself. I am grateful to Prof. J. H. Burns for kindly agreeing to revise his paper, first presented to the Political Studies Association in 1964, and to Professors Hart, Peardon and Roberts for allowing me to reprint their articles. Thanks are also due to Mr. Frank Cass for inviting me to edit the volume, and to Mrs. Ursula Owen for her editorial help.

Prof. W. H. Greenleaf has generously allowed me to draw on his vast knowledge of the period. He introduced me to the literature dealing with the nature and extent of Bentham's influence on the administrative and political reforms in the nineteenth century, and it is with regret that I had to leave out for reasons of space a number of interesting articles. My debt to him is inestimable. I am also most grateful to Mr. John Rees for commenting both on the entire collection and on my own two essays and saving me from many mistakes.

Introduction

Bentham, like any other political philosopher, can be looked at in a number of different ways. He can be seen with Mill as a one-eyed man who offered philosophy a new method of analysis.[1] Or he can be seen with Marx as an 'insipid, pedantic, leather-tongued oracle of the commonplace bourgeois intelligence of the nineteenth century' who could not 'have been made anywhere else than in England'.[2] He can also be seen, following Halévy, as a 'philosophic radical', 'almost a God with James Mill as his Saint Paul',[3] who married economic liberalism to moral and legal authoritarianism and barely managed to remain a political liberal. One might go even further and follow C. K. Ogden in regarding Bentham 'as one of the greatest figures in European thought, along with Reamur, Leibnitz, Newton, Malthus and Helmholtz'.[4] A sceptic might find that Michael Oakeshott's view of him as a credulous rationalist, as a *philosophe* who 'spent his life talking about first principles but who never once got beyond a consideration of what is secondary and dependent'[5] is perhaps more satisfactory. While the debate between these and other fascinating interpretations of Bentham goes on, I suggest that one other way of looking at him is to see him as articulating, or rather reflecting, some of the important assumptions, values and prejudices that have gone into the composition of the modern Western civilization. What follows is an attempt to explore this line of inquiry.

I

Bentham defines moral life in terms of the principle of utility. A moral action for him is one that realises the greatest amount of happiness of all those affected by it.[6] For reasons that will become clear later, Bentham argued that morally speaking human conduct can therefore fall into one of four categories. First, it may be an action in which an individual pursues the greatest happiness of all those affected even at the expense of his own happiness. Or second, it may be an action in which he pursues others' happiness only when it promotes his own happiness as well. Or third, it may be an action in which an individual pursues his own happiness, taking care not to cause pain to others, but not pursuing their happiness either. Or fourth, it may be an action in which he positively harms others. Clearly, says Bentham, the first type of conduct is morally the best;

the second is a little less so; the third is minimally moral; and the fourth is clearly immoral.

No human action is possible without a motive; and therefore motives too can be classified in their 'order of pre-eminence'[7] in this fourfold manner, with the important qualification that sometimes a good motive may lead to bad conduct, as when a son out of love helps his father escape from a prison, and a bad motive may lead to good conduct, as when a man motivated by hatred exposes the political scandals of a government. A motive that tends to inspire an individual to pursue others' interest even at the cost of his own, for example, the motive of benevolence, is a 'purely social' motive and is morally the best. A motive that tends to lead an individual to pursue others' interest in a way that also promotes his own, for example, the motive of reputation or praise, is a 'semi-social' motive, and is morally second best. It is morally inferior to the purely social motive, because the concern with self-interest is still there, and therefore there is the constant danger that the individual concerned would ignore or injure others' happiness when it is not likely to promote his own. Since, further, the individual acting on a semi-social motive is dependent on others for the way he behaves, he is likely to behave immorally in an unenlightened society where men are praised for doing things harmful to others. If, for example, his society hates Jews, his concern for reputation will lead him to beat them up. Self-interest, which is basically an asocial motive, is third in order of moral eminence. Fourthly and finally, there are 'dissocial' motives that lead an individual to harm society. They are morally the worst.

Since motives can be morally graded, disposition or character can also be morally graded. Thus a man can be said to be of a good or meritorious 'disposition' if he habitually acts on social and semi-social motives; and of a mischievous or bad disposition if he habitually acts on dissocial motives. Bentham's analysis of the concept of disposition contains a tension, largely because of the uneasy and ambiguous way in which he relates motives and consequences. As a utilitarian, he emphasizes consequences alone as important in judging and evaluating a man's character, so that a good man for him is one who habitually produces socially beneficial consequences. But then a man might do so without intending them. Since his action reveals nothing 'permanent' in his 'frame of mind',[8] it would be wrong to say that he has a good character. Or he might have been guided by dissocial motives. He might, for example, have exposed the corrupt practices of a politician because he personally hates him. We would find it odd, to say as does Bentham himself, that he is a man of good character or that his actions reveal a meritorious disposition. Seeing that consequences alone do not provide a sufficient basis for evaluating character, Bentham is inclined to take motives as a basis for evaluating it. But this too creates difficulties. In a tribal society, a man may be praised for collecting the largest number of skulls of people outside his tribe. His motive is semi-social, and therefore good, but the consequences of his action are clearly harmful. Bentham wants to say that the disposition of the person concerned is mischievous and bad. In desperation Bentham suggests that both motive and consequences should be taken into account in judging a man's disposition.[9] But such ecclecticism can hardly provide a way out. Forced to choose between the two Bentham generally inclines[10] to the view that motives alone are important in judging human disposition.

A good man then is one who habitually acts on social or semi-social motives, and a bad man is one who habitually acts on dissocial motives. The higher the motives on which a man acts, the nobler his disposition.[11] Or, since human actions are rarely guided by the purest of motives, the greater the proportion and force of social and semi-social motives to dissocial motives in a man, and the greater the ease with which he promotes social happiness, the better he is morally. And conversely, the greater the ease with which he succumbs to dissocial motives, the worse he is morally. If acting on commendable motives, a person nevertheless produces harmful consequences, as in the previous example of a tribal society, the fault is not his but his society's; and this only proves that no man can be completely good in a bad society.

Corresponding to this four-fold gradation of motives and of moral character, Bentham suggests, there is a four-fold gradation of forms of life. A life dedicated to the pursuit of the greatest happiness, a life that incarnates the principle of utility, is clearly the best and the highest form of life. A life in which self-interest and social interest are thoroughly and completely integrated, a life that incarnates the principle of reputation, is the second best. A life in which an individual pursues his interest and generally minds his own business is third best. And a form of life that thrives on harming others is the worst.

II

Before discussing in detail Bentham's views on how higher forms of life can be encouraged and who is capable of living them, there is an important question that needs to be answered first. It has often been suggested by commentators on Bentham that he takes man to be an essentially selfish being who has no interest in others' well-being and who cannot therefore be expected to want to pursue it.

Now if this is a true account of Bentham's psychology, it clearly undermines the very basis of our earlier discussion of forms of life, in that it would be psychologically impossible for man to live any but the third, self-interested, form of life. I propose to argue that this is not an accurate account of Bentham's theory of man.

Bentham takes the view that every human action must have a cause, a motive. Since man is a creature who pursues pleasure by the very necessity of his nature, every human action is motivated by a desire for pleasure. As pleasure is a uniquely subjective feeling, as a man can feel only his own feelings, he is ultimately motivated by considerations of *his own* pleasure. In other words, in whatever a man does, he seeks his own pleasure. Since what promotes pleasure, Bentham calls interest, every action, he argues, is an interested action; or to put it negatively, no human action 'ever has been or ever can be disinterested'.[12] A disinterested action, Bentham argues, is an action without a motive, an effect without a cause, and that is impossible. When I act benevolently towards another, I do so only because I am interested in him, only because I find pleasure in helping him. As Bentham remarks, 'the pleasure I feel in bestowing pleasure on my friend, whose pleasure is it but mine? The pain I feel at seeing my friend oppressed by pain, whose pain is it but mine? And if I feel no pleasure or felt no pain, where . . . would be my sympathy?'[13] As no man can ever 'cast off his own skin, or jump out of it', he goes on, 'the most disinterested of men is not less under the dominion of interest than the most interested'. Both Christ and Hitler did the things they did because they found their pleasure in them, and therefore are not fundamentally different.

This formal metaphysical fact of the egocentricity of human predicament does not, however, entail any specific substantive theory of human nature. To say that man acts in the way he does because he finds pleasure in it says nothing about what it is that he finds his pleasure in. He may be a person who finds pleasure in promoting the pleasure of others; on the other hand, he may be a person who finds pleasure only in minding his own business or even in causing harm to others. In other words, the metaphysical theory that no human being can ever escape himself, or that the source of man's action must be located in himself, is congruous both with the view that man is essentially a selfish creature who can pursue his own interest, as well as with the view that he is an altruistic being who consistently subordinates his interest to those of others.

When it comes to working out a substantive theory of human nature, Bentham is ambiguous and presents two different images of man. There are times when he maintains the crude view that man is essentially a selfish creature who pursues his own interest. 'Man from the very constitution of his nature prefers his own happiness to that of all other sentiment beings put together.'[14] Indeed 'the entire misery of mankind is nothing to a man, compared to the pain of his toothache', Bentham remarks. Except in rare moments when men act heroically, 'self is everything to which all other persons . . . are as nothing'.[15] 'Dream not,' he goes on, 'that men will move their little finger to serve you, unless their advantage in so doing be obvious to them. Men never did so, and never will, while human nature is made of its present materials.'[16] Somewhat inconsistently, Bentham argues that not only is man selfish by nature but also that it is *desirable* that he should be selfish, and offers a 'conclusive proof' of it.[17] If men were not selfish, everyone would be pursuing everybody else's happiness. Since no-one would suffer the consequences of his actions, he would have no means of checking if his actions were really giving happiness to his intended beneficiaries. The inevitable result would be that with all the good intentions in the world, human misery will increase and the species will become extinct 'in a few months, not to say a few weeks or days'. The fact that the species is not yet extinct demonstrates that selfishness has stood it in good stead.

But Bentham also has another, far more dominant, view of man. In his Letter to Fellow-Citizens of France, he remarks, 'yes, I admit the existence of disinterestedness in the sense in which you mean it. I admit philanthropy—of philanthropy even to an all-comprehensive extent. How could I do otherwise than admit it? . . . Without it how could so many papers that have preceded this letter have come into existence? I admit the existence of a disposition to self-sacrifice: How could I do otherwise?'[18] Rejecting the charge that he takes a very gloomy view of human nature and denies human capacity for self-sacrifice and disinterestedness, Bentham pleads, 'I admit all this. I do not deny it: I cannot deny it: I wish not to deny it: Sorry should I be if it were in my power to deny it.'[19] Indeed, he even admits that rulers, the worst species of men in his opinion, too are capable of benevolence and self-sacrifice. 'I admit the actual existence of a king who takes a pleasure in doing his duty—of a king who, on all occasions, does his utmost to promote the happiness and interests of his people.'[20] He once confided in his editor that he knew many men 'who held honours and riches cheap in comparison with the delight of doing useful service to their race';[21] and said that he would have his dearest friend know that if his interests came into conflict with those of the public, they 'are as nothing to me'.[22] Were it not for the human capacity for benevolence, he once remarked, 'no small portion of the good . . . which has place in human affairs would be an effect without a cause'.[23]

Not only does Bentham think man capable of social motives like benevolence and sympathy; he even believes that they are, generally more powerful than anti-social motives. As this point is of some importance Bentham deserves to be quoted at length. 'For in every-man, be his disposition ever so depraved, the social motives are those which, wherever the self-regarding ones stand neuter, regulate and determine the general tenor of his life. If the dissocial motives are put in action, it is only in particular circumstances and on particular occasions, the gentle but constant force of the social motives being for a while subdued. The general and standing bias of every man's nature is, therefore, towards that side to which the force of the social motives would determine him to adhere. This being the case, the force of the social motives tends continually to put an end to that of the dissocial ones; as, in natural bodies, the force of friction tends to put an end to that which is generated by impulse.'[24] In other words, Bentham thinks benevolence is natural to man in a way that malevolence is not, that the latter is a product of external factors that could be eliminated, and that benevolence is generally a much more powerful motive than malevolence.

As man is capable of acting on social motives, so is he capable of acting on semi-social motives. Unlike social motives, they promote an individual's interest as well, and therefore are more common. Indeed, if a man calculated his interest rationally he would see that he depends so much on the good will and services of other men that it is in his own interest that he should promote their interest. By promoting others' interest, he builds up a fund of good-will on which he can draw later. Semi-social motives ultimately are only enlightened self-interest.

For Bentham, then, man is capable of all the four types of motives discussed earlier. Of these self-interest is generally, but not necessarily, most uniform, common and powerful. Semi-social motives come next in strength and influence. Purely social motives come third, and anti-social motives are the least powerful. A Benthamite man, therefore, is not entirely selfish but has other—regarding motives as well; and when he does pursue his own interest, he takes a wider view of it, and defines it to include not only material interests but also 'moral' interests like prestige and reputation. To put it differently, his is not the selfishness of a barbarian but of a civilized man, not of a man in a Hobbesian state of nature but of a socialized man living in a settled society. It is, in other words, the selfishness of an Englishman as Bentham imagines him to be. The pursuit of self-interest in a Benthamite society therefore is not a ruthless war of one man against all. It is a civilized and urbane struggle that is moderated by sympathy and benevolence, restrained by the aware-

ness that one needs others, and generally untainted by any desire to
cause unnecessary pain to others.

III

As we saw in the first section the ideal man for Bentham is one
who incarnates in himself the principle of utility—who not only
always pursues the happiness of all sentiment beings intelligently but
does so out of love and concern for them. In Bentham's words, he is
a man to whom the spectacle of another's happiness is 'delightful'.[25]
His acts are not motivated by a desire for reputation and praise; nor
by a desire to please the Deity, since that in Bentham's view is
ultimately a desire to feather one's own otherworldly nest by in-
gratiating oneself with the Almighty. Bentham approvingly quotes
Addison's famous remark that religion is 'the highest species of
self-love'; and it is worth noting that he generally classifies religious
motives as semi-social. The ideal man is not motivated by any
coercive sense of moral duty either. Virtue and goodness have
become natural to him, his 'habit and disposition' of mind are well-
trained, and his appetites and desires are in 'complete subjection'.
As the pursuit of general happiness has become second nature to
him, as it is his supreme source of pleasure, his acts are spontaneous,[26]
natural and do not require a long, agonizing battle between spirit
and nature, that 'game of leapfrog between flesh and spirit' that
Swift had earlier ridiculed.[27]

It is because he loves his fellow-men, feels good-will towards them
and finds pleasure in pursuing their happiness that Bentham's ideal
man seeks ways and means of helping and benefiting them. As he
loves his fellow-men he is indignant that 'sinister' rulers should ignore
and harm their interests and, therefore, wages war on them. He
exposes their devious devices, ridicules their pretensions, and edu-
cates the masses to fight for a better society. His benevolence thus
is not passive but active, and extends beyond the personal moral level
to the political. He is a man dedicated to a cause, a man with 'a real
zeal for the service ... of mankind', a utilitarian in the sense not
merely of a person who theoretically subscribes to the principle of
utility, but, more significantly, as someone whose life is completely
dedicated to the realization of the principle of utility on earth, a
person who thinks and dreams of nothing but general happiness.

While it is not easy to live the life of a dedicated utilitarian, it is
not impossible. Christ, 'the first of utilitarians' as Perronet Thompson
called him, had attained it, and Bentham liked to believe that he, 'the
second utilitarian', had approximated it fairly closely. His own long
life, he later recalled, was rigorously dedicated to the fulfilment of a

vow he took at the age of eleven to cleanse the English law of all its
'abominations'. He thought of himself as a universal man, a man
who toiled all his waking hours for the happiness of his 'fellow-
citizens of the civilized world', and indeed for his 'fellow-citizens
of future ages'.[28] As he said, referring to himself and his friends,
'scarcely in my little circle will they hear any conversation which has
not the goal of mankind in some shape or other for its object'. He
even remarked, 'Is there any one of these my pages in which the
love of mankind has for a moment been forgotten? Show it me, and
this hand shall be the first to tear it out.'[29] As befits a man single-
mindedly devoted to the realization of a principle, Bentham avowed,
'I have taken the principle of utility for my guide. I will follow
wheresoever it leads me. No prejudices shall force me to quit the
road. No interest shall seduce me. No superstitions shall appal
me.'[30]

Universal benevolence, Bentham believes, can be acquired in one
of three ways. There are men to whom it comes naturally, in whom
it is 'a feeling of instinct, a gift of nature'. Why some should have
this instinct and not others Bentham does not explain. There are
others who acquire it from their religion that enjoins on them the
duty to imitate the Deity or the example of a prophet like Jesus. And
finally, universal benevolence can be acquired through education and
enlightenment, from the rational realization that since happiness
alone is good, one should aim at producing the greatest quantity of
it irrespective of who its recipients are. Of the three, the last is the
most effective and reliable. Nature is erratic and cannot always be
trusted. While encouraging benevolence, religion also encourages
hatred of those belonging to other religions. And in any case since a
religious man is motivated by the desire to please the Deity, his
benevolence is not 'pure' but tainted by self-interest. Ideally, therefore an enlightened man, a man who is fully rational, a philosopher
as Bentham calls him, is the only person capable of a life of universal
benevolence.[31]

While 'very few' men,[32] 'one in a thousand' as Mill put it later,
are capable of living a life of universal benevolence, ordinary men in
Bentham's view can be helped to acquire at least *some* degree of
benevolence. One of the most important factors responsible for
developing it, he believes, is industrialization. In an undeveloped
society where human wants are few and men can satisfy them by
their own efforts, they generally live a solitary life and have very few
interests in common. As their wants increase, they become increasingly interdependent; and as their interests become closely inter-
woven, each acquires an interest in the well-being of others. He
would not want to hurt them because that would only hurt him. In

other words, he develops sympathy for them. With the increase in international trade, different parts of the world are drawn together into a single system of interests, and human sympathy even extends to the entire species. Sympathy, which is initially generated by consideration of self-interest, gradually acquires an autonomy and independence and becomes a new principle of human nature.

Industrialization in Bentham's view develops sympathy in another way as well. In a savage, 'scarce a trace of sympathetic affection is visible.... His time is divided between pursuit of food, enjoyment of means, and reckless apathy. At which of these three times should sympathetic affection find place in his breast?... While he is tortured by hunger, while he is ... gorging himself, or while he is buried in sleep or in indolence?' Men can afford to think of their social and moral relations with their fellow-men, Bentham remarks, only when they have leisure and the tempo of their life is relatively relaxed. As industrialization creates economic security and leisure, it creates conditions in which pleasures of social life can increase in importance, giving rise eventually to sympathy and benevolence.

Sympathy and benevolence, Bentham believes, grow best in small groups bound together by ties of common interest and friendship. Gradually as such small groups multiply and expand, new ties are acquired or old ones are extended to new men, and the range of sympathy begins to widen until it extends to the entire community and even to mankind as a whole. As such social, civic, professional and other groups are best developed in a functionally differentiated industrialized society, this is another way in which industrialization leads to the growth of sympathy. Bentham believes that it is the pluralistic and club-orientated structure of British society that is largely responsible for making it the most benevolent society in the world.[33] Waxing eloquent over the benefits of industrialization, he remarks that as it advances men become 'everyday more virtuous than on the former day' and 'will continue to do so till, if ever, they naturally shall have arrived at its perfection. Shall they stop? Shall they turn back? The rivers shall as soon make a wall, and roll up the mountains to their source.'

The plant of benevolence, Bentham goes on, grows best in a social climate where the greatest possible respect is shown for life. The government should therefore abolish practices that involve cruelty to men and animals and abolish or regulate institutions that advocate violence and hatred. Religion, since it encourages antipathy to the adherents of other religions and an attitude of indifference to man's worldly well-being, is the worst culprit in this matter. If 'Louis XIV had had no religion, France would not have lost 800,000 of its most valuable subjects', Bentham remarks. While his attitude to religion is ambivalent,[34] Bentham generally takes the view that the government should educate people out of religious prejudices and, whenever possible, reinterpret religion along Benthamite utilitarian lines. As artists often plant prejudices and create hatred among different sections of the community, Bentham suggests that their activities should in some sense be regulated. How can one like the Jews after reading Voltaire? he asks.[35] Instead of ridiculing Jews, Voltaire, a man of universal benevolence, should have drawn public attention to their degraded condition and persuaded his society to take a charitable view of their less agreeable features. Bentham, however, is opposed to the censorship of 'anti-social' works of art and literature and urges no more than that artists and writers should subordinate their craft to the realization of worthwhile moral objectives. The government, he believes, can also create a climate of gentleness and universal good-will by abolishing cruel punishment and cruel sports like cock-fights, bull-baiting, hunting hares and foxes, and fishing. Bentham greatly admires 'the great people of China' for their remarkable spirit of gentleness; and while he is critical of the way they have turned politeness into 'a sort of worship', he is convinced that England has a lot to learn from them. He also holds up as exemplary the great 'simplicity' and 'innocent manners' of Africans for accounts of whose life he relies on the travels of Mungo Park.

Bentham believes that the development of benevolence is an art that should be carefully developed and ingeniously applied. Different individuals are touched by different kinds of misery: some are affected by deafness, others by blindness, and yet others by the misery of orphans, widows, the dumb, or the lame. If therefore the government could encourage the foundation of different types of charity like the French Daughters of Charity and the Maternal Society such that 'every kind of sensibility' is appealed to, the spirit of benevolence would find a constant nourishment. An attempt should especially be made to appeal to women 'among whom the sentiment of pity is stronger than among men'.

It would also help if the government were to compose 'a code of political morality' discussing in detail moral and political questions with the help of amusing examples, illustrations and historical anecdotes.[36] The code would be composed by philosophers like Bentham who would also draw on the teachings of other 'masters of truth and virtue'. Bentham used to say that it was possible to 'condense the marrow of morality into a few simple rules' that could be 'pasted on the back of an almanac'.[37] The code would mention popular prejudices on every important moral and political question and show how and why they are mistaken. It would be

compulsory reading for every citizen, and it would be the responsibility of parents and teachers to instruct their children in its basic
principles. When wisdom is 'sanctified by the touch of the sceptre'
Bentham believes, no human mind has the power to resist its
influence.

While nearly all men can be helped by these and other means to
develop some degree of benevolence, it is not likely to be very great.
We should therefore aim to cultivate the second-best semi-social
motives, of which the love of reputation is the most important.
Unlike certain other eighteenth century moralists, Bentham does
not believe that the love of reputation is natural to man. In his
view it grows out of man's desire to pursue his own interest, and is
socially acquired. When an individual realizes that his happiness
depends on others' cooperation, that he needs their services, he comes
to pursue activities that will please them and earn him moral capital
that he can later use to promote his interest. The realization that the
criticism and indifference of others is 'a burden too heavy for human
sufferance',[38] as Locke had put it, is in Bentham's view the beginning
of the love of reputation.

Bentham believes that the love of reputation, the paradigmatic
semi-social motive, can develop only under certain conditions,
mainly four.[39] First the more a man depends on others, the more
others' actions affect his happiness; and as the greater the sanctions
they have on him, the greater is bound to be his desire for their good-
will. Conversely, the less a man depends on others, the less he cares
for their opinion. A Turk whose life centres around his slaves and
women has no regard for what others think of him, since even if
they were to condemn and ostracize him, 'his women will not be
less beautiful, nor his slaves less obedient to his will'. Second, it is
not enough that a man should need the services of others; he should
be able to obtain them only by showing concern for their interest.
A despot, for example, needs the services of his subjects, but as he
can command them, he does not feel the need to promote his subjects' interest. Third, even when a man needs to earn others' services,
he might ignore their interest if they are not sufficiently intelligent
and are in the habit of praising people on wrong and irrational
grounds. Thus if a ruler in an ignorant society is admired for waging
and winning wars, his love of reputation clearly cannot lead him to
pursue the greatest happiness of his community. Fourthly, and
finally, says Bentham, even if a community was generally enlightened
and intelligent, it would have no check on its members if it did not
have an intimate knowledge of their conduct and pattern of life. As
the effectiveness of social sanction depends on the degree of its
members' visibility, publicity is 'the best guardian of virtue'. He even

wishes 'that no such thing as secrecy ever existed—that every man's house were made of glass'.[40]

Bentham believes that since semi-social motives can be best cultivated only under these conditions, they can be developed fully only in the middle classes. As the lives of their members are not totally occupied with making ends meet, they have both the time and the desire to cultivate each others' good-will. Being relatively equal in wealth and status they cannot command each others' services and have to earn them. They are educated and enlightened and are careful in how they praise and blame others. And since they are in constant contact with each other, their social visibility is much greater than that of any other class. As a fairly cohesive social body the middle class is in effect a supreme moral tribunal, a grand 'administrator of the moral sanction',[41] a 'depository of the laws and archives of honour'. Since the love of reputation and its counterpart, the love of shame, are most strongly developed in the middle classes, naturally they are the 'most virtuous classes'[42] in society.

For reasons already discussed Bentham believes that the 'lower classes' whose life is absorbed in earning their livelihood can hardly be expected to have the time, energy, desire or the need to develop social and semi-social motives. By the comparative and spatial term 'lower' classes, Bentham means all those classes that are socially and economically 'below' the middle classes who, for him as for many others, constitute a kind of social waistline of the 'body' politic. Bentham believes, apparently without any reason, that no matter how much industrial civilization advances, the working classes are unlikely to change very much. Some of their members may, of course, rise above their class, but workers as a class, Bentham believes, will always remain with us, and their condition of life will remain more or less as it is. As some men have fewer abilities and less drive than others, society, he thinks, will 'always' be divided into higher and lower classes, and 'painful labour, daily subjection, a condition nearly allied to indigence will always be the lot of numbers'.[43] This being the case, it would be 'utopian' to expect them to be guided by other motives than those of narrow self-interest.

Unlike the philosopher who can be left to be guided by his own enlightened reason, and unlike the middle classes who can be similarly left to be guided by the censorious and vigilant eye of their peers, the working classes need to be regulated by the government. The government must ensure that they pursue their interests intelligently and without causing mischief. It should devise a system of law that, by a complicated and ingenious pattern of regulations, will ensure that no member of society, but particularly no member of the working class, will ever find it in his interest to harm others. Such a system is elaborated by Bentham in many of his writings, particularly the *Constitutional Code*, and is too well-known to need repetition. As such a legal and political system presupposes that ordinary citizens, especially the lower classes, are capable of calculating the detailed consequences of their actions, it requires, Bentham maintains, a system of education along the lines he has developed in his *Chrestomathia*. It is basically a vocationally orientated system that gives its recipients essential information about life and society and aims to instil in them a spirit of frugality and self-help. Bentham also proposes a number of institutions and practices that in his view would encourage and enable the lower classes to stand on their own feet, to save, to plan their marriages and families according to their means, etc. The discussion of these proposals is not relevant to our main theme, and will not therefore be pursued further here.

On the last question, that of dealing with anti-social passions—for Bentham one of the most important questions of political theory—he has some curious and interesting things to say. The question dominated a great deal of his time and energy, and therefore his treatment of it deserves to be considered in some detail.

Man, he believes, engages in anti-social behaviour for a number of reasons, of which three are most important. They are desire for revenge, poverty and sex.[44] If a man was left free to avenge himself, his vengeance would know no limits. If therefore the law stepped in and granted him sufficient satisfaction, he would not wish to seek more; he would know that any attempt to do so would bring him into conflict with authority. When the individual offended is not content with the satisfaction offered by the law, the government might show indulgence to practices like duelling. It is worth noting, says Bentham, that the practice of poisoning and assassinating opponents was hardly heard of in societies where duelling was an established practice. Duels were less common in Italy than in France and England, but then clandestine poisoning and assassination were more common as well. Conversely, where duelling was forbidden as in Malta, assassination became common and duelling had to be permitted at specified hours and places. Duelling also preserves peace and politeness, since no one would want to quarrel if he knew he would be obliged to challenge his enemy to a duel. No doubt duelling is an evil, but the evil is comparatively light and is like 'a premium of assurance whereby a nation guarantees itself against the greater evil of other offences'.[45]

As for poverty the best way to deal with it is to prevent it by creating general economic prosperity, a task in which the government has a limited role. If poverty still exists, it could be best dealt with by private charities. In a society in which the spirit of benevolence is absent, the government must intervene and provide poor relief. To

avoid female poverty and prostitution Bentham suggests the government should reserve for women certain occupations like selling
children's toys, keeping fashion shops, making women's shoes, stays
and dresses, and midwifery.[46]

As for sex which, Bentham thinks, should be discussed 'honestly'
and without 'hypocritical reserve',[47] it is such a powerful passion
that only angels can do without it. 'What the force of steam is in the
physical world, the force of love is in the psychological—capable,
when under pressure, of opposing the strongest force' and of 'rising
beyond any height to which pecuniary interest has ever been known
to rise'.[48] Ideally sexual urge should be gratified within the matri-
monial framework, and therefore the legislator should encourage
and facilitate marriages. He should also make divorce relatively easy
both because broken marriages cause unhappiness and lead to
adultery, and because divorce would eventually lead to remarriage.
Judicial separations are undesirable, as they lead either to the
'privation of celibacy' or to 'illicit connexions'.[49] Although marriage
is generally desirable it presupposes a settled residence and a capacity
to earn and plan for the future. And this creates problems for those
like domestic servants who live in a state of dependence and for
others like soldiers and sailors who have no fixed residence. These
men are unable or unfit to marry and are 'reduced to a forced
celibacy'. Although the problem is not very acute, since in men who
are engaged in hard manual work and are forced to live a simple life
on a frugal diet, sexual passion is not likely to be very strong,[50] it is
still there and needs to be solved.

Bentham thinks one way of dealing with this problem is to legiti-
matize short-term marriages. A sailor or a soldier stationed abroad,
for example, should be able to contract a two or three year marriage
agreement. The advantage of short term marriages, in Bentham's
view, is that it would protect the woman involved, legitimize her
children, secure them parental care, and save her from humiliation
and debauchery. This is what the so-called 'left-handed marriages'
achieved in Germany, he believes. Bentham knows that such marriages have been generally disapproved of, but thinks the disapproval
mistaken. We consider marriage contracts sacred when their duration
is indefinite, but not when they are for a year or two. Bentham cannot
see how the simple fact of duration can 'change black into white'.[51]
A marriage contracted for a limited time is as 'innocent' as that
contracted for life, and the woman contracting it is entitled to as
much respect as the one married for life. Bentham is concerned to
reassure his critics that he is not proposing the new institution as
something intrinsically good but only 'as an amelioration of an evil
which exists'.[52] 'It is not proposed as a rule, but as a remedy.'[53]

Another way of resolving the problems created by sexual passion, Bentham thinks, is to legitimize prostitution.[54] Prostitution is an evil, no doubt, but prohibiting it leads to greater evil still. And even when forbidden, it generally continues to be carried on privately, and the government dare not punish it for fear of strong public reaction. Bentham realizes that prostitution does raise highly controversial moral issues; but believes that precisely for that reason it should be discussed calmly and carefully on the basis of its known advantages and disadvantages. He points to a number of examples to show the beneficial consequences of legalized prostitution. When the Empress of Hungary banned prostitution, he remarks, the result was that it corrupted conjugal life; adultery gained in respectability; and prostitution, being concealed, only became more dangerous. Ancient Greeks, on the other hand, tolerated and even encouraged prostitution, and Romans too acquiesced in it, and their public and private life was none the worse for it. Holland licensed brothels and so did the republic of Venice; and no disaster came to them. In great European towns prostitution, Bentham believes, has proved particularly useful, and its abolition extremely harmful. In England where it is prohibited, London hospitals for repentant girls in Chelsea and Greenwich have become hunting grounds for soldiers and sailors respectively. Having made out a case for prostitution to his satisfaction, Bentham suggests that as prostitution is a condition 'in which the period of harvest is necessarily short, but in which there are sometimes considerable profits', it would be desirable to institute a savings scheme so that the capital built up by prostitutes during their working life could yield annuity later when they retire.

In addition to these and other specific measures necessary to deal with the three major causes of anti-social behaviour, a more general way to deal with it, Bentham suggests, is to re-channel anti-social passions into 'innocent amusements'.[55] When a man has nothing to do and is bored, his mind turns to anti-social activities. This is why there were so many wars and so much drunkenness in feudal and other 'rude ages'. With infinite leisure at their disposal and having few 'objects of amusement', men in those days looked for action. As they lacked civilization, their sexual life lacked sentimental refinement and romantic embellishment, and soon became boring. Having nothing else to do they tended to think of avenging imaginary grievances, or simply drank themselves to sleep. Something similar happens today to the illiterate masses, Bentham remarks.

It is imperative therefore that the government, whose job it is to keep people's minds off socially harmful activities, should follow a systematic policy of developing and encouraging new sources of amusement. It should introduce or encourage the introduction of different types of culinary dishes and nutritive vegetables. It should introduce tea and coffee which, being morally more desirable than intoxicating liquors, occupy an important place 'in a catalogue of moral objects'. This is also true of the arts which 'in as much as they constitute innocent employments ... possess a species of moral utility. ... They are excellent substitutes for drunkenness, slander and the love of gaming'.[56] Bentham takes the view that no artistic taste is bad unless it leads to mischief. Indeed the whole idea of bad taste strikes him as 'fantastic', and he criticizes Addison and Hume for attacking perfectly harmless, though vulgar, amusements. These self-styled benefactors of the human race 'are really only the interrupters of their pleasure'.[57] Bentham's remark that push-pin is as good as poetry thus does not appear as bizarre or foolish as is often made out. Seen as a method of preventing people from causing mischief, both are equally valuable and effective; and therefore from the moral point of view, which is Bentham's only interest in the matter, they are equally good. Bentham thinks the government should also encourage elegance of dress and furniture, gardens, and the invention of new athletic or sedentary games 'for passing the time'. In particular it should popularize the game of chess. 'These tranquil games have brought the sexes more nearly upon an equality, and have diminished ennui, the peculiar malady of the human race, and especially of the opulent and the aged.'[58] The government should also encourage music, theatre, clubs, public amusements, arts, sciences and literature as means of diverting anti-social desires into innocent pursuits.

Bentham gives a number of examples to show that luxury is a moralizing force, a 'source of virtue'.[59] He quotes a remark of a Paris policeman that more irregularities and debaucheries were committed in Paris during the Easter fortnight when theatres were shut than during the four months of the season when they were open. He finds a further confirmation of his theory in what he takes to be the beneficial consequences of Roman dictators encouraging their subjects to go to the circus, and the indulgence the dictatorial governments of Venice showed to all kinds of innocent amusements. Bentham is convinced that if Cromwell had not been an ascetic, and had seen the moral importance of luxury, he would not have engaged England in unnecessary foreign wars. In his view those religions and governments that condemn luxury and 'inspire sadness' contain 'the germs of the greatest vices and of the most hurtful passions'. He is worried about the strong prejudice people have against luxury, and suggests this prejudice might be removed by calling it 'prosperity' instead of luxury, since sometimes 'a simple change in the name of the object suffices to change the sentiments of men'.[60] Bentham feels certain that if these and other suggestions made by 'the noble and generous political science'[61] were adopted, crimes would cease 'almost entirely', and those still occurring would be petty and inconsequential, capable of being 'repaired by a simple pecuniary compensation'.[62]

Until society becomes a vast centre of fun and amusement, however, people will continue to commit crimes, and the law has to be prepared to deal with them. Bentham's highly complex and elaborate penal theory contains a mass of proposals, some interesting and many characteristically naïve and absurd. As it is not relevant to our purpose to discuss them in detail, I shall mention only one general principle that inspires many of them.

Pain in Bentham's view is evil; and so therefore is punishment.[63] Although a necessary evil, punishment is still an evil, and ought to be used as economically as possible. In Bentham's picturesque language, it is 'a capital hazarded in expectation of profit', profit being the prevention of crime. Punishment is 'expensive' when it produces more evil than good, or when the same amount of good can be obtained by lesser punishment. Now it is the real pain inflicted on the criminal that constitutes the punishment, and therefore the expense, while it is the actual deterrent effect produced on the masses that constitutes the profit.[64] What is necessary therefore is not so much that the criminal should be punished as that he should *appear* to be punished. Ideally 'the real punishment ought to be as small and the apparent punishment as great as possible'. Bentham believes that real punishment at best helps only the criminal by reforming him, while the apparent punishment produces the much greater good of deterring thousands of potential criminals. He is convinced that 'the uninformed and unthinking part of mankind', the main breeding ground of criminals, is guided by illusions and appearances, and is incapable of detecting the difference between real and apparent punishment.

Thus if hanging a man in effigy would produce the same degree of terror as actually hanging him, it would be 'folly or cruelty' to hang him. Similarly a small quantity of real punishment can be made to appear very frightening by getting prisoners to wear masks 'more or less tragical in proportion to the enormity of the crimes', and by such other 'strong and masterly touches which strike the imagination and fill the mind with the idea of the sublime'. Or, again,[65] if the scaffold is painted black, the officers are dressed in crepe, the executioner is in a mask, and the emblems of the crime are placed above the head of the criminal who, unbeknown to the spectators, would be a dummy, and if the whole procession is to move solemnly through the city, a far greater effect can be produced far more cheaply on a far greater number of people than the actual and expensive execution of the criminal in question. Similarly a man who has poisoned another does not need to be killed. He could be administered a dose of the poison he had himself used, but keeping at hand proper remedies for 'producing an evacuation . . . after a certain interval'. In short, Bentham's penal theory is guided by crude utilitarian criteria, and relies on fraud and terror to deal with those residual anti-social passions that fun and amusement have not been able to deflect.

IV

Bentham's political strategy for creating a good society, then, is this. Every member of society is to be helped to develop benevolence and love of praise; he is to be educated to pursue his interests intelligently; and he is to be amused and terrorized out of his anti-social passions. As we have seen, these objectives are realized differently in different classes of men. Philosophers and enlightened men in general are most capable of living a life of benevolence. Middle classes are most capable of developing love of reputation. After philosophers they live the most moral life and constitute the moral and political backbone of society. The working classes are capable of living the third best kind of life, and nothing more can be expected of them than a quiet and intelligent perseverance in the pursuit of their narrow self-interest. As for the unemployed, the poor, the vagrants, the lazy lay-abouts, they are the greatest danger to society, and can only be deterred by appearances of terrifying punishment and turned into honest men by prisons modelled after the ingenious Panopticon. While it is true that Bentham does not exclude the last two classes of men from the benefits of organized life and grants them economic and political security, his basic concern is largely to prevent them from causing any mischief by a cunning combination of force, fraud and fun. As they are largely outside the mainstream of society, and are neither to be seen nor heard, they constitute a kind of inorganic background against which the middle classes play out their social game.

It is thus the middle classes on whom Bentham pins his hope. They are not only the lynch-pin of his society, but are also the only vehicle of progress and civilization. Given Bentham's philosophy of history, they are the only classes with a future, and they have a historic mission to rule and civilize the barbarians both inside and outside their community. As they regulate their members' behaviour by a delicate distribution of praise and blame, prestige and ignominy, left to themselves they would not really need the machinery of

government. Where social conventions are riveted tightly, laws are
not necessary; and when society can literally destroy a man by
denying him its cooperation, prison and punishment are superfluous.
It is only the poor, the labourers, the criminals, who make the state
necessary. But for them it could easily wither away.

The organizing principle of Bentham's society is fear, fear of law
in the case of the 'lower' classes and fear of society or, rather, of
the other person in the case of the middle classes. What the state is
to the 'lower' classes, society is to the middle classes. Bentham
attributes to society, which is largely a middle class affair, nearly all
the properties religions have traditionally ascribed to God. It is
omniscient, omnipotent, just, exacting, stern. The middle classes are
the most fearful classes in Bentham's society: fearful of not being
noticed and respected, fearful of forfeiting society's grace. They are
also the most socialized classes—socialized in their behaviour, in their
opinions, in their beliefs. They may be the most virtuous, but they
are also the least free. It is only to be expected that in such a society
the Lockean problem of law versus liberty should be replaced by the
new problem of society versus liberty and, since society for Bentham
is the main source and sanction of morality, of morality versus
liberty. This was Bentham's legacy to J. S. Mill. And as the problem
is still with us, the study of Bentham is of great value, even if
in parts negative value, for the understanding of our historical
predicament.

BHIKHU PAREKH, 1974

NOTES

1. Bentham, *Dissertations & Discussions*, vol. I.
2. *Capital*, Everyman ed., Vol. II, 671. For Marx's views on Bentham, see also
   Appendix III in Sidney Hook's *From Hegel to Marx*.
3. *The Growth of Philosophic Radicalism*, Tr. Mary Morris (London, 1927),
   XIX, and 506ff. For an interesting critique of Halévy, see Charles C.
   Gillispie's Review Article in *Journal of Modern History*, 1950.
4. *Bentham's Theory of Legislation*, ed. C. K. Ogden (Kegan Paul, 1931).
5. The New Bentham, *Scrutiny*, 1933. Mrs. Shirley Letwin in her *The Pursuit of
   Certainty* has offered an ingenious interpretation of Bentham along Oake-
   shottian lines.
6. For a detailed discussion of Bentham's principle of utility, see below, 96–119.
7. *Principles of Morals and Legislation*, ed., Wilfrid Harrison (Basil Blackwell,
   Oxford, 1960), 236 (ch. X, para. 36). This work is hereafter referred to as
   Principles. Bentham also suggests an interesting scale of duties, see, for
   example, ibid., 171.
8. *Principles*, 246.
9. Ibid., 250ff.
10. Ibid., 256.
11. Ibid., 262f.
12. Vol. I, 212.

13. *Deontology*, vol. I, 83f.
14. X, 80 and IX, 5.
15. IX, 61.
16. *Deontology*, vol. II, 133.
17. IX, 5/6. Also X, 80.
18. IV, 431.
19. IV, 430/1.
20. IV, 431.
21. XI, 77.
22. X, 73.
23. III, 292 and VII, 399.
24. *Principles*, 263–4. See also *Deontology*, vol. I, 169f. But see *Economic Writings*, ed. Stark, vol. III, 430, where Bentham refers to dissocial motives as 'under all circumstances most unhappily copious and active', and explains them in terms of natural scarcity and desire for power.
25. *Deontology*, vol. I, 193 and Box 14, pp. 16 and 88.
26. Ibid., 190.
27. MSS., UCL, Box 14, pp. 378ff.
28. IV, 449.
29. X, 142.
30. *Deontology*, vol. II, VIII. Bentham wrote in his Commonplace Book: 'Oh, Britain, Oh, my country! the object of my waking and sleeping thoughts! whose love is my first labour and greatest joy', X, 72.
31. I, 537.
32. X, 511.
33. I, 562.
34. I, 566.
35. I, 562.
36. I, 568.
37. *Deontology*, vol. II, VIII.
38. *An Essay Concerning Human Understanding*, ed. A. C. Fraser (Clarendon Press, Oxford, 1894), vol. II, XXVIII, 7–12.
39. Vol. X, 145 and I, 453f.
40. *Deontology*, vol. I, 100.
41. Sheldon Wolin in his excellent essay on liberalism in his *Politics and Vision* (Allen and Unwin, 1960) suggests that Bentham's public opinion tribunal is a neat way of translating Rousseau's general will into the language of liberalism (348). This seems to me an exaggeration since, unlike Rousseau, Bentham does not define liberty in terms of self-government and is more concerned with maximizing happiness than with safeguarding liberty.
42. I, 457.
43. I, 194.
44. I, 542f.
45. Ibid.
46. Ibid., 543.
47. I, 549.
48. I, 213f. and 544f; also VII, 581.
49. I, 544.
50. Physical work and austere existence 'divert the desires from love and maintain for a longer period a calm among the feelings and the imagination'. Ibid. Bentham believes that 'among the working classes, sexual desire develops late and remains far less intense throughout life than among the middle classes'. For Bentham's elaborate defence of sexual 'eccentricities' like homosexuality and sodomy, see UCL, Boxes 73, 74 and 161b.

51. I, 544.
52. Ibid., 545.
53. Ibid.
54. Ibid.
55. Ibid., 540.
56. II, 254.
57. Ibid.
58. I, 540.
59. Ibid., 541.
60. Ibid., 564. 'If the people were philosophers the expedient would be worth nothing.' But they are not. And in any case in such matters philosophers themselves are 'only men'. I, 562. It is worth observing that Bentham refers to such devices for changing human feelings as 'indirect legislation'.
61. Ibid., 580.
62. Ibid.
63. I, 83.
64. Ibid., 549. Also ibid., 404.
65. Ibid., 549.

Chapter 1

Bentham

J. S. Mill

[Although this is the most famous of Mill's essays on Bentham it is not the only one. Mill's first writing on Bentham was his obituary notice in *The Examiner*, 10th June, 1832. In 1833 at the request of Edward Lytton Bulwer, later 1st Baron Lytton, he wrote a critical account of Bentham's philosophy which was printed as Appendix B in Lytton's *England and the English*, London, Bentley, 1833. In August 1838 Mill published an essay on Bentham in *London and Westminster Review*. It was signed 'A' and was a review of Bowring's edition of Bentham's works. This number of the *Review* went into second edition, but Mill made no changes except to add a footnote at the end. Later in the year Mill's essay appeared as an offprint, entitled *An Estimate of Bentham's Philosophy*. It was still signed 'A', and apart from removing the running titles Mill made no other changes. When, however, he later included it in his *Dissertations and Discussions* vol. I, he revised it at several places. It is this final version that I have used here, indicating at appropriate places many of Mill's important revisions. Mill's last systematic discussion of Bentham was in his 'Dr. Whewell on Moral Philosophy', published in *Westminster Review*, October, 1852, and reprinted without substantial changes in his *Dissertations and Discussions*, vol. II. This is a shrewd and skilful essay in that having himself criticized Bentham a few years earlier, he is now required to defend him against Whewell's similar criticisms. For further comments see the editorial note on p. 41—Editor.]

There are two men, recently deceased, to whom their country is indebted not only for the greater part of the important ideas which have been thrown into circulation among its thinking men in their time, but for a revolution in its general modes of thought and investigation. These men, dissimilar in almost all else, agreed in being closet-students—secluded in a peculiar degree, by circumstances and character, from the business and intercourse of the world: and both were, through a large portion of their lives, regarded by those who took the lead in opinion (when they happened to hear of them) with feelings akin to contempt. But they were destined to renew a lesson given to mankind by every age, and always disregarded—to show that speculative philosophy, which to the superficial appears a thing so remote from the business of life and the outward interests of men, is in reality the thing on earth which most influences them, and in the long run overbears every other influence save those which it must itself obey. The writers of whom we speak have never been read by the multitude; except for the more slight of their works, their readers have been few: but they have been the teachers of the teachers; there is hardly to be found in England an individual of any importance in the world of mind, who (whatever opinions he may have afterwards adopted) did not first learn to think from one of these two; and though their influences have but begun to diffuse themselves through these intermediate channels over society at large, there is already scarcely a publication of any consequence addressed to the educated classes, which, if these persons had not existed, would not have been different from what it is. These men are, Jeremy Bentham and Samuel Taylor Coleridge—the two great seminal minds of England in their age.

No comparison is intended here between the minds or influences of these remarkable men: this was impossible unless there were first formed a complete judgment of each, considered apart. It is our intention to attempt, on the present occasion, an estimate of one of them; the only one, a complete edition of whose works is yet in progress, and who, in the classification which may be made of all writers into Progressive[1] and Conservative, belongs to the same division with ourselves. For although they were far too great men to be correctly designated by either appellation exclusively, yet in the main, Bentham was a Progressive philosopher, Coleridge a Conservative one. The influence of the former has made itself felt chiefly on minds of the Progressive class; of the latter, on those of the Conservative:[2] and the two systems of concentric circles which the shock given by them is spreading over the ocean of mind, have only just begun to meet and intersect. The writings of both contain severe lessons to their own side, on many of the errors and faults they are addicted to: but to Bentham it was given to discern more particularly those truths with which existing doctrines and institutions were at variance; to Coleridge, the neglected truths which lay *in* them.

A man of great knowledge of the world, and of the highest reputation for practical talent and sagacity among the official men of his time (himself no follower of Bentham, nor of any partial or exclusive school whatever) once said to us, as the result of his observation, that to Bentham more than to any other source might be traced the questioning spirit, the disposition to demand the *why* of everything, which had gained so much ground and was producing such important consequences in these times.[3] The more this assertion is examined, the more true it will be found. Bentham has been in this age and country the great questioner of things established. It is by the influence of the modes of thought with which his writings inoculated a considerable number of thinking men, that the yoke of authority has been broken, and innumerable opinions, formerly received on tradition as incontestable, are put upon their defence, and required to give an account of themselves. Who, before Bentham (whatever controversies might exist on points of detail) dared to speak disrespectfully, in express terms, of the British Constitution, or the English Law? He did so; and his arguments and his example together encouraged others. We do not mean that his writings caused the Reform Bill, or that the Appropriation Clause owns him as its parent: the changes which have been made, and the greater changes which will be made, in our institutions, are not the work of philosophers, but of the interests and instincts of large portions of society recently grown into strength. But Bentham gave voice to those interests and instincts: until he spoke out, those who found our institutions unsuited to them did not dare to say so, did not dare consciously to think so; they had never heard the excellence of those institutions questioned by cultivated men, by men of acknowledged intellect; and it is not in the nature of uninstructed minds to resist the united authority of the instructed. Bentham broke the spell. It was not Bentham by his own writings; it was Bentham through the minds and pens which those writings fed—through the men in more direct contact with the world, into whom his spirit passed. If the superstition about ancestorial wisdom has fallen into decay; if the public are grown familiar with the idea that their laws and institutions are in great part not the product of intellect and virtue, but of modern corruption grafted upon ancient barbarism; if the hardiest innovation is no longer scouted because it is an innovation—establishments no longer considered sacred because they are establishments—it will be found that those who have accustomed the public mind to these ideas have learnt them in Bentham's school, and that the assault on ancient institutions has been, and is, carried on for the most part with his weapons. It matters not although these thinkers, or indeed thinkers of any description, have been but scantily found among the persons prominently and ostensibly at the head of the Reform movement. All movements, except directly revolutionary ones, are headed, not by those who originate them, but by those who know best how to compromise between the old opinions and the new. The father of English innovation both in doctrines and in institutions, is Bentham: he is the great *subversive*, or, in the language of continental philosophers, the great *critical*, thinker of his age and country.

We consider this, however, to be not his highest title to fame. Were this all, he were only to be ranked among the lowest order of the potentates of mind—the negative, or destructive philosophers; those who can perceive what is false, but not what is true; who awaken the human mind to the inconsistencies and absurdities of time-sanctioned opinions and institutions, but substitute nothing in the place of what they take away. We have no desire to undervalue

the services of such persons: mankind have been deeply indebted to
them; nor will there ever be a lack of work for them, in a world in
which so many false things are believed, in which so many which
have been true, are believed long after they have ceased to be true.
The qualities, however, which fit men for perceiving anomalies,
without perceiving the truths which would rectify them, are not
among the rarest of endowments. Courage, verbal acuteness, command over the forms of argumentation, and a popular style, will
make, out of the shallowest man, with a sufficient lack of reverence,
a considerable negative philosopher. Such men have never been
wanting in periods of culture; and the period in which Bentham
formed his early impressions was emphatically their reign, in proportion to its barrenness in the more noble products of the human
mind. An age of formalism in the Church and corruption in the
State, when the most valuable part of the meaning of traditional
doctrines[4] had faded from the minds even of those who retained
from habit a mechanical belief in them, was the time to raise up all
kinds of sceptical philosophy. Accordingly, France had Voltaire,
and his school of negative thinkers, and England (or rather Scotland) had the profoundest negative thinker on record, David Hume:
a man, the peculiarities of whose mind qualified him to detect failure
of proof, and want of logical consistency, at a depth which French
sceptics, with their comparatively feeble powers of analysis and
abstraction, stopt far short of,[5] and which German subtlety alone
could thoroughly appreciate, or hope to rival.

If Bentham had merely continued the work of Hume, he would
scarcely have been heard of in philosophy; for he was far inferior to
Hume in Hume's qualities, and was in no respect fitted to excel as
a metaphysician. We must not look for subtlety, or the power of
recondite analysis, among his intellectual characteristics. In the
former quality, few great thinkers have ever been so deficient; and to
find the latter, in any considerable measure, in a mind acknowledging
any kindred with his, we must have recourse to the late Mr. Mill—a
man who united the great qualities of the metaphysicians of the
eighteenth century, with others of a different complexion, admirably
qualifying him to complete and correct their work. Bentham had not
these peculiar gifts; but he possessed others, not inferior, which were
not possessed by any of his precursors; which have made him a
source of light to a generation which has far outgrown their influence,
and, as we called him, the chief subversive thinker of an age which
has long lost all that they could subvert.

To speak of him first as a merely negative philosopher—as one
who refutes illogical arguments, exposes sophistry, detects contradiction and absurdity; even in that capacity there was a wide field

left vacant for him by Hume, and which he has occupied to an unprecedented extent; the field of practical abuses. This was Bentham's peculiar province: to this he was called by the whole bent of his disposition: to carry the warfare against absurdity into things practical. His was an essentially practical mind. It was by practical abuses that his mind was first turned to speculation—by the abuses of the profession which was chosen for him, that of the law. He has himself stated what particular abuse first gave that schock to his mind, the recoil of which has made the whole mountain of abuse totter; it was the custom of making the client pay for three attendances in the office of a Master in Chancery, when only one was given. The law, he found, on examination, was full of such things. But were these discoveries of his? No; they were known to every lawyer who practised, to every judge who sat on the bench, and neither before nor for long after did they cause any apparent uneasiness to the consciences of these learned persons, nor hinder them from asserting, whenever occasion offered, in books, in parliament, or on the bench, that the law was the perfection of reason. During so many generations, in each of which thousands of educated young men were successivly placed in Bentham's position and with Bentham's opportunities, he alone was found with sufficient moral sensibility and self-reliance to say to himself that these things, however profitable they might be, were frauds, and that between them and himself there should be a gulf fixed. To this rare union of self-reliance and moral sensibility we are indebted for all that Bentham has done. Sent to Oxford by his father at the unusually early age of fifteen—required, on admission, to declare his belief in the Thirty-nine Articles—he felt it necessary to examine them; and the examination suggested scruples, which he sought to get removed, but instead of the satisfaction he expected was told that it was not for boys like him to set up their judgment against the great men of the Church. After a struggle, he signed; but the impression that he had done an immoral act, never left him; he considered himself to have committed a falsehood, and throughout life he never relaxed in his indignant denunciations of all laws which command such falsehoods, all institutions which attach rewards to them.

By thus carrying the war of criticism and refutation, the conflict with falsehood and absurdity, into the field of practical evils, Bentham, even if he had done nothing else, would have earned an important place in the history of intellect. He carried on the warfare without intermission. To this, not only many of his most piquant chapters, but some of the most finished of his entire works, are entirely devoted: the 'Defence of Usury'; the 'Book of Fallacies'; and the onslaught upon Blackstone, published anonymously under the title of 'A Fragment on Government', which, though a first production, and of a writer afterwards so much ridiculed for his style, excited the highest admiration no less for its composition than for its thoughts, and was attributed by turns to Lord Mansfield, to Lord Camden, and (by Dr. Johnson) to Dunning, one of the greatest masters of style among the lawyers of his day. These writings are altogether original; though of the negative school, they resemble nothing previously produced by negative philosophers; and would have sufficed to create for Bentham, among the subversive thinkers of modern Europe, a place peculiarly his own. But it is not these writings that constitute the real dinstinction between him and them. There was a deeper difference. It was that they were purely negative thinkers, he was positive: they only assailed error, he made it a point of conscience not to do so until he thought he could plant instead the corresponding truth. Their character was exclusively analytic, his was synthetic. They took for their starting-point the received opinion on any subject, dug round it with their logical implements, pronounced its foundations defective, and condemned it: he began *de novo*, laid his own foundations deeply and firmly, built up his own structure, and bade mankind compare the two; it was when he had solved the problem himself, or thought he had done so, that he declared all other solutions to be erroneous. Hence, what they produced will not last; it must perish, much of it has already perished, with the errors which it exploded: what he did has its own value, by which it must outlast all errors to which it is opposed. Though we may reject, as we often must, his practical conclusions, yet his premises, the collections of facts and observations from which his conclusions were drawn, remain for ever, a part of the materials of philosophy.

A place, therefore, must be assigned to Bentham among the masters of wisdom, the great teachers and permanent intellectual ornaments of the human race. He is among those who have enriched mankind with imperishable gifts; and although these do not transcend all other gifts, nor entitle him to those honours 'above all Greek, above all Roman fame', which by a natural reaction against the neglect and contempt of the ignorant, many[6] of his admirers were once disposed to accumulate upon him, yet to refuse an admiring recognition of what he was, on account of what he was not, is a much worse error, and one which, pardonable in the vulgar, is no longer permitted to any cultivated and instructed mind.

If we were asked to say, in the fewest possible words, what we conceive to be Bentham's place among these great intellectual benefactors of humanity; what he was, and what he was not; what kind of service he did and did not render to truth; we should say—he was not a great philosopher, but he was a great reformer in philosophy. He brought into philosophy something which it greatly needed, and for want of which it was at a stand. It was not his doctrines which did this, it was his mode of arriving at them. He introduced into morals and politics those habits of thought and modes of investigation, which are essential to the idea of science; and the absence of which made those departments of inquiry, as physics had been before Bacon, a field of interminable discussion, leading to no result. It was not his opinions, in short, but his method, that constituted the novelty and the value of what he did; a value beyond all price, even though we should reject the whole, as we unquestionably must a large part, of the opinions themselves.

Bentham's method may be shortly described as the method of detail; of treating wholes by separating them into their parts, abstractions by resolving them into Things, classes and generalities by distinguishing them into the individuals of which they are made up; and breaking every question into pieces before attempting to solve it. The precise amount of originality of this process, considered as a logical conception—its degree of connexion with the methods of physical science, or with the previous labours of Bacon, Hobbes or Locke—is not an essential consideration in this place. Whatever originality there was in the method—in the subjects he applied it to, and in the rigidity with which he adhered to it, there was the greatest. Hence his interminable classifications. Hence his elaborate demonstrations of the most acknowledged truths. That murder, incendiarism, robbery, are mischievous actions, he will not take for granted without proof; let the thing appear ever so self-evident, he will know the why and the how of it with the last degree of precision; he will distinguish all the different mischiefs of a crime, whether of the *first*, the *second* or the *third* order, namely, 1. the evil to the sufferer, and to his personal connexions; 2. the *danger* from example, and the *alarm* or painful feeling of insecurity; and 3. the discouragement to industry and useful pursuits arising from the *alarm*, and the trouble and resources which must be expended in warding off the *danger*. After this enumeration, he will prove from the laws of human feeling, that even the first of these evils, the sufferings of the immediate victim, will on the average greatly outweigh the pleasure reaped by the offender; much more when all the other evils are taken into account. Unless this could be proved, he would account the infliction of punishment unwarrantable; and for taking the trouble to prove it formally, his defence is, 'there are truths which it is necessary to prove, not for their own sakes, because they are acknowledged, but that an opening may be made for the reception of other truths which depend upon them. It is in this manner we provide for the reception of first principles, which, once received, prepare the way for admission of all other truths.'[7] To which may be added, that in this manner also we discipline the mind for practising the same sort of dissection upon questions more complicated and of more doubtful issue.

It is a sound maxim, and one which all close thinkers have felt, but which no one before Bentham ever so consistently applied, that error lurks in generalities: that the human mind is not capable of embracing a complex whole, until it has surveyed and catalogued the parts of which that whole is made up; that abstractions are not realities *per se*, but an abridged mode of expressing facts, and that the only practical mode of dealing with them is to trace them back to the facts (whether of experience or of consciousness) of which they are the expression. Proceeding on this principle, Bentham makes short work with the ordinary modes of moral and political reasoning. These, it appeared to him, when hunted to their source, for the most part terminated in *phrases*. In politics, liberty, social order, constitution, law of nature, social compact, etc., were the catchwords: ethics had its analogous ones. Such were the arguments on which the gravest questions of morality and policy were made to turn; not reasons, but allusions to reasons; sacramental expressions, by which a summary appeal was made to some general sentiment of mankind, or to some maxim in familiar use, which might be true or not, but the limitations of which no one had ever critically examined. And this satisfied other people; but not Bentham. He required something more than opinion as a reason for opinion. Whenever he found a *phrase* used as an argument for or against anything, he insisted upon knowing what it meant; whether it appealed to any standard, or gave intimation of any matter of fact relevant to the question; and if he could not find that it did either, he treated it as an attempt on the part of the disputant to impose his own individual sentiment on other people, without giving them a reason for it; a 'contrivance for avoiding the obligation of appealing to any external standard, and for prevailing upon the reader to accept of the author's sentiment and opinion as a reason, and that a sufficient one, for itself'. Bentham shall speak for himself on this subject: the passage is from his first systematic work, 'Introduction to the Principles of Morals and Legislation', and we could scarcely quote anything more strongly exemplifying both the strength and weakness of his mode of philosophizing.

It is curious enough to observe the variety of inventions men have hit upon, and the variety of phrases they have brought forward, in order to conceal from the world, and, if possible, from themselves, this very general and therefore very pardonable self-sufficiency.

1. One man says, he has a thing made on purpose to tell him what is right and what is wrong; and that is called a 'moral sense': and then he

goes to work at his ease, and says, such a thing is right, and such a thing is wrong—why? 'Because my moral sense tells me it is.'

2. Another man comes and alters the phrase: leaving out *moral*, and putting in *common* in the room of it. He then tells you that his common sense tells him what is right and wrong, as surely as the other's moral sense did; meaning by common sense a sense of some kind or other, which, he says, is possessed by all mankind: the sense of those whose sense is not the same as the author's being struck out as not worth taking. This contrivance does better than the other; for a moral sense being a new thing, a man may feel about him a good while without being able to find it out: but common sense is as old as the creation; and there is no man but would be ashamed to be thought not to have as much of it as his neighbours. It has another great advantage: by appearing to share power, it lessens envy; for when a man gets up upon this ground, in order to anathematize those who differ from him, it is not by a *sic volo sic jubeo*, but by a *velitis jubeatis*.

3. Another man comes, and says, that as to a moral sense indeed, he cannot find that he has any such thing: that, however, he has an *understanding*, which will do quite as well. This understanding, he says, is the standard of right and wrong: it tells him so and so. All good and wise men understand as he does: if other men's understandings differ in any part from his, so much the worse for them: it is a sure sign they are either defective or corrupt.

4. Another man says, that there is an eternal and immutable Rule of Right: that that rule of right dictates so and so: and then he begins giving you his sentiments upon anything that comes uppermost: and these sentiments (you are to take for granted) are so many branches of the eternal rule of right.

5. Another man, or perhaps the same man (it is no matter), says that there are certain practices conformable and others repugnant, to the Fitness of Things; and then he tells you, at his leisure, what practices are conformable, and what repugnant: just as he happens to like a practice or dislike it.

6. A great multitude of people are continually talking of the Law of Nature; and then they go on giving you their sentiments about what is right and what is wrong: and these sentiments, you are to understand, are so many chapters and sections of the Law of Nature.

7. Instead of the phrase, Law of Nature, you have sometimes Law of Reason, Right Reason, Natural Justice, Natural Equity, Good Order. Any of them will do equally well. This latter is most used in politics. The three last are much more tolerable than the others, because they do not very explicitly claim to be anything more than phrases: they insist but feebly upon the being looked upon as so many positive standards of themselves, and seem content to be taken, upon occasion, for phrases expressive of the conformity of the thing in question to the proper standard, whatever that may be. On most occasions, however, it will be better to say *utility*: *utility* is clearer, as referring more explicitly to pain and pleasure.

8. We have one philosopher, who says, there is no harm in anything in

the world but in telling a lie; and that if, for example, you were to murder your own father, this would only be a particular way of saying, he was not your father. Of course when this philosopher sees anything that he does not like, he says, it is a particular way of telling a lie. It is saying, that the act ought to be done, or may be done, when, *in truth*, it ought not be done.

9. The fairest and openest of them all is that sort of man who speaks out, and says, I am of the number of the Elect: now God himself takes care to inform the Elect what is right: and that with so good effect, and let them strive ever so, they cannot help not only knowing it but practising it. If therefore a man wants to know what is right and what is wrong, he has nothing to do but to come to me.

Few will contend that this is a perfectly fair representation of the *animus* of those who employ the various phrases so amusingly animadverted on; but that the phrases contain no argument, save what is grounded on the very feelings they are adduced to justify, is a truth which Bentham had the eminent merit of first pointing out.[8]

It is the introduction into the philosophy of human conduct, of this method of detail—of this practice of never reasoning about wholes until they have been resolved into their parts, nor about abstractions until they have been translated into realities—that constitutes the originality of Bentham in philosophy, and makes him the great reformer of the moral and political branch of it. To what he terms the 'exhaustive method of classification', which is but one branch of this more general method, he himself ascribes everything original in the systematic and elaborate work from which we have quoted. The generalities of his philosophy itself have little or no novelty: to ascribe any to the doctrine that general utility is the foundation of morality, would imply great ignorance of the history of philosophy, of general literature, and of Bentham's own writings. He derived the idea, as he says himself, from Helvetius;[9] and it was the doctrine no less, of the religious philosophers of that age, prior to Reid and Beattie. We never saw an abler defence of the doctrine of utility than in a book written in refutation of Shaftesbury, and now little read—Brown's[10] 'Essays on the Characteristics'; and in Johnson's celebrated review of Soame Jenyns, the same dotrine is set forth as that both of the author and of the reviewer. In all ages of philosophy one of its schools has been utilitarian—not only from the time of Epicurus, but long before. It was by mere accident that this opinion became connected in Bentham with his peculiar method. The utilitarian philosophers antecedent to him had no more claims to the method than their antagonists. To refer, for instance, to the Epicurean philosophy, according to the most complete view we have of the moral part of it, by the most accomplished scholar of antiquity, Cicero; we ask any one who has read his philosophical writings,

the 'De Finibus' for instance, whether the arguments of the Epicureans do not, just as much as those of the Stoics or Platonists,
consist of mere rhetorical appeals to common notions, to $\dot{\epsilon}\iota\kappa\acute{o}\tau\alpha$ and
$\sigma\eta\mu\epsilon\hat{\iota}\alpha$ instead of $\tau\epsilon\kappa\mu\acute{\eta}\rho\iota\alpha$, notions picked up as it were casually,
and when true at all, never so narrowly looked into as to ascertain
in what sense and under what limitations they are true. The application of a real inductive philosophy to the problems of ethics, is as
unknown to the Epicurean moralists as to any of the other schools;
they never take a question to pieces, and join issue on a definite
point.[11] Bentham certainly did not learn his sifting and anatomizing
method from them.

   This method Bentham has finally installed in philosophy; has made
it henceforth imperative on philosophers of all schools. By it he has
formed the intellects of many thinkers, who either never adopted, or
have abandoned, many of his peculiar opinions. He has taught the
method to men of the most opposite schools to his; he has made
them perceive that if they do not test their doctrines by the method
of detail, their adversaries will. He has thus, it is not too much to say,
for the first time introduced precision of thought into moral and
political philosophy. Instead of taking up their opinions by intuition,
or by ratiocination from premises adopted on a mere rough view,
and couched in language so vague that it is impossible to say exactly
whether they are true or false, philosophers are now forced to understand one another, to break down the generality of their propositions, and join a precise issue in every dispute. This is nothing less
than a revolution in philosophy. Its effect is gradually becoming
evident in the writings of English thinkers of every variety of opinion,
and will be felt more and more in proportion as Bentham's writings
are diffused, and as the number of minds to whose formation they
contribute is multiplied.

   It will naturally be presumed that of the fruits of this great philosophical improvement some portion at least will have been reaped
by its author. Armed with such a potent instrument, and wielding it
with such singleness of aim; cultivating the field of practical philosophy with such unwearied and such consistent use of a method right
in itself, and not adopted by his predecessors; it cannot be but that
Bentham by his own inquiries must have accomplished something
considerable. And so, it will be found, he has; something not only
considerable, but extraordinary; though but little compared with
what he has left undone, and far short of what his sanguine and
almost boyish fancy made him flatter himself that he had accomplished. His peculiar method, admirably calculated to make clear
thinkers, and sure ones to the extent of their materials, has not equal

efficacy for making those materials complete. It is a security for accuracy, but not for comprehensiveness; or rather, it is a security for one sort of comprehensiveness, but not for another.

Bentham's method of laying out his subject is admirable as a preservative against one kind of narrow and partial views.[12] He begins by placing before himself the whole of the field of inquiry to which the particular question belongs, and divides down till he arrives at the thing he is in search of; and thus by successively rejecting all which is not the thing, he gradually works out a definition of what it is. This, which he calls the exhaustive method, is as old as philosophy itself. Plato owes everything to it, and does everything by it; and the use made of it by that great man in his Dialogues, Bacon, in one of those pregnant logical hints scattered through his writings, and so much neglected by most of his pretended followers, pronounces to be the nearest approach to a true inductive method in the ancient philosophy. Bentham was probably not aware that Plato had anticipated him in the process to which he too declared that he owed everything. By the practice of it, his speculations are rendered eminently systematic and consistent; no question, with him, is ever an insulated one; he sees every subject in connexion with all the other subjects with which in his view it is related, and from which it requires to be distinguished; and as all that he knows, in the least degree allied to the subject, has been marshalled in an orderly manner before him, he does not, like people who use a looser method, forget and overlook a thing on one occasion to remember it on another. Hence there is probably no philosopher of so wide a range, in whom there are so few inconsistencies. If any of the truths which he did not see, had come to be seen by him, he would have remembered it everywhere and at all times, and would have adjusted his whole system to it. And this is another admirable quality which he has impressed upon the best of the minds trained in his habits of thought: when those minds open to admit new truths, they digest them as fast as they receive them.

But this system, excellent for keeping before the mind of the thinker all that he knows, does not make him know enough; it does not make a knowledge of some of the properties of a thing suffice for the whole of it, nor render a rooted habit of surveying a complex object (though ever so carefully) in only one of its aspects, tantamount to the power of contemplating it in all. To give this last power, other qualities are required: whether Bentham possessed those other qualities we now have to see.

Bentham's mind, as we have already said, was eminently synthetical. He begins all his inquiries by supposing nothing to be known on the subject, and reconstructs all philosophy *ab initio*, without reference to the opinions of his predecessors. But to build either a philosophy or anything else, there must be materials. For the philosophy of matter, the materials are the properties of matter; for moral and political philosophy, the properties of man, and of man's position in the world. The knowledge which any inquirer possesses of these properties, constitutes a limit beyond which, as a moralist or a political philosopher, whatever be his powers of mind, he cannot reach.[13] Nobody's synthesis can be more complete than his analysis. If in his survey of human nature and life he has left any element out, then, wheresoever that element exerts any influence, his conclusions will fail, more or less, in their application. If he has left out many elements, and those very important, his labours may be highly valuable; he may have largely contributed to that body of partial truths which, when completed and corrected by one another, constitute practical truth; but the applicability of his system to practice in its own proper shape will be of an exceedingly limited range.

Human nature and human life are wide subjects,[14] and whoever would embark in an enterprise requiring a thorough knowledge of them, has need both of large stores of his own, and of all aids and appliances from elsewhere. His qualifications for success will be proportional to two things: the degree in which his own nature and circumstances furnish him with a correct and complete picture of man's nature and circumstances; and his capacity of deriving light from other minds.

Bentham failed in deriving light from other minds. His writings contain few traces of the accurate knowledge of any schools of thinking but his own; and many proofs of his entire conviction that they could teach him nothing worth knowing. For some of the most illustrious of previous thinkers, his contempt was unmeasured. In almost the only passage of the 'Deontology'[15] which, from its style, and from its having before appeared in print, may be known to be Bentham's, Socrates, and Plato are spoken of in terms distressing to his greatest admirers; and the incapacity to appreciate such men, is a fact perfectly in unison with the general habits of Bentham's mind. He had a phrase, expressive of the view he took of all moral speculations to which his method had not been applied, or (which he considered as the same thing) not founded on a recognition of utility as the moral standard; this phrase was 'vague generalities'. Whatever presented itself to him in such a shape, he dismissed as unworthy of notice, or dwelt upon only to denounce as absurd. He did not heed, or rather the nature of his mind prevented it from occurring to him, that these generalities contained the whole un-analysed experience of the human race.

Unless it can be asserted that mankind did not know anything until logicians taught it to them—that until the last hand has been put to a moral truth by giving it a metaphysically precise expression, all the previous rough-hewing which it has undergone by the common intellect at the suggestion of common wants and common experience is to go for nothing; it must be allowed, that even the originality which can, and the courage which dares, think for itself, is not a more necessary part of the philosophical character than a thoughtful regard[16] for previous thinkers, and for the collective mind of the human race. What has been the opinion of mankind, has been the opinion of persons of all tempers and dispositions, of all partialities and prepossessions, of all varieties in position, in education, in opportunities of observation and inquiry. No one inquirer is all this; every inquirer is either young or old, rich or poor, sickly or healthy, married or unmarried, meditative or active, a poet or a logician, an ancient or a modern, a man or a woman; and if a thinking person, has, in addition, the accidental peculiarities of his individual modes of thought. Every circumstance which gives a character to the life of a human being, carries with it its peculiar biases; its peculiar facilities for perceiving some things, and for missing or forgetting others. But, from points of view different from his, different things are perceptible; and none are more likely to have seen what he does not see, than those who do not see what he sees. The general opinion of mankind is the average of the conclusions of all minds, stripped indeed of their choicest and most recondite thoughts, but freed from their twists and partialities: a net result, in which everybody's point of view is represented, nobody's predominant. The collective mind does not penetrate below the surface, but it sees all the surface; which profound thinkers, even by reason of their profundity, often fail to do:[17] their intenser view of a thing in some of its aspects diverting their attention from others.

The hardiest assertor, therefore, of the freedom of private judgment—the keenest detector of the errors of his predecessors, and of the inaccuracies of current modes of thought—is the very person who most needs to fortify the weak side of his own intellect, by study of the opinions of mankind in all ages and nations, and of the speculations of philosophers of the modes of thought most opposite to his own. It is there that he will find the experiences denied to himself—the remainder of the truth of which he sees but half—the truths, of which the errors he detects are commonly but the exaggerations. If, like Bentham, he brings with him an improved instrument of investigation, the greater is the probability that he will find ready prepared a rich abundance of rough ore, which was merely waiting for that instrument. A man of clear ideas errs grievously if he imagines that whatever is seen confusedly does not exist: it belongs to him, when he meets with such a thing, to dispel the mist, and fix the outlines of the vague form which is looming through it.

Bentham's contempt, then, of all other schools of thinkers; his determination to create a philosophy wholly out of the materials furnished by his own mind, and by minds like his own; was his first disqualification as a philosopher. His second, was the incompleteness of his own mind as a representative of universal human nature. In many of the most natural and strongest feelings of human nature he had no sympathy; from many of its graver experiences he was altogether cut off; and the faculty by which one mind understands a mind different from itself, and throws itself into the feelings of that other mind, was denied him by his deficiency of Imagination.

With Imagination in the popular sense, command of imagery and metaphorical expression, Bentham was, to a certain degree, endowed. For want, indeed, of poetical culture, the images with which his fancy supplied him were seldom beautiful, but they were quaint and humorous, or bold, forcible, and intense: passages might be quoted from him both of playful irony, and of declamatory eloquence, seldom surpassed in the writings of philosophers. The Imagination which he had not, was that to which the name is generally appropriated by the best writers of the present day; that which enables us, by a voluntary effort, to conceive the absent as if it were present, the imaginary as if it were real, and to clothe it in the feelings which, if it were indeed real, it would bring along with it. This is the power by which one human being enters into the mind and circumstances of another. This power constitutes the poet, in so far as he does anything but melodiously utter his own actual feelings. It constitutes the dramatist entirely. It is one of the constituents of the historian; by it we understand other times; by it Guizot interprets to us the middle ages; Nisard, in his beautiful Studies on the later Latin poets, places us in the Rome of the Cæsars; Michelet disengages the distinctive characters of the different races and generations[18] of mankind from the facts of their history. Without it nobody knows even his own nature, further than circumstances have actually tried it and called it out; nor the nature of his fellow-creatures, beyond such generalizations as he may have been enabled to make from his observation of their outward conduct.

By these limits, accordingly, Bentham's knowledge of human nature is bounded. It is wholly empirical; and the empiricism of one who has had little experience. He had neither internal experience nor external; the quiet, even tenor of his life, and his healthiness of mind, conspired to exclude him from both. He never knew prosperity and adversity, passion nor satiety: he never had even the experiences which sickness gives; he lived from childhood to the age of eighty-five in boyish health. He knew no dejection, no heaviness of heart. He never felt life a sore and a weary burthen. He was a boy to the last. Self-consciousness, that dæmon of the men of genius of our time, from Wordsworth to Byron, from Goethe to Chateaubriand, and to which this age owes so much both of its cheerful and its mournful wisdom, never was awakened in him. How much of human nature slumbered in him he knew not, neither can we know. He had never been made alive to the unseen influences which were acting on himself, nor consequently on his fellow-creatures. Other ages and other nations were a blank to him for purposes of instruction. He measured them but by one standard; their knowledge of facts, and their capability to take correct views of utility, and merge all other objects in it. His own lot was cast in a generation of the leanest and barrenest men whom England had yet produced, and he was an old man when a better race came in with the present century. He saw accordingly in man little but what the vulgarest eye can see; recognized no diversities of character but such as he who runs may read. Knowing so little of human feelings, he knew still less of the influences by which those feelings are formed: all the more subtle workings both of the mind upon itself, and of external things upon the mind, escaped him; and no one, probably, who, in a highly instructed age, ever attempted to give a rule to all human conduct, set out with a more limited conception[19] either of the agencies[20] by which human conduct *is*, or of those by which it *should* be, influenced.

This, then, is our idea of Bentham. He was a man both of remarkable endowments for philosophy, and of remarkable deficiences for it: fitted, beyond almost any man, for drawing from his premises, conclusions not only correct, but sufficiently precise and specific to be practical: but whose general conception of human nature and life furnished him with an unusually slender stock of premises. It is obvious what would be likely to be achieved by such a man; what a thinker, thus gifted and thus disqualified, could do in philosophy. He could, with close and accurate logic, hunt half-truths to their consequences and practical applications, on a scale both of greatness and of minuteness not previously exemplified; and this is the character which posterity will probably assign to Bentham.

We express our sincere and well-considered conviction when we say, that there is hardly anything positive in Bentham's philosophy which is not true: that when his practical conclusions are erroneous, which in our opinion they are very often, it is not because the considerations which he urges are not rational and valid in themselves, but because some more important principle, which he did not perceive, supersedes those considerations, and turns the scale. The bad part of his writings is his resolute denial of all that he does not see, of all truths but those which he recognizes. By that alone has he exercised any bad influence upon his age; by that he has, not created a school of deniers, for this is an ignorant prejudice, but put himeslf at the head of the school which exists always, though it does not always find a great man to give it the sanction of philosophy: thrown the mantle of intellect over the natural tendency of men in all ages to deny or disparage all feelings and mental states[21] of which they have no consciousness in themselves.

The truths which are not Bentham's, which his philosophy takes no account of, are many and important; but his non-recognition of them does not put them out of existence; they are still with us, and it is a comparatively easy task that is reserved for us, to harmonize those truths with his. To reject his half of the truth because he overlooked the other half, would be to fall into his error without having his excuse. For our own part, we have a large tolerance for one-eyed men, provided their one eye is a penetrating one: if they saw more, they probably would not see so keenly, nor so eagerly pursue one course of inquiry. Almost all rich veins of original and striking speculation have been opened by systematic half-thinkers: though whether these new thoughts drive out others as good, or are peacefully superadded to them, depends on whether these half-thinkers are or are not followed in the same track by complete thinkers. The field of man's nature and life cannot be too much worked, or in too many directions; until every clod is turned up the work is imperfect; no whole truth is possible but by combining the points of view of all the fractional truths, nor, therefore, until it has been fully seen what each fractional truth can do by itself.

What Bentham's fractional truths could do, there is no such good means of showing as by a review of his philosophy: and such a review, though inevitably a most brief and general one, it is now necessary to attempt.

The first question in regard to any man of speculation is, what is his theory of human life? In the minds of many philosophers, whatever theory they have of this sort is latent, and it would be a revelation to themselves to have it pointed out to them in their writings as others can see it, unconsciously moulding everything to its own likeness. But Bentham always knew his own premises, and made his reader know them: it was not his custom to leave the theoretic grounds of his practical conclusions to conjecture. Few great thinkers have afforded the means of assigning with so much certainty the exact conception which they had formed of man and of man's life. Man is conceived by Bentham as a being susceptible of pleasures and pains, and governed in all his conduct partly by the different modifications of self-interest, and the passions commonly classed as selfish, partly by sympathies, or occasionally antipathies, towards other beings. And here Bentham's conception of human nature stops. He does not exclude religion; the prospect of divine rewards and punishments he includes under the head of 'self-regarding interest', and the devotional feeling under that of sympathy with God. But the whole of the impelling or restraining principles, whether of this or of another world, which he recognizes, are either self-love, or love or hatred towards other sentient beings. That there might be no doubt of what he thought on the subject, he has not left us to the general evidence of his writings, but has drawn out a 'Table of the Springs of Action', an express enumeration and classification of human motives, with their various names, laudatory, vituperative, and neutral: and this table, to be found in Part I. of his collected works, we recommend to the study of those who would understand his philosophy.

Man is never recognized by him as a being capable of pursuing spiritual perfection as an end; of desiring, for its own sake, the conformity of his own character to his standard of excellence, without hope of good or fear of evil from other source than his own inward consciousness. Even in the more limited form of Conscience, this great fact in human nature escapes him. Nothing is more curious than the absence of recognition in any of his writings of the existence of conscience, as a thing distinct from philanthropy, from affection for God or man, and from self-interest in this world or in the next. There is a studied abstinence from any of the phrases which, in the mouths of others, import the acknowledgment of such a fact.[22] If we find the words 'Conscience', 'Principle', 'Moral Rectitude', 'Moral Duty', in his Table of the Springs of Action, it is among the synonymes of the 'love of reputation'; with an intimation as to the two former phrases, that they are also sometimes synonymous with the *religious* motive, or the motive of *sympathy*. The feeling of moral approbation or disapprobation properly so called, either towards ourselves or our fellow-creatures, he seems unaware of the existence of; and neither the word *self-respect*, nor the idea to which that word is appropriated, occurs even once, so far as our recollection serves us, in his whole writings.

Nor is it only the moral part of man's nature, in the strict sense of the term—the desire of perfection, or the feeling of an approving or of an accusing conscience—that he overlooks; he but faintly recognizes, as a fact in human nature, the pursuit of any other ideal end for its own sake. The sense of *honour*, and personal dignity—that feeling of personal exaltation and degradation which acts independently of other people's opinion, or even in defiance of it; the love of *beauty*, the passion of the artist; the love of *order*, of congruity, of consistency in all things, and conformity to their end; the love of *power*, not in the limited form of power over other human beings, but abstract power, the power of making our volitions effectual; the love of *action*, the thirst for movement and activity, a principle scarcely of less influence in human life than its opposite, the love of ease: None of these powerful constituents of human nature are thought worthy of a place among the 'Springs of Action'; and though there is possibly no one of them of the existence of which an acknowledgment might not be found in some corner of Bentham's writings, no conclusions are ever founded on the acknowledgment. Man, that most complex being, is a very simple one in his eyes. Even under the head of *sympathy*, his recognition does not extend to the more complex forms of the feeling—the love of *loving*, the need of a sympathizing support, or of objects of admiration and reverence. If he thought at all of any of the deeper feelings of human nature, it was but as idiosyncrasies of taste, with which the moralist no more than the legislator had any concern, further than to prohibit such as were mischievous among the actions to which they might chance to lead. To say either that man should, or that he should not, take pleasure in one thing, displeasure in another, appeared to him as much an act of despotism in the moralist as in the political ruler.

It would be most unjust to Bentham to surmise (as narrow-minded and passionate adversaries are apt in such cases to do) that this picture of human nature was copied from himself; that all those constituents of humanity which he rejected from his table of motives, were wanting in his own breast. The unusual strength of his early feelings of virtue, was, as we have seen, the original cause of all his speculations; and a noble sense of morality, and especially of justice, guides and pervades them all. But having been early accustomed to keep before his mind's eye the happiness of mankind (or rather of the whole sentient world), as the only thing desirable in itself, or which rendered anything else desirable, he confounded all disinterested feelings which he found in himself, with the desire of general happiness: just as some religious writers, who loved virtue for its own sake as much perhaps as men could do, habitually confounded their love of virtue with their fear of hell. It would have required greater subtlety than Bentham possessed, to distinguish from each other, feelings which, from long habit, always acted in the same direction; and his want of imagination prevented him from reading the distinction, where it is legible enough, in the hearts of others.

Accordingly, he has not been followed in this grand oversight by any of the able men who, from the extent of their intellectual obligations to him, have been regarded as his disciples. They may have followed him in his doctrine of utility, and in his rejection of a moral sense as the test of right and wrong: but while repudiating it as such, they have, with Hartley, acknowledged it as a fact in human nature; they have endeavoured to account for it, to assign its laws: nor are they justly chargeable either with undervaluing this part of our nature, or with any disposition to throw it into the background of their speculations. If any part of the influence of this cardinal error has extended itself to them, it is circuitously, and through the effect on their minds of other parts of Bentham's doctrines.

Sympathy, the only disinterested motive which Bentham recognized, he felt the inadequacy of, except in certain limited cases, as a security for virtuous action. Personal affection, he well knew, is as liable to operate to the injury of third parties, and requires as much to be kept under government, as any other feeling whatever: and general philanthropy, considered as a motive influencing mankind in general, he estimated at its true value when divorced from the feeling of duty—as the very weakest and most unsteady of all feelings. There remained, as a motive by which mankind are influenced, and by which they may be guided to their good, only personal interest. Accordingly, Bentham's idea of the world is that of a collection of persons pursuing each his separate interest or pleasure, and the prevention of whom from jostling one another more than is unavoidable, may be attempted by hopes and fears derived from three sources—the law, religion and public opinion. To these three powers, considered as binding human conduct, he gave the name of *sanctions*: the *political* sanction, operating by the rewards and penalties of the law; the *religious* sanction, by those expected from the Ruler of the Universe; and the *popular*, which he characteristically calls also the *moral* sanction, operating through the pains and pleasures arising from the favour or disfavour of our fellow-creatures.

Such is Bentham's theory of the world. And now, in a spirit neither of apology nor of censure, but of calm appreciation, we are to inquire how far this view of human nature and life will carry any one: how much it will accomplish in morals, and how much in political and social philosophy: what it will do for the individual, and what for society.

It will do nothing for the conduct of the individual, beyond prescribing some of the more obvious dictates of worldly prudence, and outward probity and beneficence. There is no need to expatiate on the deficiencies of a system of ethics which does not pretend to aid individuals in the formation of their own character; which recognizes no such wish as that of self culture, we may even say no such power, as existing in human nature; and if it did recognize, could furnish little assistance to that great duty, because it overlooks the existence of about half of the whole number of mental feelings which human beings are capable of, including all those of which the direct objects are states of their own mind.

Morality consists of two parts. One of these is self-education; the training, by the human being himself, of his affections and will. That department is a blank in Bentham's system. The other and co-equal part, the regulation of his outward actions, must be altogether halting and imperfect without the first; for how can we judge in what manner many an action will affect even the worldly interests of ourselves or others, unless we take in, as part of the question, its influence on the regulation of our, or their, affections and desires? A moralist on Bentham's principles may get as far as this, that he ought not to slay, burn, or steal; but what will be his qualifications for regulating the nicer shades of human behaviour, or for laying down even the greater moralities as to those facts in human life which tend to influence the depths of the character quite independently of any influence on worldly circumstances—such, for instance, as the sexual relations, or those of family in general, or any other social and sympathetic connexions of an intimate kind? The moralities of these questions depend essentially on considerations which Bentham never so much as took into the account; and when he happened to be in the right, it was always, and necessarily, on wrong or insufficient grounds.[23]

It is fortunate for the world that Bentham's taste lay rather in the direction of jurisprudential than of properly ethical inquiry. Nothing expressly of the latter kind has been published under his name, except the 'Deontology'—a book scarcely ever, in our experience, alluded to by any admirer of Bentham without deep regret that it ever saw the light. We did not expect from Bentham correct systematic views of ethics, or a sound treatment of any question the moralities of which require a profound knowledge of the human heart; but we did anticipate that the greater moral questions would have been boldly plunged into, and at least a searching criticism produced of the received opinions; we did not expect that the *petite morale* almost alone would have been treated, and that with the most pedantic minuteness, and on the *quid pro quo* principles which regulate trade. The book has not even the value which would belong to an authentic exhibition of the legitimate consequences of an erroneous line of thought; for the style proves it to have been so entirely rewritten, that it is impossible to tell how much or how little of it is Bentham's. The collected edition, now in progress, will not, it is said, include Bentham's religious writings; these, although we think most of them of exceedingly small value, are at least his, and the world has a right to whatever light they throw upon the constitution of his mind. But the omission of the 'Deontology' would be an act of editorial discretion which we should deem entirely justifiable.

If Bentham's theory of life can do so little for the individual, what can it do for society?

It will enable a society which has attained a certain state of spiritual development, and the maintenance of which in that state is otherwise provided for, to prescribe the rules by which it may protect its material interests. It will do nothing (except sometimes as an instrument in the hands of a higher doctrine) for the spiritual interests of society; nor does it suffice of itself even for the material interests. That which alone causes any material interests to exist, which alone enables any body of human beings to exist as a society, is national character: *that* it is, which causes one nation to succeed in what it attempts, another to fail; one nation to understand and aspire to elevated things, another to grovel in mean ones; which makes the greatness of one nation lasting, and dooms another to early and rapid decay. The true teacher of the fitting social arrangements for England, France, or America, is the one who can point out how the English, French or American character can be improved, and how it has been made what it is. A philosophy of laws and institutions, not founded on a philosophy of national character, is an absurdity. But what could Bentham's opinion be worth on national character? How could he, whose mind contained so few and so poor types of individual character, rise to that higher generalization? All he can do is but to indicate means by which, in any given state of the national mind, the material interests of society can be protected; saving the question, of which others must judge, whether the use of those means would have, on the national character, any injurious influence.

We have arrived, then, at a sort of estimate of what a philosophy like Bentham's can do. It can teach the means of organizing and regulating the merely *business* part of the social arrangements. Whatever can be understood or whatever done without reference to moral influences, his philosophy is equal to; where those influences require to be taken into account, it is at fault. He committed the mistake of supposing that the business part of human affairs was the whole of them; all at least that the legislator and the moralist had to do with. Not that he disregarded moral influences when he perceived them; but his want of imagination, small experience of human feelings, and ignorance of the filiation and connexion of feelings with one another, made this rarely the case.

The business part is accordingly the only province of human affairs which Bentham has cultivated with any success; into which he has introduced any considerable number of comprehensive and luminous practical principles. That is the field of his greatness; and there he is indeed great. He has swept away the accumulated cobwebs of centuries—he has untied knots which the efforts of the ablest thinkers, age after age, had only drawn tighter; and it is no exaggeration to say of him that over a great part of the field he was the first to shed the light of reason.

We turn with pleasure from what Bentham could not do, to what he did. It is an ungracious task to call a great benefactor of mankind to account for not being a greater—to insist upon the errors of a man who has originated more new truths, has given to the world more sound practical lessons, than it ever received, except in a few glorious instances, from any other individual. The unpleasing part of our work is ended. We are now to show the greatness of the man; the grasp which his intellect took of the subjects with which it was fitted to deal; the giant's task which was before him, and the hero's courage and strength with which he achieved it. Nor let that which he did be deemed of small account because its province was limited: man has but the choice to go a little way in many paths, or a great way in only one. The field of Bentham's labours was like the space between two parallel lines; narrow to excess in one direction, in another it reached to infinity.

Bentham's speculations, as we are already aware, began with law; and in that department he accomplished his greatest triumphs. He found the philosophy of law a chaos, he left it a science: he found the practice of the law an Augean stable, he turned the river into it which is mining and sweeping away mound after mound of its rubbish.

Without joining in the exaggerated invectives against lawyers, which Bentham sometimes permitted to himself, or making one portion of society alone accountable for the fault of all, we may say that circumstances had made English lawyers in a peculiar degree liable to the reproach of Voltaire, who defines lawyers the 'conservators of ancient barbarous usages'. The basis of the English law was, and still is, the feudal system. That system, like all those which existed as custom before they were established as law, possessed a certain degree of suitableness to the wants of the society among whom it grew up—that is to say, of a tribe of rude soldiers, holding a conquered people in subjection, and dividing its spoils among themselves. Advancing civilization had, however, converted this armed encampment of barbarous warriors in the midst of enemies reduced to slavery, into an industrious, commercial, rich, and free people. The laws which were suitable to the first of these states of society, could have no manner of relation to the circumstances of the second; which could not even have come into existence unless something had been done to adapt those laws to it. But the adaptation was not the result of thought and design; it arose not from any comprehensive consideration of the new state of society and its exigencies. What was done, was done by a struggle of centuries between the old barbarism and the new civilization; between the feudal aristocracy of conquerors, holding fast to the rude system they had established, and the conquered effecting their emancipation. The last was the growing power, but was never strong enough to break its bonds, though ever and anon some weak point gave way. Hence the law came to be like the costume of a full-grown man who had never put off the clothes made for him when he first went to school. Band after band had burst, and, as the rent widened, then, without removing anything except what might drop off of itself, the hole was darned, or patches of fresh law were brought from the nearest shop and stuck on. Hence all ages of English history have given one another rendezvous in English law; their several products may be seen all together, not interfused, but heaped one upon another, as many different ages of the earth may be read in some perpendicular section of its surface—the deposits of each successive period not substituted but superimposed on those of the preceding. And in the world of law no less than in the physical world, every commotion and conflict of the elements has left its mark behind in some break or irregularity of the strata: every struggle which ever rent the bosom of society is apparent in the disjointed condition of the part of the field of law which covers the spot: nay, the very traps and pitfalls which one contending party set for another are still standing, and the teeth not of hyenas only, but of foxes and all cunning animals, are imprinted on the curious remains found in these antediluvian caves.

In the English law, as in the Roman before it, the adaptations of barbarous laws to the growth of civilized society were made chiefly by stealth. They were generally made by the courts of justice, who could not help reading the new wants of mankind in the cases between man and man which came before them; but who, having no authority to make new laws for those new wants, were obliged to do the work covertly, and evade the jealousy and opposition of an ignorant, prejudiced, and for the most part brutal and tyrannical legislature. Some of the most necessary of these improvements, such as the giving force of law to trusts, and the breaking up of entails, were effected in actual opposition to the strongly-declared will of Parliament, whose clumsy hands, no match for the astuteness of judges, could not, after repeated trials, manage to make any law which the judges could not find a trick for rendering inoperative. The whole history of the contest about trusts may still be read in the words of a conveyance, as could the contest about entails, till the abolition of fine and recovery by a bill of the present Attorney-General; but dearly did the client pay for the cabinet of historical curiosities which he was obliged to purchase every time that he made a settlement of his estate. The result of this mode of improving social institutions was, that whatever new things were done had to be done in consistency with old forms and names; and the laws were improved with much the same effect as if, in the improvement of agriculture, the plough could only have been introduced by making it look like a spade; or as if, when the primeval practice of ploughing by the horse's tail gave way to the innovation of harness, the tail, for form's sake, had still remained attached to the plough.

When the conflicts were over, and the mixed mass settled down into something like a fixed state, and that state a very profitable and therefore a very agreeable one to lawyers, they, following the natural tendency of the human mind, began to theorize upon it, and, in obedience to necessity, had to digest it and give it a systematic form. It was from this thing of shreds and patches, in which the only part that approached to order or system was the early barbarous part, already more than half superseded, that English lawyers had to construct, by induction and abstraction, their philosophy of law; and without the logical habits and general intellectual cultivation which the lawyers of the Roman empire brought to a similar task. Bentham found the philosophy of law what English practising lawyers had made it; a jumble, in which *real* and *personal* property, *law* and *equity*, *felony*, *præmunire*, *misprision* and *misdemeanour*, words without a vestige of meaning when detached from the history of English institutions—mere tide-marks to point out the line which the sea and the shore, in their secular struggles, had adjusted as their mutual boundary—all passed for distinctions inherent in the nature of things; in which every absurdity, every lucrative abuse, had a reason found for it—a reason which only now and then even pretended to be drawn from expediency; most commonly a technical reason, one of mere form, derived from the old barbarous system. While the theory of the law was in this state, to describe what the practice of it was would require the pen of a Swift, or of Bentham himself. The whole progress of a suit at law seemed like a series of contrivances for lawyers' profit, in which the suitors were regarded as the prey; and if the poor were not the helpless victims of every Sir Giles Overreach who could pay the price, they might thank opinion and manners for it, not the law.

It may be fancied by some people that Bentham did an easy thing in merely calling all this absurd, and proving it to be so. But he began the contest a young man, and he had grown old before he had any followers. History will one day refuse to give credit to the intensity of the superstition which, till very lately, protected this mischievous mess from examination or doubt—passed off the charming representations of Blackstone for a just estimate of the English law, and proclaimed the shame of human reason to be the perfection of it. Glory to Bentham that he has dealt to this superstition its deathblow —that he has been the Hercules of this hydra, the St. George of this pestilent dragon! The honour is all his—nothing but his peculiar qualities could have done it. There were wanted his indefatigable perseverance, his firm self-reliance, needing no support from other men's opinion; his intensely practical turn of mind, his synthetical habits—above all, his peculiar method. Metaphysicians, armed with vague generalities, had often tried their hands at the subject, and left it no more advanced than they found it. Law is a matter of business; means and ends are the things to be considered in it, not abstractions: vagueness was not to be met by vagueness, but by definiteness and precision: details were not to be encountered with generalities, but with details. Nor could any progress be made, on such a subject, by merely showing that existing things were bad; it was necessary also to show how they might be made better. No great man whom we read of was qualified to do this thing except Bentham. He has done it, once and for ever.[24]

Into the particulars of what Bentham has done we cannot enter: many hundred pages would be required to give a tolerable abstract of it. To sum up our estimate under a few heads. First: he has expelled mysticism from the philosophy of law, and set the example of viewing laws in a practical light, as means to certain definite and precise ends. Secondly: he has cleared up the confusion and vagueness attaching to the idea of law in general, to the idea of a body of laws, and the various general ideas[25] therein involved. Thirdly: he demonstrated the necessity and practicability of *codification*, or the conversion of all law into a written and systematically arranged code: not like the Code Napoleon, a code without a single definition, requiring a constant reference to anterior precedent for the meaning of its technical terms; but one containing within itself all that is necessary for its own interpretation, together with a perpetual provision for its own emendation and improvement. He has shown of what parts such a code would consist; the relation of those parts to one another; and by his distinctions and classifications has done very much towards showing what should be, or might be, its nomenclature and arrangement. What he has left undone, he has made it comparatively easy for others to do. Fourthly: he has taken a systematic view* of the exigencies of society for which the civil code is intended to provide, and of the principles of human nature by which its provisions are to be tested: and this view, defective (as we have already intimated) wherever spiritual interests require to be taken into account, is excellent for that large portion of the laws of any country which are designed for the protection of material interests. Fifthly: (to say nothing of the subject of punishment, for which something considerable had been done before) he found the philosophy of judicial procedure, including that of judicial establishments and of evidence, in a more wretched state than even any other part of the philosophy of law; he carried it at once almost to perfection. He left it with every one of its principles established, and little remaining to be done even in the suggestion of practical arrangements.

These assertions in behalf of Bentham may be left, without fear for the result, in the hands of those who are competent to judge of them. There are now even in the highest seats of justice, men to whom the claims made for him will not appear extravagant. Principle after principle of those propounded by him is moreover making its way by infiltration into the understandings most shut against his influence, and driving nonsense and prejudice from one corner of them to another. The reform of the laws of any country according to his principles, can only be gradual, and may be long ere it is accomplished; but the work is in progress, and both parliament and the judges are every year doing something, and often something not inconsiderable, towards the forwarding of it.

It seems proper here to take notice of an accusation sometimes made both against Bentham and against the principle of codification —as if they required one uniform suit of ready-made laws for all times and all states of society. The doctrine of codification, as the word imports, relates to the form only of the laws, not their substance; it does not concern itself with what the laws should be, but declares that whatever they are, they ought to be systematically arranged, and fixed down to a determinate form of words. To the accusation, so far as it affects Bentham, one of the essays in the collection of his works (then for the first time published in English) is a complete answer: that 'On the Influence of Time and Place in Matters of Legislation'. It may there be seen that the different exigencies of different nations with respect to law, occupied his attention as systematically as any other portion of the wants which render laws necessary: with the limitations, it is true, which were set to all his speculations by the imperfections of his theory of human nature.

* See the 'Principles of Civil Law,' contained in Part II of his collected works.

For, taking, as we have seen, next to no account of national character and the causes which form and maintain it, he was precluded
from considering, except to a very limited extent, the laws of a
country as an instrument of national culture: one of their most
important aspects, and in which they must of course vary according
to the degree and kind of culture already attained; as a tutor gives
his pupil different lessons according to the progress already made in
his education. The same laws would not have suited our wild ancestors, accustomed to rude independence, and a people of Asiatics
bowed down by military despotism: the slave needs to be trained to
govern himself, the savage to submit to the government of others.
The same laws will not suit the English, who distrust everything
which emanates from general principles, and the French, who
distrust whatever does not so emanate.[26] Very different institutions
are needed to train to the perfection of their nature, or to constitute
into a united nation and social polity, an essentially *subjective* people
like the Germans, and an essentially *objective* people like those of
Northern and Central Italy; the one affectionate and dreamy, the
other passionate and worldly; the one trustful and loyal, the other
calculating and suspicious; the one not practical enough, the other
overmuch; the one wanting individuality, the other fellow-feeling;
the one failing for want of exacting enough for itself, the other for
want of conceding enough to others. Bentham was little accustomed
to look at institutions in their relation to these topics. The effects of
this oversight must of course be perceptible throughout his speculations, but we do not think the errors into which it led him very
material in the greater part of civil and penal law: it is in the department of constitutional legislation that they were fundamental.

The Benthamic theory of government has made so much noise in
the world of late years; it has held such a conspicuous place among
Radical philosophies, and Radical modes of thinking have partici-
pated so much more largely than any others in its spirit, that many
worthy persons imagine there is no other Radical philosophy extant.
Leaving such people to discover their mistake as they may, we shall
expend a few words in attempting to discriminate between the truth
and error of this celebrated theory.

There are three great questions in government. First, to what
authority is it for the good of the people that they should be subject?
Secondly, how are they to be induced to obey that authority? The
answers to these two questions vary indefinitely, according to the
degree and kind of civilization and cultivation already attained by a
people, and their peculiar aptitudes for receiving more. Comes next
a third question, not liable to so much variation, namely, by what
means are the abuses of this authority to be checked? This third

question is the only one of the three to which Bentham seriously
applies himself, and he gives it the only answer it admits of—
Responsibility: responsibility to persons whose interest, whose
obvious and recognizable interest, accords with the end in view—
good government. This being granted, it is next to be asked, in what
body of persons this identity of interest with good government, that
is, with the interest of the whole community, is to be found? In
nothing less, says Bentham, than the numerical majority: nor, say
we, even in the numerical majority itself; of no portion of the community less than all, will the interest coincide, at all times and in all
respects, with the interest of all. But since power given to all, by a
representative government, is in fact given to a majority; we are
obliged to fall back upon the first of our three questions, namely,
under what authority is it for the good of the people that they be
placed? And if to this the answer be, under that of a majority among
themselves, Bentham's system cannot be questioned. This one
assumption being made, his 'Constitutional Code' is admirable.
That extraordinary power which he possessed, of at once seizing
comprehensive principles, and scheming out minute details, is
brought into play with surpassing vigour in devising means for
preventing rulers from escaping from the control of the majority;
for enabling and inducing the majority to exercise that control un-
remittingly; and for providing them with servants of every desirable
endowment, moral and intellectual, compatible with entire sub-
servience to their will.

But *is* this fundamental doctrine of Bentham's political philosophy an universal truth? Is it, at all times and places, good for
mankind to be under the absolute authority of the majority of themselves? We say the authority, not the political authority merely,
because it is chimerical to suppose that whatever has absolute power
over men's bodies will not arrogate it over their minds—will not
seek to control (not perhaps by legal penalties, but by the persecu-
tions of society) opinions and feelings which depart from its standard; will not attempt to shape the education of the young by its
model, and to extinguish all books, all schools, all combinations of
individuals for joint action upon society, which may be attempted
for the purpose of keeping alive a spirit at variance with its own. Is it,
we say, the proper condition of man, in all ages and nations, to be
under the despotism of Public Opinion?

It is very conceivable that such a doctrine should find acceptance
from some of the noblest spirits, in a time of reaction against the
aristocratic governments of modern Europe; governments founded
on the entire sacrifice (except so far as prudence, and sometimes
humane feeling interfere) of the community generally, to the

self-interest and ease of a few. European reformers have been accustomed to see the numerical majority everywhere unjustly depressed,
everywhere trampled upon, or at the best overlooked, by governments; nowhere possessing power enough to extort redress of their
most positive grievances, provision for their mental culture, or even
to prevent themselves from being taxed avowedly for the pecuniary
profit of the ruling classes. To see these things, and to seek to put an
end to them, by means (among other things) of giving more political
power to the majority, constitutes Radicalism; and it is because so
many in this age have felt this wish, and have felt that the realization
of it was an object worthy of men's devoting their lives to it, that
such a theory of government as Bentham's has found favour with
them. But, though to pass from one form of bad government to
another be the ordinary fate of mankind, philosophers ought not
to make themselves parties to it, by sacrificing one portion of important truth to another.

The numerical majority of any society whatever, must consist of
persons all standing in the same social position, and having, in the
main, the same pursuits, namely, unskilled manual labourers; and
we mean no disparagement to them: whatever we say to their
disadvantage, we say equally of a numerical majority of shopkeepers,
or of squires. Where there is identity of position and pursuits, there
also will be identity of partialities, passions, and prejudices; and to
give to any one set of partialities, passions and prejudices, absolute
power, without counter-balance from partialities, passions and
prejudices of a different sort, is the way to render the correction of
any of those imperfections hopeless; to make one narrow, mean type
of human nature universal and perpetual, and to crush every influence
which tends to the further improvement of man's intellectual and
moral nature. There must, we know, be some paramount power in
society; and that the majority should be that power, is on the whole
right, not as being just in itself, but as being less unjust than any
other footing on which the matter can be placed. But it is necessary
that the institutions of society should make provision for keeping up,
in some form or other, as a corrective to partial views, and a shelter
for freedom of thought and individuality of character, a perpetual
and standing Opposition to the will of the majority. All countries
which have long continued progressive, or been durably great, have
been so because there has been an organized opposition to the ruling
power, of whatever kind that power was: plebeians to patricians,
clergy to kings, freethinkers to clergy, kings to barons, commons to
king and aristocracy. Almost all the greatest men who ever lived
have formed part of such an Opposition. Wherever some such quarrel
has not been going on—wherever it has been terminated by the

complete victory of one of the contending principles, and no new contest has taken the place of the old—society has either hardened into a Chinese stationariness, or fallen into dissolution. A centre of resistance, round which all the moral and social elements which the ruling power views with disfavour may cluster themselves, and behind whose bulwarks they may find shelter from the attempts of that power to hunt them out of existence, is as necessary where the opinion of the majority is sovereign, as where the ruling power is a hierarchy or an aristocracy. Where no such *point d'appui* exists, there the human race will inevitably degenerate; and the question, whether the United States, for instance, will in time sink into another China (also a most commercial and industrious nation), resolves itself, to us, into the question, whether such a centre of resistance will gradually evolve itself or not.

These things being considered, we cannot think that Bentham made the most useful employment which might have been made of his great powers, when, not content with enthroning the majority as sovereign, by means of universal suffrage without king or house of lords, he exhausted all the resources of ingenuity in devising means for riveting the yoke of public opinion closer and closer round the necks of all public functionaries, and excluding every possibility of the exercise of the slightest or most temporary influence either by a minority, or by the functionary's own notions of right. Surely when any power has been made the strongest power, enough has been done for it; care is thenceforth wanted rather to prevent that strongest power from swallowing up all others. Wherever all the forces of society act in one single direction, the just claims of the individual human being are in extreme peril. The power of the majority is salutary in so far as it is used defensively, not offensively—as its exertion is tempered by respect for the personality of the individual, and deference to superiority of cultivated intelligence. If Bentham had employed himself in pointing out the means by which institutions fundamentally democratic might be best adapted to the preservation and strengthening of those two sentiments, he would have done something more permanently valuable, and more worthy of his great intellect. Montesquieu, with the lights of the present age, would have done it; and we are possibly destined to receive this benefit from the Montesquieu of our own times, M. de Tocqueville.

Do we then consider Bentham's political speculations useless? Far from it. We consider them only one-sided. He has brought out into a strong light, has cleared from a thousand confusions and misconceptions, and pointed out with admirable skill the best means of promoting, one of the ideal qualities of a perfect government— identity of interest between the trustees and the community for whom they hold their power in trust. This quality is not attainable in its ideal perfection, and must moreover be striven for with a perpetual eye to all other requisites; but those other requisites must still more be striven for without losing sight of this: and when the slightest postponement is made of it to any other end, the sacrifice, often necessary, is never unattended with evil.[27] Bentham has pointed out how complete this sacrifice is in modern European societies: how exclusively, partial and sinister interests are the ruling power there, with only such check as is imposed by public opinion—which being thus, in the existing order of things, perpetually apparent as a source of good, he was led by natural partiality to exaggerate its intrinsic excellence. This sinister interest of rulers Bentham hunted through all its disguises, and especially through those which hide it from the men themselves who are influenced by it. The greatest service rendered by him to the philosophy of universal human nature, is, perhaps, his illustration of what he terms 'interest-begotten prejudice'—the common[28] tendency of man to make a duty and a virtue of following his self-interest. The idea, it is true, was far from being peculiarly Bentham's: the artifices by which we persuade ourselves that we are not yielding to our selfish inclinations when we are, had attracted the notice of all moralists, and had been probed by religious writers to a depth as much below Bentham's, as their knowledge of the profundities and windings of the human heart was superior to his. But it is selfish interest in the form of class-interest, and the class morality founded thereon, which Bentham has illustrated: the manner in which any set of persons who mix much together, and have a common interest, are apt to make that common interest their standard of virtue, and the social feelings of the members of the class are made to play into the hands of their selfish ones; whence the union so often exemplified in history, between the most heroic personal disinterestedness and the most odious class-selfishness. This was one of Bentham's leading ideas, and almost the only one by which he contributed to the elucidation of history: much of which, except so far as this explained it, must have been entirely inexplicable to him. The idea was given him by Helvetius, whose book, 'De l'Esprit', is one continued and most acute commentary on it; and, together with the other great idea of Helvetius, the influence of circumstances on character, it will make his name live by the side of Rousseau, when most[29] of the other French metaphysicians[30] of the eighteenth century will be extant as such only in literary history.

In the brief view which we have been able to give of Bentham's philosophy, it may surprise the reader that we have said so little about the first principle of it, with which his name is more identified than with anything else; the 'principle of utility', or, as he afterwards named it, 'the greatest-happiness principle'. It is a topic on which much were to be said, if there were room, or if it were in reality necessary for the just estimation of Bentham. On an occasion more suitable for a discussion of the metaphysics of morality, or on which the elucidations[31] necessary to make an opinion on so abstract a subject intelligible could be conveniently given, we should be fully prepared to state what we think on this subject. At present we shall only say, that while, under proper explanations, we entirely agree with Bentham in his principle, we do not hold with him that all right thinking on the details of morals depends on its express assertion.[32] We think utility, or happiness, much too complex and indefinite an end to be sought except through the medium of various secondary ends, concerning which there may be, and often is, agreement among persons who differ in their ultimate standard; and about which there does in fact prevail a much greater unanimity among thinking persons, than might be supposed from their diametrical divergence on the great questions of moral metaphysics. As mankind are much more nearly of one nature, than of one opinion about their own nature, they are more[33] easily brought to agree in their intermediate principles, *vera illa et media axiomata*, as Bacon says, than in their first principles: and the attempt to make the bearings of actions upon the ultimate end more evident than they can be made by referring them to the intermediate ends, and to estimate their value by a direct reference to human happiness, generally terminates in attaching most importance, not to those effects which are really the greatest, but to those which can most easily be pointed to and individually identified. Those who adopt utility as a standard can seldom apply it truly except through the secondary principles; those who reject it, generally do no more than erect those secondary principles into first principles.[34] It is when two or more of the secondary principles conflict, that a direct appeal to some first principle becomes necessary; and then commences the practical importance of the utilitarian controversy; which is, in other respects, a question of arrangement and logical subordination rather than of practice; important principally in a purely scientific point of view, for the sake of the systematic unity and coherency of ethical philosophy.[35] It is probable, however, that to the principle of utility we owe all that Bentham did; that it was necessary for him to find a first principle which he could receive as self-evident, and to which he could attach all his other doctrines as logical consequences: that to him systematic unity was an indispensable condition of his confidence in his own intellect. And there is something further to be remarked. Whether happiness be or be not the end to which morality should be referred—that it be referred to an *end* of some sort, and not left in the dominion of vague feeling or inexplicable internal conviction, that it be made a matter of reason and calculation, and not merely of sentiment, is essential to the very idea of moral philosophy; is, in fact, what renders argument or discussion on moral questions possible. That the morality of actions depends on the consequences which they tend to produce, is the doctrine of rational persons of all schools; that the good or evil of those consequences is measured solely by pleasure or pain, is all of the doctrine of the school of utility, which is peculiar to it.

In so far as Bentham's adoption of the principle of utility induced him to fix his attention upon the consequences of actions as the consideration determining their morality, so far he was indisputably in the right path: though to go far in it without wandering, there was needed a greater knowledge of the formation of character, and of the consequences of actions upon the agent's own frame of mind, than Bentham possessed. His want of power to estimate this class of consequences, together with his want of the degree of modest deference which, from those who have not competent experience of their own, is due to the experience of others on that part of the subject, greatly limit the value of his speculations on questions of practical ethics.[36]

He is chargeable also with another error, which it would be improper to pass over, because nothing has tended more to place him in opposition to the common feelings of mankind, and to give to his philosophy that cold, mechanical and ungenial air which characterizes the popular idea of a Benthamite. This error, or rather one-sidedness, belongs to him not as a utilitarian, but as a moralist by profession, and in common with almost all professed moralists, whether religious or philosophical: it is that of treating the *moral* view of actions and characters, which is unquestionably the first and most important mode of looking at them, as if it were the sole one: whereas it is only one of three, by all of which our sentiments towards the human being may be, ought to be, and without entirely crushing our own nature cannot but be, materially influenced. Every human action has three aspects: its *moral* aspect, or that of its *right* and *wrong*; its *æsthetic* aspect, or that of its beauty; its *sympathetic* aspect, or that of its *loveableness*. The first addresses itself to our reason and conscience; the second to our imagination; the third to our human fellow-feeling. According to the first, we approve or disapprove; according to the second, we admire, or despise; according to the third, we love, pity or dislike. The morality of an action depends on its foreseeable consequences; its beauty, and its loveableness, or the reverse, depend on the qualities which it is evidence of. Thus, a lie is *wrong*, because its effect is to mislead, and because it tends to destroy the confidence of man in man; it is also *mean*, because it is cowardly—because it proceeds from not daring to face the consequences of telling the truth—or at best is evidence of want of that *power* to compass our ends by straightforward means, which is conceived as properly belonging to every person not deficient in energy or in understanding. The action of Brutus in sentencing his sons was *right*, because it was executing a law essential to the freedom of his country, against persons of whose guilt there was no doubt: it was *admirable*, because it evinced a rare degree of patriotism, courage and self-control; but there was nothing *loveable* in it; it affords either no presumption in regard to loveable qualities, or a presumption of their deficiency. If one of the sons had engaged in the conspiracy from affection for the other, his action would have been loveable, though neither moral nor admirable. It is not possible for any sophistry to confound these three modes of viewing an action; but it is very possible to adhere to one of them exclusively, and lose sight of the rest. Sentimentality consists in setting the last two of the three above the first; the error of moralists in general, and of Bentham, is to sink the two latter entirely. This is pre-eminently the case with Bentham: he both wrote and felt as if the moral standard ought not only to be paramount (which it ought), but to be alone; as if it ought to be the sole master of all our actions, and even of all our sentiments; as if either to admire or like, or despise or dislike a person for any action which neither does good nor harm, or which does not do a good or a harm proportioned to the sentiment entertained, were an injustice and a prejudice. He carried this so far, that there were certain phrases which, being expressive of what he considered to be this groundless liking or aversion, he could not bear to hear pronounced in his presence. Among these phrases were those of *good* and *bad taste*. He thought it an insolent piece of dogmatism in one person to praise or condemn another in a matter of taste: as if men's likings and dislikings, on things in themselves indifferent, were not full of the most important inferences as to every point of their character; as if a person's tastes did not show him to be wise or a fool, cultivated or ignorant, gentle or rough, sensitive or callous, generous or sordid, benevolent or selfish, conscientious or depraved.

Connected with the same topic are Bentham's peculiar opinions on poetry. Much more has been said than there is any foundation for, about his contempt for the pleasures of imagination, and for the fine arts.[37] Music was throughout life his favourite amusement; painting, sculpture and the other arts addressed to the eye, he was so far from holding in any contempt, that he occasionally recognizes them as means employable for important social ends; though his ignorance of the deeper springs of human character prevented him (as it prevents most Englishmen)[38] from suspecting how profoundly such things enter into the moral nature of man, and into the education both of the individual and of the race. But towards poetry in the narrower sense, that which employs the language of words, he entertained no favour. Words, he thought, were perverted from their proper office when they were employed in uttering anything but precise logical truth. He says, somewhere in his works, that, 'quantity of pleasure being equal, push-pin is as good as poetry': but this is only a paradoxical way of stating what he would equally have said of the things which he most valued and admired. Another aphorism is attributed to him, which is much more characteristic of his view of this subject: 'All poetry is misrepresentation'. Poetry, he thought, consisted essentially in exaggeration for effect: in proclaiming some one view of a thing very emphatically, and suppressing all the limitations and qualifications. This trait of character seems to us a curious example of what Mr. Carlyle strikingly calls 'the completeness of limited men'. Here is a philosopher who is happy within his narrow boundary as no man of indefinite range ever was: who flatters himself that he is so completely emancipated from the essential law of poor human intellect, by which it can only see one thing at a time well, that he can even turn round upon the imperfection and lay a solemn interdict upon it. Did Bentham really suppose that it is in poetry only that propositions cannot be exactly true, cannot contain in themselves all the limitations and qualifications with which they require to be taken when applied to practice? We have seen how far his own prose propositions are from realizing this Utopia: and even the attempt to approach it would be incompatible not with poetry merely, but with oratory, and popular writing of every kind. Bentham's charge is true to the fullest extent; all writing which undertakes to make men feel truths as well as see them, does take up one point at a time, does seek to impress that, to drive that home, to make it sink into and colour the whole mind of the reader or hearer. It is justified in doing so, if the portion of truth which it thus enforces be that which is called for by the occasion. All writing addressed to the feelings has a natural tendency to exaggeration; but Bentham should have remembered that in this, as in many things, we must aim at too much, to be assured of doing enough.

From the same principle in Bentham came the intricate and involved style, which makes his later writings books for the student only, not the general reader. It was from his perpetually aiming at impracticable precision. Nearly all his earlier and many parts of his later writings, are models, as we have already observed, of light, playful and popular style: a Benthamiana might be made of passages worthy of Addison or Goldsmith. But in his later years and more advanced studies, he fell into a Latin or German structure of sentence, foreign to the genius of the English language. He could not bear, for the sake of clearness and the reader's ease, to say, as ordinary men are content to do, a little more than the truth in one sentence, and correct it in the next. The whole of the qualifying remarks which he intended to make, he insisted upon imbedding as parentheses in the very middle of the sentence itself. And thus the sense being so long suspended, and attention being required to the accessory ideas before the principal idea had been properly seized, it became difficult, without some practice, to make out the train of thought. It is fortunate that so many of the most important parts of his writings are free from this defect. We regard it as a *reductio ad absurdum* of his objection to poetry. In trying to write in a manner against which the same objection should not lie, he could stop nowhere short of utter unreadableness, and after all attained no more accuracy than is compatible with opinions as imperfect and one-sided as those of any poet or sentimentalist breathing. Judge then in what state literature and philosophy would be, and what chance they would have of influencing the multitude, if his objection were allowed, and all styles of writing banished which would not stand his test.

We must here close this brief and imperfect view of Bentham and his doctrines; in which many parts of the subject have been entirely untouched, and no part done justice to, but which at least proceeds from an intimate familiarity with his writings, and is nearly the first attempt at an impartial estimate of his character as a philosopher, and of the result of his labours to the world.

After every abatement, and it has been seen whether we have made our abatements sparingly—there remains to Bentham an indisputable place among the great intellectual benefactors of mankind. His writings will long form an indispensable part of the education of the highest order of practical thinkers; and the collected edition of them ought to be in the hands of everyone who would either understand his age, or take any beneficial part in the great business of it.[39]

NOTES

1. In *London and Westminster Review* (hereafter called *LWR*) 'progressive' read 'movement'.
2. In *LWR*, the sentence up to this point read: 'The influence of the former has made itself felt chiefly upon Movement minds, of the latter on Conservative ones'.
3. In *LWR* 'in these times' read 'in these later days'.
4. In the original version, 'traditional doctrines' read 'spiritual truths'.

5. In the *LWR* version the sentence ended here and was followed by the following passage: 'Hume, the Prince of *dilettanti*; from whose writings one will hardly learn that there is such a thing as truth, far less that it is attainable; but only that pro and con or everything may be argued with infinite ingenuity, and furnishes a fine intellectual exercise. This absolute scepticism very naturally brought him round to Toryism in practice; for if no faith can be had in the operations of human intellect, and one side of every question is about as likely as another to be true, a man will commonly be inclined to prefer that order of things which, being no more wrong than every other, he has hitherto found compatible with his private comforts. Accordingly Hume's scepticism agreed very well with the comfortable classes, until it began to reach the uncomfortable: when the discovery was made that, although men would be content to be rich without a faith, men would not be content to be poor without it, and religion and morality came into fashion again as the cheap defence of rents and tithes.'
6. In *LWR*, 'many' read 'some few'.
7. Part I. 161–162, of the collected edition.
8. In the *LWR* the entire paragraph read as follows: 'Few, we believe, are now of opinion that these phrases and similar ones have nothing more in them than Bentham saw. But it will be as little pretended, now-a-days, by any person of authority as a thinker, that the phrases can pass as reasons, till after their meaning has been completely analysed, and translated into more precise language: until the standard they appeal to is ascertained, and the *sense* in which, and the *limits* within which, they are admissible as arguments, clearly marked out.'
9. The original version had 'from Hume and Helvetius'.
10. Author of another book which made no little sensation when it first appeared, 'An Estimate of the Manners of the Times.'
11. The two sentences, from 'we ask any one . . .' to '. . . on a definite point' read is *LWR* as: 'we ask any one who has read his philosophical writings, the "De Finibus" for instance, whether the arguments of the Epicureans are not as perfect a specimen of σκιαμαχία as those of the Stoics or Platonists— vague phrases which different persons may understand in different senses and no person in any definite sense; rhetoric appeals to common notions, to εἰκότα and σημεῖα instead of τεκμήρια notions never narrowly looked into and seldom exactly true, or true at all in the sense necessary to support the conclusion. Of any systematic appeal to facts and experience, which might seem to be their peculiar province, the Epicurean moralists are devoid as any of the other schools; they never take a question to pieces and join issue on a definite point'.
12. In *LWR* this sentence read as follows: 'It is not to be denied that Bentham's method of laying out his subject is admirable as a preservative against one kind of narrow and partial views.'
13. In *LWR* 'reach' read 'go'.
14. In *LWR* 'wide subjects' read 'a wide subject'.
15. In *LWR* 'the "Deontology"' read 'Bowring's "Deontology"'.
16. In *LWR*, 'a thoughtful regard' read 'reverence'.
17. In *LWR* 'often fail to do' read 'seldom do'.
18. In *LWR* 'generations' read 'nations'.
19. In *LWR* 'conception' read 'knowledge'.
20. In *LWR* 'agencies' read 'things'.
21. In *LWR* 'to deny or disparage all feelings and mental state' read 'to deny the existence of all spiritual influences'.
22. In a passage in the last volume of his book on Evidence, and possibly in one

or two other places, the 'love of justice' is spoken of as a feeling inherent in almost all mankind. It is impossible, without explanations now unattainable, to ascertain what sense is to be put upon casual expressions so inconsistent with the general tenor of his philosophy.

23. In the original version the last sentence read as follows: 'The moralities of these questions depend on considerations of which Bentham not only was not a competent judge, but which he never even took into the account.'

24. In *LWR* the sentence continued 'witness these volumes, and the others by which they are to be followed'.

25. In *LWR* 'the various general ideas' read 'all the general ideas'.

26. In *LWR* this sentence read as: 'The same laws will not suit the English, who place their habitual reliance in themselves, and the French, who place theirs in leaders.'

27. [For further illustrations of this point, see the Appendix to *Dissertations and Discussions*.]

28. In the original version 'common' read 'inherent'.

29. In the original version 'most' read 'all'.

30. In the original version 'metaphysicians' read 'philosophers'.

31. In the *LWR* version 'elucidations' read 'explanations'.

32. In the original version this sentence read as follows: 'All we intend to say at present is, that we are much nearer to agreeing with Bentham in his principle, than in the degree of importance which he attached to it.'

33. In the original version 'more' read 'much more'.

34. In the original version a new paragraph began here and read as follows: 'We consider, therefore, the utilitarian controversy as a question of arrangement and logical subordination rather than of practice; important principally in a purely scientific point of view, for the sake of the systematic unity and coherency of ethical philosophy. Whatever be our own opinion on the subject, it is from no such source that we look for the great improvements which we believe are destined to take place in ethical doctrine.'

35. This sentence does not exist in the original version.

36. In the original version this sentence reads as follows: 'His want of power to estimate this class of consequences, together with his want of the degree of modest respect (a far different thing from blind deference) due to the traditionary opinions and feelings in which the experience of mankind on that part of the subject lies embodied, renders him, we conceive, a most unsafe guide on questions of practical ethics.'

37. In *LWR* the sentence read as follows: 'Much has been said, for which there is no foundation about his contempt for the pleasures of imagination and for the fine arts.'

38. The clause in the bracket did not exist in the *LWR* version.

39. NB. This footnote did not exist in the original. Since the first publication of this paper, Lord Brougham's brilliant series of characters has been published, including a sketch of Bentham. Lord Brougham's view of Bentham's characteristics agrees in the main points, so far as it goes, with the result of our more minute examination, but there is an imputation cast upon Bentham, of a jealous and splenetic disposition in private life, of which we feel called upon to give at once a contradiction and an explanation. It is indispensable to a correct estimate of any of Bentham's dealings with the world, to bear in mind that in everything except abstract speculation he was to the last, what we have called him, essentially a boy. He had the freshness, the simplicity, the confidingness, the liveliness and activity, all the delightful qualities of boyhood, and the weaknesses which are the reverse side of those qualities—the undue importance attached to trifles, the habitual mismeasurement of the

practical bearing and value of things, the readiness to be either delighted or offended on inadequate cause. These were the real sources of what was unreasonable in some of his attacks on individuals, and in particular on Lord Brougham, on the subject of his Law Reforms; they were no more the effect of envy or malice, or any really unamiable quality, than the freaks of a pettish child, and are scarcely a fitter subject of censure or criticism.

Chapter 2

Bentham

William Whewell

[The following pages are taken from Whewell's *Lectures on the History of Moral Philosophy*, Cambridge, 1862. Only the first few pages that are largely of biographical interest have been omitted. Whewell, one of Mill's most distinguished and eminent contemporaries, wrote extensively on logic, ethics, metaphysics and philosophy of science. His *Lectures* is a perceptive analysis of various moral theories and made considerable impact at the time.

Mill replied to Whewell's criticisms in his 'Dr. Whewell on Moral Philosophy'. For reasons of consistency and loyalty, as well as to correct the impression that he was 'in sympathy with the reaction of the nineteenth century against the eighteenth' Mill felt he had to reject many of Whewell's criticisms. However a discerning reader cannot fail to notice how Mill's defence of Bentham is less than whole-hearted and how he subtly dissociates utilitarianism from Benthamism. It is also worth observing that the Whewell-Mill controversy bears a not unexpected resemblance to the famous Hart-Devlin controversy. See, for example, p. 505ff in *Dissertations and Discussions*, vol. II—Editor.]

I

In considering Bentham's system of Morality, I by no means wish to make it my sole business to point out the errors and defects of it. On the contrary, it will be very important to my purpose to show what amount of truth there resides in it; since by so doing, I shall both account for the extensive acceptance which it has found, and shall be advancing towards that system which contains all that is true in all preceding systems: and *that* is plainly the system at which we of this day ought to aim.

Of Bentham's system, indeed, we have in a great measure spoken, in speaking of Paley's: for as I have said, the two systems are in principle the same; and the assertions of Bentham's followers as to the great difference of the two systems, vanish on examination. The basis of Paley's scheme is Utility: Utility for the promotion of Human Happiness. Human Happiness is composed of Pleasures: Pleasures are to be estimated by their intensity and Duration. All this Paley has. Has Bentham anything more? He has nothing more which is essential in the scheme of Morality, so far as this groundwork goes. For though in enumerating the elements in the estimate of pleasures, Bentham adds to Intensity and Duration, others, as Certainty, Propinquity, Fecundity, Purity (in the sense which I have spoken of); these do not much alter the broad features of the scheme. But undoubtedly Bentham attempts to build upon this groundwork more systematically than Paley does. If there is to be a Morality erected on such a basis as that just described, the pleasures (and the pains as well) which are the guides and governors of human action must be enumerated, classed, weighed and measured. It is by determining the value of a *lot* of pleasure (the phrase is Bentham's) resulting from an act, that the moral value of an act is known, in this system. We must therefore have all the pleasures which man can feel, passed in review; and all the ways in which these pleasures can increase or diminish by human actions. This done, we shall be prepared to pass judgment on human actions, and to assign to each its rank and value in the moral scale; its title to reward or punishment on these principles.

Can this be done? Has Bentham done this? If he has, is it not really a valuable task performed? These questions naturally occur.

In reply, I may say that the task would undoubtedly be a valuable one, if it were possible; but that, so far as the moral value of actions is concerned, it is not possible, for reasons which I will shortly state; that even for the appropriation of punishment in the construction of laws, the purpose for which the author mainly intended it, it is far from completely executed, or perhaps capable of being completely executed; but that the attempt to execute it in a complete and systematic manner, over the whole field of human action, led to many useful and important remarks on schemes of law and of punishment; and that these, along with the air of system, which has always a great effect upon men, not unnaturally won for Bentham great attention, and even gave a sort of ascendancy to the rough and distorting pleasantry which he exercised towards opponents. I may afterwards speak of his merits as a jural and political philosopher, but I must first explain why, as I conceive, his mode of estimating the moral value of actions cannot suffice for the purposes of Morality.

Let it be taken for granted, as a proposition which is true, if the terms which it involves be duly understood, that actions are right and virtuous in proportion as they promote the happiness of mankind; the actions being considered upon the whole, and with regard to all their consequences. Still, I say, we cannot make this truth the basis of morality, for two reasons: first, we cannot calculate all the consequences of any action, and thus cannot estimate the degree in which it promotes human happiness; second, happiness is derived from moral elements, and therefore we cannot properly derive morality from happiness. The calculable happiness resulting from actions cannot determine their virtue; first, because the resulting happiness is not calculable; and secondly, because the virtue is one of the things which determines the resulting happiness.

These assertions are, I think, tolerably evident of themselves; but we may dwell upon them a little longer. First, I say the amount of happiness resulting from any action is not calculable. If we ask whether a given action will increase or diminish the total amount of human happiness, it is impossible to answer with any degree of certainty. Take ordinary cases. I am tempted to utter a flattering falsehood: to gratify some sensual desire contrary to ordinary moral rules. How shall I determine, on the greatest happiness-principle, whether the act is virtuous or the contrary? In the first place, the direct effect of each act is to give pleasure, to another by flattery, to myself by sensual gratification: and pleasure is the material of happiness, in the scheme we are now considering. But by the flattering lie, I promote falsehood, which is destructive of confidence, and so, of human comfort. Granted that I do this, in some degree, although I may easily say, that I shall never allow myself to speak falsely, except when it will give pleasure, and thus, I may maintain that I shall not shake confidence in any case in which it is of any value; but granted that I do in some degree shake the general fabric of mutual human confidence, by my flattering lie, still the question remains, *how much* I do this; whether in such a degree as to overbalance the pleasure, which is the primary and direct consequence of the act. How small must be the effect of my solitary act upon the whole scheme of human action and habit! How clear and decided is the direct effect of increasing the happiness of my hearer! And in the same way we may reason concerning the sensual gratification. The pleasure is evident and certain; the effect on other men's habits obscure and uncertain. Who will know it? Who will be influenced by it of those who do know it? What appreciable amount of pain will it produce in its consequences, to balance the palpable pleasure, which, according to our teachers, is the only real good? It appears to me that it is impossible to answer these questions in any way which will prove, on these principles, mendacious flattery, and illegitimate sensuality, to be vicious and immoral. They may possibly produce, take in all their effects, a balance of evil; but if they do, it is by some process which we cannot trace with any clearness, and the result is one which we cannot calculate with any certainty or even probability; and therefore, on this account, because the resulting evil of such falsehood and sensuality is not calculable or appreciable, we cannot, by calculation of resulting evil, show falsehood and sensuality to be vices; and the like is true of other vices; and on this ground the construction of a scheme of Morality on Mr. Bentham's plan is plainly impossible.[1]

But the disciples of Bentham will perhaps urge that falsehood is wrong, even if it produce immediate pleasure, because the violation of a general rule is an evil which no single pleasurable consequence can counterbalance; and because, by acts of falsehood, we weaken and destroy our own habit of truth. And the like might be said in the other case. Now when men speak in this manner, they are undoubtedly approaching to a sound and tenable morality. I say *approaching* to it; for they are still at a considerable distance from a really moral view, as I shall have to show. But though when men speak in this manner, they are approaching to sound morality, they are receding from the fundamental principle of Bentham. For on that principle, how does it appear that the evil, that is the pain, arising from violating a general rule once, is too great to be overbalanced by the pleasurable consequences of that single violation? The actor says, I acknowledge the general rule? I do not deny its value; but I do not intend that this one act should be drawn into consequence. I assert my right to look at the special case, as well as at the general rule. I have weighed one against the other: I see that the falsehood gives a clear balance of pleasure: therefore on our Master's principles, it is right and virtuous. What does the Master say to this? If he say, 'you must be wrong in violating the general rule of truth—of veracity: no advantage can compensate for that evil'; if he say this, he speaks like a moralist; but not like a Benthamite. He interposes, with an imperative dogma drawn from the opposite school, to put down the manifest consequences of his own principles. If, on the other hand, he allow the plea; if he say, Be sure that your lie brings more pleasure than pain, and then lie, and know that you are doing a virtuous act; then indeed he talks like a genuine assertor of Mr. Bentham's principles, but he ceases to be a moralist in any ordinary sense of the term.

But let us look at the other reason against an act of falsehood, that by such acts we weaken and destroy our habit of truth. To this, the person concerned might reply, that a habit of truth, absolute and unconditional, is, on Bentham's principles, of no value; that if there be cases in which the pleasure arising from falsehood is greater than the pleasure arising from truth, then, in these cases, falsehood is virtuous and veracity is vicious; that, on these principles, the habit to be cultivated is not a habit of telling truth *always*, but a habit of telling truth *when* it produces pleasure more than pain. To this I do not know what our Benthamite could reply, except that a habit of telling truth so limited, is not a habit of veracity at all; that the only way to form a habit of veracity is, to tell truth always, and without limiting conditions; that is, to tell truth if we tell anything; not to tell falsehood. This again is teaching quite consistent in the mouth of a moralist: but not consistent in the mouth of a Benthamite. It makes the regulation of our own habits, our own desires, paramount over anything which can be gained, pleasure or profit, by the violation and transgression of such regulation. Veracity comes first; pleasure and gain are subordinate. And this is our morality. But the Benthamist doctrine is, pleasure first of all things: veracity, good it may be; but good only because, and only so far as, it is an instrument of pleasure.

The other branch of the argument will be pursued in the next Lecture.

II
OBJECTIONS TO HIS SYSTEM

In the last Lecture, I stated that the Benthamite scheme of determining the morality of actions by the amount of happiness which they produce, is incapable of being executed for two reasons; first, that we cannot calculate all the pleasure or pain resulting from any one action; and next, that the happiness produced by actions depends on their morality. I have attempted to illustrate the former argument. I now proceed to the latter.

In the last lecture I tried to show that the Benthamite doctrine, that acts are virtuous in proportion as they calculably produce happiness, that is, again, according to the Benthamite analysis, pleasure, cannot be made the basis of morality, because we cannot for such purposes calculate the amount of pleasure which acts produce: and if we attempt to remedy the obvious defects of calculations on such subjects, by taking into account rules and habits, we run away from the declared fundamental principle altogether.

To show further how impossible it is to found morality on the Benthamite basis, I now proceed to observe that we cannot derive the moral value of actions from the happiness which they produce, because the happiness depends upon the morality. Why should a man be truthful and just? Because acts of veracity and justice, even if they do not produce immediate gratification to him and his friends in other ways (and it may easily be that they do not) at least produce pleasure in this way; that they procure him his own approval and that of all good men. To us, this language is intelligible and significant; but the Benthamite must analyse it further. What does it mean according to him? A man's own approval of his act, means that he thinks it virtuous. And therefore, the matter stands thus. He (being a Benthamite) thinks it virtuous, because it gives him pleasure: and it gives him pleasure because he thinks it virtuous. This is a vicious circle, quite as palpable as any of those in which Mr. Bentham is so fond of representing his adversaries as revolving. And in like manner, with regard to the approval of others. The action is virtuous, says the Benthamite, because it produces pleasure; namely the pleasure arising from the approval of neighbours; they approve it, and think it virtuous, he also says, because it gives pleasure. The virtue depends upon the pleasure, the pleasure depends upon the virtue. Here again is a circle from which there is no legitimate egress. We may grant that, taking into account all the elements of happiness, the pleasures of self-approval, of peace of mind and harmony within us, and of the approval of others, of the known sympathy of all good men; we may grant that including these elements, virtue always does produce an overbalance of happiness; but then we cannot make this moral truth the basis of morality, because we cannot extricate the happiness and the virtue, the one from the other, so as to make the first, the happiness, the foundation of the second, the virtue.

This consideration of virtue itself as one of the sources of pleasure, one of the elements of happiness, is a point at which, as appears to me, the Benthamite doctrine loses all the clearness which, in its early steps, it so ostentatiously puts forward. Considering the pretensions of the system to rigorous analysis, I cannot but think there is something robustly rude in the mode in which these matters of self-approval and approval from others are disposed of. That self-approval, and the approbation of neighbours, are pleasures, cannot be denied. Accordingly, they are reckoned by Bentham in his list of pleasures. But these sentiments involve morality—the very thing we are analysing into its elements: how are we to give an account of this ingredient of pleasure? How does Bentham make these into *elementary* pleasures? or if not elementary, whence does he take the moral *element* of these pleasures, having already professed to resolve morality into pleasures? As I have said, I think the answer to these questions is one which deprives Bentham's analysis of Morality of all coherence and completeness. In order to make an opening, by which Morality may find its way into the mind of the actor and of the spectators, he throws the theatre open to an unbounded and undefined range of external influences. He has recourse to the dimness of childhood and to the confusion of the crowd, to conceal his defect of logic. Whence does man get his grounds of self-approval and self-condemnation? 'From *Education*.' Where reside the rules by which his neighbours applaud or condemn? 'In *Public Opinion*.' And thus these two wide and loose abstractions, *Education* and *Public Opinion*, become the real sources of Morality. They are really the elements into which all Morality is analysed by Bentham: those, which themselves need analysis far more than the subjects which he began to analyse, Virtues and Vices. For is not Education (moral Education) the process by which we learn what are Virtues and what are Vices? Is not Public Opinion the Opinion which decides what acts are virtuous and what are vicious? What an analysis then is this!

Virtue is what gives pleasure. Among the principal pleasures so produced are self-approval and public approval. Self-approval is governed by what we have been taught to think virtuous: Public approval, by what the Public thinks virtuous. Surely we are here again in a palpable circle; as indeed we must be, if we want to have a Morality which does not depend on a moral basis.

That Bentham really does recur to Public Opinion, however loose and insecure a foundation that may be, for the basis of Morality, is indeed abundantly evident from the general course of his discussion of the subject. Among the *Sanctions* by which the laws of human conduct are enforced, he puts in a prominent place, and constantly and emphatically refers to, what he calls the *Popular or Moral* Sanction; that is his often-repeated phrase, the *Popular or Moral* Sanction, as an enforcing power, which stands side by side with legal punishment, physical pain, and the like. *Popular* and *Moral* with him, then, are, in this application at least, synonymous, or coincident. He cannot tell us what is moral, except he first know what is popular. Popular Opinion is, with him, an ultimate fact, upon which Morality depends. He cannot correct Popular Opinion in any authoritative manner, for it supplies one of his ruling principles; namely, one of the pleasures by which he determines what is right and what is wrong. If murder, sensuality, falsehood, oppression, be in any cases popular, this popularity tends to make them virtues, for it gives them the *reward* of virtue; and his virtue looks only *to* reward, and to such reward among others. True, he may, in certain cases, say that the pain produced by such acts overweighs the pleasure, even including the pleasure of popular applause. But then, if the applause bestowed by popular opinion be strong enough, if the pleasure which it gives becomes still greater, the opposite pain may thus be overbalanced, and those acts are still virtues. That murder, sensuality, falsehood, oppression, may, by many men, be practised as virtues, on account of such applause, is, no doubt, true; but it cannot but sound strange to us, to hear *that* doctrine called Morality, which approves of them on this account. All mankind include in their notion of moral rules this condition; that such rules, when delivered by a person who, being a moralist, cannot allow himself to assent to popular errors and vices, shall correct and rebuke such errors and such vices. But this he cannot do if he depend upon Popular Opinion for one of the Sanctions of his Morality; and not only for one of these sanctions, but for the only one which is specially called *moral*.

Bentham does indeed attempt to make some stand against popular judgment, at one period of his progress: for he warns his disciples against the general tendency to decide the character of actions and springs of action, by giving to them names implying approval and disapproval; what he calls *eulogistic* and *dyslogistic* names. But these eulogistic and dyslogistic names are part of the expression of public opinion; part of the machinery by which the 'popular or moral sanction' works. Men are deterred from actions that have a bad name; led to actions that have a good name. It is surely, on his grounds, fit that they should be so. If they were not, where would be the effect of this popular sanction? If men were not eulogistic and dyslogistic in their way of speaking of actions, how should they express that moral judgment which is an essential part of Bentham's system—which is the broadest foundation stone of his edifice of Morality?

Of course, we too know that such names have their influence, and that, a very powerful one. We know that the popular voice on subjects of morality produces a mighty effect upon men. We rejoice in this influence, when it is on the side of true morality. We rejoice, too, to think that in general it *is so*; that truth, kindness, justice, purity, orderliness, are generally approved by men; and that, in general, the popular voice enforces the moralist's precepts. But we do not take from the popular voice our judgment as to what actions are truthful, kind, just, pure, orderly. Bentham might perhaps reply, but neither does *he* thus form his judgments of actions; that he too has grounds on which he can correct the popular prejudices respecting actions. But still, he cannot but allow that, according to him, the popular prejudice does much to make those actions virtuous which it approves, those actions vicious which it condemns: since it can award to the one class, honour, to the other, infamy: and where are there pleasures and pains greater than honour, and than infamy? Now by the greatness of the pleasures, and the pains, resulting from actions, their virtuous or vicious character according to him is determined. So that, as we have said, virtue and vice depending upon pleasures and pain, and pleasures and pain again depending upon the popular opinion of right and wrong, we cannot here find any independent basis for virtue and vice, and right and wrong.

But it may be asked, does not the popular judgment of certain classes of actions as right, and certain others as wrong, depend upon an apprehension, however obscure and confused, that the former class are advantageous to the community, the latter disadvantageous? To this I reply, that if by advantage be meant external tangible advantage, independent of mental pleasures, I conceive that they do not so depend: and if we take in mental pleasures, we are brought back to that independent moral element which the utilitarians wish to exclude. But if it be alleged that this (namely, general advantage) is the ground of the public opinion of the rightness and wrongness of actions, let it be shown that it is so. Let the Benthamite begin by analysing public opinion into such elements; and let him use, in his system, those elements, and not the unanalysed opinion in that compound and concrete form in which he calls it 'the popular or moral sanction'. If Morality depend upon external advantage, both directly, and through the popular apprehension of it, let this advantage be made, once for all, the basis of the system, and not brought in both directly in its manifest form, and indirectly, disguised as popular or moral opinion. But I think that Bentham has not so analysed public opinion; and has been unable to do so. And that he despaired of so doing, I judge from the impatience with which he speaks of the eulogistic and dyslogistic phraseology by which such opinion is conveyed. If he could have said, 'the eulogistic terms imply a supposed tendency to the increase of human pleasure, and I will show you how far they are right'; these terms would have been useful steps to the exposition of his doctrine: instead of which, he everywhere speaks of them as impediments in the way of the truths which he wishes to disclose; as disguises which tend to conceal the true bearing of actions upon the promotion of happiness. I conceive therefore that Bentham saw that public opinion concerning virtues and vices included some other element than that which he wished alone to recognize; and that he therefore accepted public opinion as implying something in addition to the elementary pleasures and pains which he expressly enumerates.

But again: It may be said that the public opinion of men, and of communities, as to what is right and wrong, is a fact in man's nature; and an important fact, of which all moralists must recognize the influence: and it may be asked whether Bentham ascribes to it more influence than justly belongs to it. And to this I reply, that the public opinion as to what is right and wrong, is undoubtedly a very important fact in man's nature; and that the most important lesson to be learnt from it appears to be this: that man cannot help judging of actions, as being right or wrong; and that men universally reckon this as the supreme difference of actions; the most important character which they can have. I add, that this characteristic of human nature marks man as a moral being; as a being endowed with a faculty or faculties by which he does thus judge; that is, by which he considers that right and wrong are the supreme and paramount distinctions of actions. That this is an important point we grant, or rather we proclaim, as the beginning of all Morality: and we say that if Bentham accepts the fact in this way, he gives it no more than its just importance. We do not require that this *Faculty* or those Faculties by which man thus judges of right and wrong should be anything peculiar and ultimate, but only that the *distinction* should be a peculiar and ultimate one. And if Bentham, finding that men do so judge of actions, and perceiving that he could not, consistently with the state of their minds, analyse this their judgment into any perception of advantage and disadvantage, was willing to leave it as he found it, and to make the fact of such a judgment one of the bases of his system; so far he was right, and did not ascribe too much importance to this judgment, to this public opinion. But then, if taking the moral judgments of mankind in this aspect, Bentham puts side by side with this element, the other advantages, say bodily pleasure or wealth, which certain actions may produce, we say that he makes an incongruous scheme, which cannot pass for Morality. If he say, for instance, 'public opinion declares lying to be wrong, and I have nothing to say against that; for I cannot analyse this opinion of a thing being *wrong* into any thing else. But recollect, that though it be what they call *wrong*, it may be very pleasant and profitable, and therefore you may still have good reasons for lying; and you *will* have such, if the pleasure and profit which your lie produces, to you and other persons, outweighs that disagreeable thing, *infamy*, which public opinion inflicts upon the liar'; if he were to say this, he would hardly win any one to look upon him as a moralist. Yet this, as appears to me, is a rigorous deduction from the Benthamite doctrine, that the proper and ultimate ground for our acting is the amount of pleasure and advantage which the action will produce, including popular approval as one among other advantages.

As I have said, the real importance of the great fact of the universal and perpetual judgments of mankind concerning actions, as being right and wrong, is, that such judgments are thus seen to be a universal property of human nature: a constant and universal act, which man performs as being man. And it is because man does thus perpetually and universally form such judgments, that he is a moral creature, and that his actions are the subjects of morality; not because he is susceptible of pleasure and pain. And this is the reason why animals are not the subjects of morality; they have no idea of right and wrong; their acts are neither moral nor immoral. Animals may be indeed the *objects* of morality. We may treat them with kindness or with unkindness; and cruelty to animals is a vice, as well as cruelty to men. But cruelty to animals and cruelty to men stand upon a very different footing in morality. The pleasures of animals are elements of a very different order from the pleasures of men. We are bound to endeavour to augment the pleasures of men, not only because they are pleasures, but because they are *human* pleasures. We are bound to men by the universal tie of humanity, of human brotherhood. We have no such tie to animals. We are to be *humane* to them, because *we* are *human*, not because we and they alike feel *animal* pleasures. The Morality which depends upon the increase of pleasure alone would make it our duty to increase the pleasures of pigs or of geese rather than those of men, if we were sure that the pleasure we could give *them* were greater than the pleasures of men.

Such is the result of the doctrine which founds Morality upon the increase of pleasure. Such is a fair deduction from Bentham's principles. Do you think this an exaggerated statement? an argument carried too far? Not so. He has himself accepted this consequence of his system. Thus he says (chap. XLX. §iv.) 'Under the Gentoo and Mahometan religion the interests of the rest of the animal kingdom seem to have met with some attention. Why have they not, universally, with *as much as those of human* creatures, allowance made for the difference in point of *sensibility*? Because the laws that are, have been the work of mutual fear; a sentiment which the less rational animals have not had the same means as man has of turning to account. Why *ought* they not? No reason can be given. . . . The day *may* come when the rest of the animal creation may acquire those rights which never could have been withholden from them but by the hand of tyranny. . . . It may come one day to be recognized that the number of the legs, the villosity of the skin, or the termination of the *os sacrum*, are reasons insufficient for abandoning a sensitive being to the caprice of a tormentor. What else is it that should trace the insuperable line? Is it the faculty of reason, or perhaps the faculty of discourse? But a full-grown horse or dog is beyond comparison a more rational, as well as a more conversable animal than an infant of a day, a week, or even a month old. But suppose the case were otherwise, what would it avail? The question is not, can they *reason*? nor, can they *speak*? but, can they *suffer*?'

This appears to me a very remarkable passage, for the light which it throws upon Bentham's doctrine, as he found himself bound by the nature of his principle to accept it, when logically unfolded. When he had not only made pleasure his guide, but rejected all that especially made it *human* pleasure, allowing no differences but those of intensity and duration; he had, and could have, no reason for stopping at the pleasures of man. And thus his principle became, not the greatest amount of *human* happiness, as he had arbitrarily stated it, with a baseless limitation, which he here rejects; but the greatest amount of animal gratification, including man among animals, with, it may be, peculiar forms of pleasure, but those forms having no peculiar value on account of their kind. But when the principle is thus stated, we are surely entitled to ask, *why* it is to be made our guide? why utility for such an end is to be made the measure of the value of our actions? For certainly, that we are to regulate our actions so as to give the greatest pleasure to the whole animal creation, is not a self-evident principle. It is not only not our obvious, but to most persons not a tolerable doctrine, that we may sacrifice the happiness of men, provided we can in that way produce an overplus of pleasure to cats, dogs and hogs, not to say lice and fleas. Even those who, in the regions of Oriental superstition, have felt and enjoined the greatest tenderness towards animals, have done so, it would seem, in all cases, not because they considered that the pleasures of mere brutes were obviously as sacred as that of men, but because they imagined some mysterious community of nature between man and the animals which they wished to save from pain. That we are to increase human happiness where we can, may be asserted, with some truth, to be universally allowed, and in some measure self-evident: but that we are to make it an object equally important in kind, to increase the pleasures of animals, is not generally accepted as a rule of human conduct; still less as a basis of all rules. If we are asked to take this as the ground of our morality, we must at least require some reason why we should adopt such a foundation principle. No such answer is given: and thus, the whole Benthamite doctrine rests, it seems, on no visible foundation at all. It is, as we hold, false to make even human pleasure the source of all virtue. We think that we have other things to look at as our guides, not overlooking this. But in order to estimate the value of this standard, we have begun by allowing it to be true; and by denying only that it is either applicable or independent. But when we are required to take the pleasures of all creatures, brute and human, into our account, and forbidden to take account of anything else, we cannot submit. Such a standard appears to us not only false, but false without any show of truth. We can see no reason for it, and Mr. Bentham himself does not venture to offer us any. Why, then, are we to take his standard at all? He himself shows us what its true nature is; and so doing shows, as I conceive, that it is absurd, as well as inapplicable and self-assuming.

I say nothing further of Mr. Bentham's assumption in the above passage, that because a child cannot *yet* take care of itself, and cannot converse with us, its pleasures are therefore of no more import to the moralist than those of a kitten or a puppy. We hold that there is a tie which binds together all human beings, quite different from that which binds them to cats and dogs; and that a man, at any stage of his being, is to be treated according to his human capacity, not according to his mere animal condition. It would be easy to show what strange results would follow from estimating the value of children in men's eyes by Mr. Bentham's standard as here stated; but I shall not pursue the subject.

There is another remark which I wish to make on Mr. Bentham's mode of proceeding, which is exemplified in this passage, among many other places. Mr. Bentham finding in the common judgments and common language of men a recognition of a supreme distinction of right and wrong, which does not yield to his analysis, is exceedingly disposed to quarrel with the terms which imply this distinction while at the same time he cannot really exclude this distinction from his own reasonings (as no man can); nor avoid using the terms which imply it, and which he so vehemently condemns in others. The term *ought* is one of these. In the *Deontology*, he says,[2] 'The talisman of arrogance, indolence and ignorance is to be found in a single word, an authoritative imposture, which in these pages it will be frequently necessary to unveil. It is the word "ought"—"ought or ought not", as the case may be. In deciding "you ought to do this"—"you ought not to do it"—is not every question of morals set at rest?' 'If', he goes on, 'the use of the word be admissible at all, it *ought* to be banished from the vocabulary of morals.' Yet he finds it quite impossible to banish it from his own vocabulary; and not only uses it, but uses it in the way in which it is so commonly used by others, as representing a final and supreme rule, opposed, it may be, to the existing actual habits of action. Thus, in the passage on the treatment of animals just quoted: 'They are not treated as well as men. True as to the fact. But *ought* they not?' And he puts the word in italics to show how much he rests upon it. So in giving a description of an altercation between an ancient and a modern—he makes the former, with whom he obviously sympathizes—say, 'Our business was to inquire not what people *think*, but what they *ought to think*': again italicizing the word. Numerous, almost innumerable, other examples might be produced.[3]

Perhaps it may be worth while considering for a moment what may appear to be the reason for the extraordinary manner in which Bentham and the Benthamites have been in the habit of treating their opponents; for their perpetual assertions that the opponents' principles are unmeaning—are mere assumptions—perpetual beggings of the question—ipse dixits—vicious rounds of baseless reasons: for this is their usual mode of speaking of opponents. They rarely quote them; and appear to conceive that men so extremely in error could not have injustice done them; that any assertion might be made about them, for their absurdity was so broad that the most random shot must hit it. This appears to be the mood in which Bentham speaks of all opposing moralists. Now you may ask, whether any probable reason can be given why he should allow himself such liberties; why he should be so incapable of seeing any sense or reason in any previous scheme of ethics. I do not pretend to explain the matter: but I think we may go as far as this: That his mind was so completely possessed by his own system of thought, that he could not see any sense or reason in any differing system: and that it was this want of any sense or reason apparent to him in the opinions of others which raised him into his strange mood of arrogance, his intoxication of self-complacent contempt for adverse systems and arguments, which his admiring disciples held to be so overwhelming to all opponents. I think we may go further. We may see a little nearer why it was that he found no meaning in opposite systems. It appears to me to have been thus. He had set himself to discover and lay down a general principle of human action by which all rules of action must be determined. His principle was, that we must aim at a certain *external* end: at happiness, as it is first stated: but happiness is plainly not altogether external; happiness depends upon the mind itself. Divest, then, the object of this condition; make it wholly external to the mind: it then becomes pleasure. Pleasure, then, must be the sole object of human action; and Pleasure variously trans-formed must give rise to all the virtues. If you are not satisfied with this, he cries, show me any other external object which men either do care for or can care for. *Summum Bonum, Honestum, καλόν*, why should they care for these if they give them no pleasure? And if they do, say so boldly, and have done with it. Of course the answer is, that we are so made that we do care for things on other grounds than are expressed, in any common and simple way, by saying they give us pleasure. Men's care for justice, honesty, truth, and female purity, is not expressed in any appropriate or intelligible or adequate way, by saying that these give them pleasure. Men are so *constituted* as to care for these things. But this idea of a constitution in man, an internal condition of morality, was quite out of Bentham's field of view. No, he said: I want you to point out the thing which men get, and try to get, by virtuous action. If you will not do this, I cannot understand you. If you do this, you must come to my standard. And this habit of mind was, I conceive, in him, not affected, but real: and after a while, broke out, as I have said, in the most boisterous ridicule of all who differed from him.

In quitting these general considerations, and turning to detail, it would be unjust to Bentham not to allow that in that portion of Ethics in which his principle is really applicable, there is a great deal of felicity, and even of impressiveness, in the manner in which he follows out his doctrine. I speak of the virtues and duties which depend directly upon Benevolence. He enjoins kindness, gentleness, patience, meekness, good humour, in a manner which makes him conspicuous among the kindlier moralists. He has for instance such precepts as this: 'Never do evil for mere ill desert',[4] with many other like precepts (209), etc. At the same time, it must be said that a great many of the precepts which he thus gives are rather rules of good manners than rules of morality. And though he extends his injunctions to the subjects of discourse and action in a wider view, he appears to be most at home in pointing out what Civility, or, as he calls it, negative efficient Benevolence, requires us to do, and to refrain from, in the very rudest provinces of good manners; and this he traces with a gravity and a technical physiological detail which are truly astounding.[5]

III

BENTHAM—DEFECT OF HIS SYSTEM.

Having thus noticed one great defect and error in Bentham's system, his depreciation of *historical law*, I must now notice another point in which I think him also altogether defective and erroneous; namely in not fully recognizing the *moral object* of Law. According to our views, Law has for its object to promote, not merely the pleasure of man, but his moral nature; not merely to preserve and gratify, but to teach him: not to enable him to live a comfortable animal life, but to raise him above mere animal life: in short, to conform to his nature as man: not merely as a sentient, not merely a gregarious, not merely a social creature, but a moral creature; a creature to whose moral being and agency all mere material possessions, enjoyments, and advantages are instruments, means and occasions. Punishment is to be, not merely a means of preventing suffering, but is also to be a moral Lesson (*Morality*, Art. 988). Bentham, on the other hand, professes to make the promotion of human happiness—such happiness as can be resolved into mere pleasure or absence of pain—the sole object of punishment. On this view, there is no difference between laws restraining men in consequence of some calamity in which they are involved with no fault of theirs, and punishments for crime. Quarantine is not distinguishable from imprisonment for theft. Restraints imposed on those afflicted with contagious diseases are punishments, as much as restraints on those who try to break into a house. Now this is contrary to all common notions, and to all real jural philosophy. But the fact is, that such a view cannot be consistently carried through. And Bentham himself is obliged to defend laws which have no solid ground except their moral tendency; their effect in teaching men good morality.

As an example of the results of Bentham's attempt to exclude morality, as such, in his legislation, let us look at what he says respecting the Laws of Marriage.

On this subject he argues strongly in favour of a liberty of Divorce by common consent. He condemns the law which makes marriages indissoluble, in the strongest terms: he calls it cruel and absurd: he says this law 'surprises the contracting parties in the tenderness of their youth, in the moments which open all the vistas of happiness. It says to them, "You unite in the hope of being happy, but I tell you, you only enter a prison whose door will be closed against you. I shall be inexorable to the cries of your grief, and when you dash yourselves against your fetters I shall not permit you to be delivered".' And as decisively condemnatory of this policy he says, 'The government which interdicts them [divorces] takes upon itself to decide that it understands the interests of individuals better than they do themselves.' (*Civil Code*, Pt. III.c.v.)

Now upon this we may remark, that undoubtedly, in this and in many other cases, government, both in its legislation and administration, does assume that it understands the interests of individuals, and the public interest as affected by them, better than they do themselves. What is the meaning of restraints imposed for the sake of public health, cleanliness and comfort? Why are not individuals left to do what they like with reference to such matters? Plainly because carelessness, ignorance, indolence, would prevent their doing what is most for their own interest. Is there anything strange in assuming that legislation, looking at all the consequences of marriage to the individuals and to society, to their comfort, fortune, and moral being, should judge better of the conditions under which it ought to be contracted than the parties in that delirium of feeling which Mr. Bentham describes? Does not indeed almost the whole of law suppose the government to understand men's interests on many points better than they do themselves? Mr. Bentham is very fond of using this sarcasm, (for such it is rather than an argument,) when he is disposed to disparage a particular law: but it is rather a sarcasm against laws in general.

But is Mr. Bentham ready to apply consistently the principle which he thus implies, that in such matters individuals are the best judges of their own interests? Will he allow divorce to take place whenever the two parties agree in desiring it? As I understand him, he would not. Indeed such a facility of divorce as this, leaves hardly any difference possible between marriage and concubinage. If a pair may separate when they please, why does the legislator take the trouble to recognize their being together? Such an extension of Divorce seems to be inconsistent with the existence of Families. Accordingly it does not appear that Mr. Bentham would carry divorce so far as this; although, for aught I can see, his argument just mentioned would. But he has other arguments on the other side.[6] He allows that the comfort and advantage of the parties, and especially of the woman and her children, requires that the duration of the connexion should be indefinite. Marriage for life is, he says, the most natural marriage: if there were no laws except the ordinary law of contracts, this would be the most ordinary arrangement.

So far, good. But Mr. Bentham having carried his argument so far, does not go on with it. What conclusion are we to suppose him to intend? This arrangement would be very *general* without law, therefore the legislator should pass a law to make it *universal*? This is not at all like his usual style of reasoning. The more general it would be without the law, the less need of the law, it would seem; and Mr. Bentham, of all persons, is the last to deem constraint a good when it is not needed. Or shall we supply an additional step in the argument, and say that the general tendency of men to make the marriage contract a contract for life, shows that such a contract is most for their happiness? This, again, is not in the usual style of Bentham's reasoning. He is not wont to estimate the happiness resulting from a rule by any opinion of persons under special circumstances, this opinion being only implied and conjectured, not expressed. His method is rather to show how happiness is increased or diminished, by resolving it into its elements, and showing how these are affected. I say therefore that I cannot see how Bentham goes on from this point, or what his conclusion is as to the restraints which ought to be placed upon Divorce. 'Love', he says, 'on the part of the man, love and foresight on the part of the woman, all concur with enlightened freedom and affection on the part of parents in impressing the character of perpetuity upon the contract of this alliance.' But what then? Does he say, 'Let it be perpetual'? No. The very next sentence is employed in showing the absurdity of making the engagement one from which the parties cannot liberate themselves by mutual consent. And there is no attempt to reduce these two arguments, or their results, to a consistency: no indication how marriages are to be perpetual, and yet dissoluble at will: no provision for the case in which the fickleness may come on while the children still need the cares of both parents. The general good of families points one way: the inclinations of the man and woman may point the opposite way. There is no rule given or suggested, as to which influence shall prevail in any given case.

But suppose that one party wish for a separation while the other does not. Shall divorce then be permitted? Not, it would seem, without the consent of the other. But suppose the consent to be obtained by ill-treatment. Suppose the stronger party to maltreat the weaker for this very purpose. Is it fit that the legislator should aid him in carrying his purpose into effect? Is it fit that he should liberate the man because he has by cruelty, or fear, or importunity, induced the woman to allow him to abandon her?

Mr. Bentham's answer to this case shows, it seems to me, how difficult it is for any writer, however strictly he may try to follow out the results of a theory—to get rid of the ordinary moral impressions with which men look at actions. Mr. Bentham's decision on this point is, that in such a case, liberty should be allowed to the party maltreated, and not to the other. If a husband wish for a divorce from a wife whom he hates, and ill use her so that she gives her consent to the divorce, she may marry again, but he may not. Now to this decision I have nothing to object: but I must remark, that the view which makes it tolerable, is its being a decision on moral grounds, such as Mr. Bentham would not willingly acknowledge. The man may not take advantage of his own wrong: *that* is a maxim which quite satisfies *us*. But Mr. Bentham, who only regards wrong as harm, would, I think, find it difficult to satisfy the man that he was fairly used. The man would say, 'You allow every one else to separate from ill-sorted partners on grounds of repugnance: you care for their happiness; you have no regard for mine. I cannot live with this woman without misery. By your own principle, that is a reason why I should not live with her at all. My happiness requires my union with another. My present wife has consented. Why do you interpose to make us all wretched? You say I obtained my wife's consent by ill usage. I did no more than was requisite to obtain it. I gave her no pain which was not necessary for this purpose, and so, for my own happiness: and in truth, for hers also, for what happiness can she have in clinging to one whom she makes wretched? But if she have aught to accuse me of in the way of ill usage, let that be punished in the ordinary way, not by this cruel prohibition; a refinement of cruelty worthy of the great leaders of the ascetic school, rather than of the professed promoters of human happiness.' To this appeal, I do not see what reply Mr. Bentham could make. We, as I have said, have no such difficulty. We say to the man, We cannot allow you to take advantage of your own wrong. His having ill-used his wife steels our hearts to his complaints. His having thought only of *his own* happiness makes his happiness of small account in our eyes. We exhort him to try to find consolation and relief in promoting the happiness of others: to bend to the yoke of duty, instead of merely aiming at self-gratification.

Of course, no one can deny that such cases as this, and many other cases, are questions of great difficulty: nor do we say that the indissolubility of marriage is a rule which, on mere human grounds, must necessarily be the best. But we say that no good rule can be established on this subject without regarding the marriage union in a moral point of view; without assuming it as one great object of the law to elevate and purify men's idea of marriage; to lead them to look upon it as an entire union of interests and feelings, enjoyments and hopes, between the two parties. With this view, the law prohibits polygamy, denies rights to concubines and illegitimate children, invests the Family with honours and advantages; and with the same view, it only in cases of extreme necessity allows Divorce.[7]

But let us consider Bentham's argument against divorce on one-sided application a moment longer. He says that such a law as he proposes would prevent the husband who wishes for a divorce from ill-treating the wife; he would try to get her consent by fair means. But what I urge is, that if he fails in this, he has just the same reason to complain, which, on Bentham's grounds, both parties have who wish for a divorce and are not allowed by the law to obtain one. It is no fault of his that he is not odious to his wife, and that he tries in vain to make himself so.

In truth, I believe Bentham in this case, as in some others, to have been seduced by the apparently happy thought of finding an appropriate punishment for an offence, and thus, turning the edge of an adverse argument.

Indeed this part of Bentham's writings—the discovery of appropriate and effective punishments—the *Rationale of Punishment*, as he calls it, has been the work of great labour. It is full of invention and ingenuity, and, as I have already said, by being systematic, it necessarily brings into view a number of instructive relations among the matters considered. It is one of Bentham's great titles to consideration as a jural writer, though disfigured in some degree with his usual faults. But this part of his writings does not bear upon our subject, Morality, with so much closeness as to make it suitable to dwell upon them.

I have said that Bentham's system of law is defective in not giving due prominence to the moral purpose of laws. Still, we must not forget that his principle, that the promotion of human happiness is the object of good laws, is really in almost every case a valuable guide to legislation, even in its direct Benthamite interpretation, where happiness is understood as consisting merely of pleasures. The legislator, though not the moralist, may take this principle for his guide. The legislator will hardly be wrong if he makes his laws with an intelligent and comprehensive regard to the promotion of general happiness and the prevention of misery; though the moralist is very likely to be understood as teaching a low and scanty morality, if he tell men they must always aim solely at their own happiness. This I say on the Benthamite analysis of happiness. But if we take that wider sense of *happiness*, which agrees with the common feeling of mankind, and into which our Utilitarians have a perpetual tendency to slide—the happiness which includes moral elements—the happiness which arises from knowing that we neither do nor suffer wrong—the happiness which arises from the promotion of virtue in ourselves and others—the happiness of kindness, justice, honesty, veracity, purity, order—then indeed happiness becomes a perfect and unerring guide—if only we can discover which way her guidance points. But then, we invert the Benthamite analysis, and make happiness depend upon virtue, rather than virtue upon happiness. Yet to this way of understanding the term *happiness*, the Utilitarian, if he be really a kind and virtuous man, is perpetually prone to recur, swept away by the sympathy of the general feelings of man. Thus when Bentham has to speak of the reasons why there should be laws against marriages between near relations, he says (*Principles of Civil Code*, Pt. III.c.v.), 'If there were not an insurmountable barrier against marriages between near relations, called to live together in the closest intimacy, this close connexion, these continual opportunities, even friendship itself and its innocent caresses, might kindle the most disastrous passions. Families, those retreats in which repose ought to be found in the bosom of order, and where the emotions of the soul, agitated in the scenes of the world, ought to sink to rest—families themselves would become the prey of all the inquietudes, the rivalries, and the fury of love. Suspicion would banish confidence; the gentlest feelings would be extinguished; and eternal enmities and revenges, of which the idea alone makes one tremble, would usurp their place. The opinion of the chastity of young women, so powerful an attraction to marriage, would not know upon what to repose, and the most dangerous snares in the education of youth would be found even in the asylum where they could be least avoided.'

Here we find that the good to be aimed at has taken a moral tinge, and derives all its force from that. Friendship, innocence, repose in the bosom of order, rest for the emotions of the soul; the calamities of rivalry, passion, suspicion, mistrust, enmity, revenge; and finally, the opinion of female purity, are put forwards as the grounds of such a rule. I do not say that, even in this form, they appear to me to give a sufficient basis for his views; and still less when he carries them into detail. But they show, and especially the last phrase, how large a share moral considerations must have in such questions; as, in truth, such considerations must enter into the view of the moralist at one point or other. If morality is not to be a direct object of the law, it must still be an object of the law on this account, that men care much about it. If the legislator can see no positive and independent value in female purity, still he must legislate to preserve it, since the opinion of it is so highly prized by men, and its loss is a ground of such bitter grief and indignation. If the legislator will not be himself an independent moralist, at least he has to make laws for moral creatures; for creatures who think moral good and evil the most important and weighty form of good and evil. If he will not hear a moral voice in his own bosom, he cannot shut his ears to the moral voice which proceeds from the people at large; and thus, by refusing to give morality an independent place in his system, he makes his system depend upon the popular cry. If he will not acknowledge the moral rule as something which ought to command and control the popular prejudice, he must take moral elements from popular prejudices: if he will not place a moral monitor above the applause and vituperation of the popular voice, he must find one in the popular voice. If he has no moral sanction properly so called, he must have a *moral or popular* sanction as identical: and this, we have seen, Bentham has.

I have thus again brought my views of Bentham's morality to the same point to which I formerly conducted them; and this is, I conceive, the principal view which it behoves us to take of Bentham's morality. I shall not now think further consideration of this celebrated writer necessary.

NOTES

1. The impossibility of really applying the principle that we are to estimate the virtue of actions by calculating the amount of pleasure which they will produce, appears further, by looking at the rude and loose manner in which Bentham makes such calculations. Among the consequences of acts of robbery, for instance, which make them vicious, he reckons the alarm which such an act produces in other persons, and the danger in which it places them. And this alarm and danger are carefully explained, as to their existence (chap. XII, §viii.). But the probability of each is not at all estimated. This however is rather where he is looking at the grounds of judicial punishment than of moral condemnation.
2. I, 31.
3. So, *Principles*, chap. XVIII, Art. i. Classes of Offences, Art. i. 'It is necessary at the outset to make a distinction between such acts as *are* or *may* be, and such as *ought* to be offences.'

   So, same chap. Art. xxv note, he would call the person benefitted by a trust, the beneficiendary, 'to put it more effectually out of doubt that the party meant was the party who *ought* to receive the benefit, whether he actually receives it or no.'

   So, same chap. Art. xxvii text and note: 'The trust is either of the number of those which ought by law to subsist . . . or is not.' 'What articles ought to be created [property], etc.' The whole page and note swarms with *oughts*.

   So same chap. Par. XLII. 'Whether any and what modes of servitude ought to be established and kept on foot?' Again, Par. XLVI, LIX.
4. *Deontol*, II, 193.
5. Ibid., 237, etc.
6. *Civil Code*, Part III.c.v.
7. I need not discuss Bentham's other arguments on this subject. They all, I think, admit of answer on the same principles as those to which I have referred. I have considered the principal of them in the *Morality*, Bk. V.c.13.

Chapter 3

Bentham

John Watson*

It may be safely said that no hedonistic system subsequent to Hume has added anything to the general doctrine, but has either introduced distinctions belonging to an earlier stage of its development or has ennobled it by the introduction of conceptions that are inconsistent with its fundamental principle. That all actions are determined by the desire for pleasure; that the pleasure which to the individual at the moment seems strongest determines the will; that reason has no power to originate, to retard, or to prevent action, but is a purely formal, or theoretical activity; that there is no 'innate faculty' or 'moral sense' belonging to man in his natural state, but that moral judgments are resolvable into a peculiar form of pleasure; that justice is a means of obtaining security for life and property, and so of securing the greatest pleasure of society as a whole; and that a man's motive in doing a benevolent or just act is ultimately a regard for his own pleasure; these are the main features of a hedonism that is as self-consistent as hedonism can be made, and they are all clearly set forth by Hume.

Jeremy Bentham is a thinker rather of the type of Hobbes, than of the type of Hume. His predominant interest is in the advancement of social well-being, and keeping this end ever before him, he presents us with a doctrine having in it much higher elements than any of his predecessors, but higher elements which logically have no place in a hedonistic theory of conduct. Destitute of the speculative subtlety of Hume, he tries not so much to reconcile his hedonism with the principle that morality consists in doing actions which secure the greatest good of the greatest number, as to show how hedonism may be practically applied in the regulation of the actions of private individuals, and to the improvement of legislation. Especially in the latter respect his writings have been of great practical value, a value which, as it may be fairly said, is independent of what he believed to be the motive of all actions, the desire for one's own pleasure.

We shall, I think, best appreciate the strength and the weakness of Bentham by viewing him as a writer who above all things was interested in an analysis of the springs of human conduct, with a view

---

* This essay forms chapter VII in John Watson's interesting and sadly rather neglected *Hedonistic Theories from Aristippus to Spencer*, (Macmillan, London, 1895) (ed.).

to finding the most effective means of improving society by acting upon them. Hence his elaborate classification of the various pleasures which serve as motives, his endless divisions and subdivisions, and his continual insistence on the principle that 'every one is to count for one and no one for more than one'. Bentham is really attempting to construct a system of conduct that shall serve as a guide in actual life. Whether such a system can be constructed or not, we are at least entitled to demand that it should not be based upon inconsistent principles.

Let us look at the main points in Bentham's doctrine.

1. He has no hesitation in rejecting as false all other principles except that of 'utility', the principle which 'approves or disapproves of every action whatsoever, according to the tendency which it appears to have to augment or diminish the happiness of the party whose interest is in question'. The adverse principles which he criticizes are those of *asceticism* and *sympathy and antipathy*.

(*a*) Asceticism he defines as 'that principle, which, like the principle of utility, approves or disapproves of any action, according to the tendency which it appears to have to augment or diminish the happiness of the party whose interest is in question; but in an inverse manner, approving of actions in as far as they tend to diminish his happiness; disapproving of them in as far as they tend to augment it'. Such a representation, or rather misrepresentation, of asceticism is a curious instance of the extraordinary want of intellectual sympathy which is characteristic of Bentham. That the end of life is to get as much pain as possible is a mere caricature of ascetic morality. What has given that mode of thought a peculiar fascination to many minds is that it opposes the higher or spiritual life to the lower, and maintains that the former can only be obtained by the complete sacrifice of the latter. The end is therefore from the ascetic point of view, not the production of pain, but the transcendence of the pleasures of the flesh by means of self-mortification, which is believed to be the only 'way to the blessed life'.

(*b*) Bentham is more successful in detecting the weakness of the second principle to which he objects. The principle of 'sympathy and antipathy', is, as he contends, 'rather a principle in name than in reality'. To say that an action is good merely because it is *felt* to be good is the negation of all principle. One man says that a thing is right because his 'moral sense' tells him so; another appeals to 'common sense', and conveniently leaves out 'the sense of those whose sense is not the same' as his own; a third speaks of an 'eternal and immutable rule of right', but when he comes to particulars you find that he really means what *he* thinks to be right; others appeal to the 'law of nature' or 'natural justice' or 'right reason'. In all these cases recourse is had to one's own feeling, which affords no standard of conduct at all.

2. Having thus cleared away the rubbish, Bentham goes to work with great energy to construct an edifice of morals on the basis of hedonism.

The end is the securing of pleasure and the avoidance of pain. It is necessary, therefore, if we are to determine action in conformity with this end, to know how pleasures vary in value. Considered by itself a pleasure or pain is greater or less according to (a) intensity, (b) duration, (c) certainty or uncertainty, (d) propinquity or remoteness; to which must be added, when we are estimating the value of an *act* (e) fecundity, or the chance it has of being followed by sensations of the *same* kind, (f) its purity, or the chance it has of not being followed by sensations of the opposite kind. When we are estimating the pleasures of a number of persons, we must add (g) extent, i.e. the number of persons who are affected by it. To determine the general tendency of an act, is to strike a balance between the pleasures and pains associated with it. If the pleasure is in excess the act is good, if the pain is in excess the act is bad. As an illustration of the method of determining value by a calculation of pleasures and pains, Bentham cites the instance of a landed estate, which a man values for the pleasures it will bring and the pain it will enable him to avoid, while its value rises according to the *length of time* he is to have possession and the *nearness* of the time he is to come into possession of it. The other circumstances which go to make up the quantity of the man's pleasure, the *intensity, fecundity* and *purity* of the pleasures, are not considered beforehand because they vary with the use which each person may come to make of the estate. This process of calculation is not pursued in every case, but it may always be kept in view, and the more fully it is carried out the nearer will it approach to the character of an exact one.

Not only do pleasures differ in quantity, but they are distinguished according to their exciting causes, and these are subdivided into (a) single, (b) complex. Fourteen different sorts or kinds of pleasure are mentioned, viz., pleasures of sense, wealth, skill, amity, good name, power, piety, benevolence, malevolence, memory, imagination, expectation, association, relief. A further division of even greater importance is into (1) self-regarding, (2) extra-regarding, the latter comprehending the pleasures of benevolence and the pleasures of malevolence, all the rest belonging to the former class. It is admitted by Bentham that the quantity of pleasure and pain is not excited by a given cause, is not the same in different persons. One man may be most affected by the pleasures of the taste; another by those of the ear. The various circumstances which influence the sensibility are enumerated by Bentham, and are such as health, strength, hardness, bodily imperfection, knowledge, moral sensibility, etc.

3. Bentham's next attempt is to determine what enters into and constitutes the character of human actions; and here he distinguishes, (*a*) the *act* itself, (*b*) the *circumstances* in which it is done, (*c*) the *intentionality* that may have accompanied it, (*d*) the *consciousness* that may have accompanied it, (*e*) the *motive* which gives rise to it, (*f*) the *disposition* which it indicates.

The *intention* may regard either the act itself or its consequences. The act may be intentional but not the consequences, as when you may intend to touch a man without intending to hurt him, and yet as a matter of fact you may chance to hurt him. But the consequences cannot be intentional without the act being intentional. If you do not intend the act, the consequences are not intended. People often speak of a good or bad intention, but this is an imperfect way of speaking. Nothing is either good or bad but pain or pleasure, or things that are the causes or preventives of pain and pleasure. A man certainly intends his act, but he cannot strictly speaking be said to intend the consequences. He may be *conscious* or not conscious of them, but he does not intend them. If I take a prescription which is furnished me by a physician, I *intend* to take it, but I cannot be said to intend the consequences; I can only *know* or not know what the consequences will be. No intention therefore can be called either good or bad, since goodness and badness are dependent upon the consequences in the way of pleasure or pain.

The *motive* to an act must be distinguished from the intention. The only motives with which we are concerned are those which act upon the will. Now, to be governed by any motive a man must look beyond his action to the consequences of it. 'A fire breaks out in your neighbour's house; you are under apprehension of its extending to your own; you are apprehensive that if you stay in it you will be burnt; you accordingly run out of it. This then is the act, the others are all motives to it.' A motive is 'substantially nothing more than pleasure or pain, operating in a certain manner'. Now, 'pleasure is in *itself* a good; nay, even setting aside freedom from pain, the only good; pain is in itself an evil; and indeed, without exception, the only evil. And this is alike true of every sort of pain, and of every sort of pleasure. It follows, therefore, that *there is no such thing as any sort of motive that is in itself a bad one*'. If motives are good or bad it is only on account of their effects; good, on account of their tendency to produce pleasure, or avert pain; bad, on account of their tendency to produce pain, or avert pleasure. The various motives correspond to the different sorts of pleasure. Frequently a man is acted upon by different motives at the same time: 'one motive or set of motives, acting in one direction; another motive, or set of motives, acting as it were in an opposite direction.'

Is there nothing, then, about a man that can properly be termed good or bad? Yes, certainly; his *disposition*. But the disposition is good or bad according to its effects in the production of pleasure and pain. When a man is accustomed to do acts which bring more pleasure than pain to the community, we say that he has a good disposition.

4. Bentham, then, places goodness and badness entirely in the disposition of the agent, as determined by the view which is taken of the tendency of his act combined with his view of its consequences. The question arises whether there is any difference between pleasures such as entitles us to speak of the disposition of a man as good or bad in a moral sense. A man's disposition is good when the tendency of his act is good, i.e. when it produces pleasure, and when he acts from an extra-regarding motive. But is the distinction of motives into the two classes of self-regarding and extra-regarding tenable? Bentham virtually admits that it is not. The only motive that can be brought to bear upon a man is 'his own pain and pleasure'. 'On the occasion of every act he exercises every human being is led to pursue that line of conduct which, according to his view of the case taken by him at the moment, will be in the highest degree contributory to his own happiness.' Whether, therefore, the man's motive is called self-regarding or extra-regarding, the motive is ultimately a desire for his own greatest pleasure.

5. Bentham distinguishes, however, between 'private ethics' and the 'art of legislation', endeavouring to determine the limits of each. 'Ethics at large may be defined as the art of directing men's actions to the production of the greatest possible quantity of happiness.' Private ethics is the art of self-government, or 'the art of directing a man's own actions'. Government or legislation is the art of directing the actions of other agents so as to produce a maximum of pleasure in the whole community. The quality which a man manifests in discharging his duty to himself ('if duty it is to be called') is that of *prudence*. In so far as his behaviour may affect the interests of those about him, it may be said to depend upon his *duty to others*. To forbear from diminishing the happiness of one's neighbour is *probity*; to add something to his happiness is *beneficence*. If it is asked, why should I obey the dictates of *probity* and *beneficence*? Bentham answers that, while 'the only interests which a man at all times and upon all occasions is sure to find *adequate* motives for consulting are his own', yet, 'there are no occasions in which a man has not some motives for consulting the happiness of other men. In

the first place, he has, on all occasions, the purely social motive of sympathy or benevolence; in the next place, he has, on most occasions, the semi-social motives of love, of amity, and love of reputation. The motive of sympathy will act upon him with more or less effect, according to the bias of his sensibility; the two other motives, according to a variety of circumstances, principally according to the strength of his intellectual powers, the firmness and steadiness of his mind, the quantum of his moral sensibility, and the characters of the people he has to deal with.' As private ethics and legislation have the same end in view, viz., the happiness of every member of the community, to a certain extent they go hand in hand. How then do they differ? They differ in so far as the acts with which they are concerned are 'not *perfectly and throughout* the same'. 'There is no case in which a private man ought not to direct his own conduct to the production of his own happiness, and of that of his fellow creatures; but there are cases in which the legislation ought not to attempt to direct the conduct of the several other members of the community. Every act which promises to be beneficial upon the whole to the community (himself included) each individual ought to perform of himself; but it is not every such act that the legislator ought to compel him to perform.' There are, then, actions with which legislation may not interfere, but which are left to private ethics. What are these cases?

(*a*) Legislation should not interfere where punishment would be inefficacious. It is useless, for example, to punish a man for not obeying a law that has not been duly announced beforehand; and yet, admitting the law to be a wise one, the action prohibited is pernicious in its consequences, and is, therefore, contrary to 'private ethics'. Where no law would be of any efficacy, as in the case of an insane person, neither is there any private law. But the main region in which private ethics operates of itself is in cases where punishment would be unprofitable. Thus, when the guilty person will in all likelihood escape detection, especially if the temptation to commit the offence is very strong, or when there is danger of the innocent being punished, the matter is one that private ethics alone should deal with. An instance of the latter is treachery or ingratitude.

(*b*) 'Of the rules of moral duty, those which stand least in need of the assistance of legislation are the rules of *prudence*. It can only be through some defect on the part of the understanding, if a man be ever deficient in point of duty to himself.' All that the legislator can hope to do is 'to increase the efficacy of private ethics, by giving strength and direction to the influence of the moral sanction. With what chance of success, for example, would a legislator go about to extirpate drunkenness and fornication by dint of legal punishment?

Not all the tortures which ingenuity could invent would compass it; and, before he had made any progress worth regarding, such a mass of evil would be produced by the punishment, as would exceed a thousandfold the utmost possible mischief of the offence. The great difficulty would be in the procuring evidence; an object which could not be attempted with any probability of success, without spreading dismay through every family, tearing the bonds of sympathy asunder, and rooting out the influence of all the social motives.' Legislative interference is even worse in matters of religion. Louis XIV, for example, out of pure sympathy and loving kindness was led into coercive measures which produced 'all the miseries which the most determined malevolence could have devised'.

(c) The rules of *probity* are those which stand most in need of assistance on the part of the legislator, and in which, in point of fact, his interference has been most extensive. 'There are few cases, if any, in which it would not be expedient to punish a man for injuring his neighbour.' Here, in fact, 'we must first know what are the dictates of legislation, before we can know what are the dictates of private ethics'.

(d) The rules of *beneficence* must necessarily be left in great measure to private ethics; for, as a rule, the beneficial quality of the act depends upon its being free and voluntary. To sum up: 'Private ethics teaches how each man may dispose himself to pursue the course most conducive to his own happiness, by means of such motives as offer of themselves; the act of legislation teaches how a multitude of men, composing a community, may be disposed to pursue that course which, upon the whole, is the most conducive to the happiness of the whole community, by means of motives to be applied by the legislator.' Bentham adds, that social opinion and religion have also sanctions of their own, but the former not infrequently runs counter to the public good, while the influence of the latter is weak and uncertain in its action.

Through the whole of Bentham's ethical theory there runs an ambiguity which imparts to it a delusive air of plausibility and consistency. The founder of the modern school of Utilitarianism has fixed for it the main outlines of the common creed, and his doctrine, like that of his disciples, rests upon two distinct and even contradictory principles.

(1) Bentham's attempt to show that pleasures and pains may be balanced against one another by being separately summed up, rests upon a confusion between pleasure and pain as feelings and as objects of thought. Let us take Bentham's own instance of the man who thinks of buying an estate. He calls up in imagination the various pleasures which are associated with it, and the quantity of each of

these he multiplies by the time he expects to enjoy them, adding to the sum the extra amount of pleasure connected with immediate possession. Now, it is here implied that each of the pleasures that go to form the whole sum has a certain precise degree of intensity which can be, at least approximately, determined beforehand. But Bentham himself points out that pleasures vary according to the susceptibility of the individual. Now, surely that means that no pleasure has any quantity apart from its relation to the idea of one's self as the subject of the pleasure. Thus the quantity of the pleasure means the thought of a certain object as a means of bringing satisfaction to the man who anticipates it. What the man really does is to compare different means of self-satisfaction, and to pronounce that certain objects will, as he believes, judging from his own past experience, be a better means of realizing himself than certain other objects. He is not contrasting feelings of pleasure as such, but he is comparing himself in one ideal set of circumstances with himself in another ideal set of circumstances. Take away this conception of himself, and he is unable to say that any one pleasure has more or less quantity than another. Always, when he says that one pleasure is greater than another, he tacitly adds, greater *for me*, and for those of like nature with me. But if the conception of himself as a permanent subject capable of satisfaction in various defined ways is what gives meaning to the supposed calculus of pleasures, is it not plain that not pleasure as a mere feeling, but pleasure as the possible satisfaction of his ideal self, is what really determines whether, in the case mentioned, he shall buy the estate?

(2) It follows from this that not pleasure, as Bentham supposes, but the realization of man's nature in its ideal perfection is the end of all action. When we set aside as inconsistent with the highest conduct anything with which a man may, as a matter of fact, seek to satisfy himself, we can justify our judgment only on the ground that it is incompatible with the idea of perfect manhood. The man, we say, is trying to violate his true nature. The idea of himself which he is seeking to realize is incompatible with the idea of himself of which he is at least obscurely conscious. The prodigal wastes his substance in riotous living, but at last 'he comes to himself'. Contrasting what he has been trying to realize with the ideal of himself, he is visited with repentance, as he becomes aware of how poor is his real as compared with his ideal self. Thus arises the idea of what he ought to be, as contrasted with what he is. At first the notion of moral obligation is negative. 'I have not done', he says, 'what I ought to have done'. And so he condemns himself in the presence of the unrealized self. But this is only the beginning of a change of life. What he *ought* to do is not merely the negative idea that what

he *is* is inconsistent with what he *ought* to be, but in this negation there is already the 'promise and potency' of what he may become. Thus he goes on to fill up the ideal of himself as he should be, and he adds, 'I will arise and go to my father.'

(3) Bentham's account of intentionality or will is beset with a similar imperfection. A man intends to do an act, but his intention has nothing to do with the consequences of his act, to himself or others. Now, if we thus separate an act from its consequences it ceases to have any moral character, and hence Bentham naturally says that no intention is either good or bad. The truth is that an act which is isolated in this way is not an act at all, but is simply a physical movement. The act of taking a physician's prescription, viewed in itself, is not viewed as a distinctively human act. But no one takes a prescription without some end in view. He desires the removal of something which interferes with the healthy discharge of the bodily functions, and he desires health because that is included in his idea of himself as he ought to be. Thus the intention is properly the willing of a certain act as the *means* to a given end. But there can be no willing of an act as a means, unless there is the consciousness of the end to which it is the means. The intention, therefore, is just the willing of the means by which a preconceived end is sought to be obtained.

(4) Bentham makes a similar separation between motive and consequences. The motive, he says, is always a desire for pleasure, and as pleasure is always a good, no motive is in itself bad. Now, certainly if we separate a motive from the consequences of an act, the motive is not bad, and neither is it good; it simply has no moral character. What this shows is that a feeling of pleasure as such is not a motive at all. The motive is always the desire for the realization of one's self. Apart from such an ideal self, a motive can only be regarded as a feeling that arises spontaneously in the mind, and is followed by a certain external movement. But no motive is of this character. When a man acts from the motive of benevolence, he does so because he has set before himself this end as one of the ways in which his ideal nature may be realized. Thus from the very character of the motive, it involves the consequences; only the consequences must not be conceived, as they are by Bentham, as merely the relation of an external movement to other external movements which follow as its effects. The consequences which a man sets before himself are consequences in the way of fulfilling his ideal of himself, and which, therefore, enter into and form his character; and these are good or bad according as they do or do not make for that end. Thus the motive and the consequences are the same thing, viewed, the former from the side of the willing agent, and the latter from the

side of the object which he wills. So regarded, every motive has a distinct moral character as good or bad.

(5) Bentham holds that the only thing that can be called good is a man's disposition. By this he means that a man's act is good if, on the whole, his acts tend to produce more pleasure than pain. This is another way of saying that no intention is properly either good or bad. This is almost expressly said by Bentham when he tells us that a man's disposition is 'the sum of his intentions', and it is implied in his virtual definition of a 'good' disposition as one which is 'beneficial', and of a 'bad' disposition as one which is 'mischievous'. Thus a man's disposition is not strictly good or bad in any sense conveying moral praise or blame. That this should follow from Bentham's view of the will is not in the least surprising. It follows, as a matter of course, from the doctrine that will is merely the effect of certain motives that depend upon 'the degree of a man's sensibility'.

(6) We now come to that part of Bentham's system, in which his false analysis of human nature exhibits itself in an almost open conflict of two diverse principles. Granting that pleasure is at once the end and the motive to action, the question still remains: Whose pleasure? Is the end the production of the greatest amount of pleasure to each individual, or to the greatest number of individuals? Is the motive desire for one's own pleasure, or desire for the pleasure of the community as a whole? Here Bentham plays fast and loose with language in a way that makes all clear thinking on the question impossible.

(a) Both private ethics and legislation have the same end in view, the happiness of every member of the community. Now there is here a manifest ambiguity. If each man seeks his own good, no doubt we may say that the good of every member of the community is made the end. But it is the good of each *separately* that is sought. The legislator, on the other hand, does not seek the good of any one man, or set of men, but the good of all men; and this good may involve the taking pleasure from some that others may have more.

(b) To say that the motive of each man is desire for his own pleasure is certainly to say that every member of the community acts out of regard for pleasure. But the legislator is not seeking the good of men individually but collectively. How, then, is he to act upon individuals so as to make them choose the good of all? Bentham admits that he can only do so by convincing each man that his own good is bound up with the good of others; in other words, the motive to action of the individual is always a regard for his own pleasure. Clearly, therefore, the distinction of self-regarding and extra-regarding motives is a distinction without a difference. All motives are self-regarding.

(7) This objection is not one that can be got rid of without completely recasting the whole system. When we see that the aim is always the realization of the higher self, we also see that the opposition of self-regarding and other-regarding motives is a false one. A man best realizes himself in seeking the good of others, and he cannot truly seek the good of others without seeking to realize himself. There are not two discrepant sets of motives. From the moral point of view the distinction of self and others is annulled and transcended; and what popular language calls selfishness is seen to be contradictory at once of individual and of common good.

Chapter 4

Bentham*

H. L. A. Hart

I

In 1838 when John Stuart Mill wrote his famous essay on Bentham,[1] Bowring's edition of Bentham's works, which included much not previously published, was still in progress. Mill says that at this time 'except for the more slight of his works' Bentham's readers had been few. It seems that the completion in 1843 of the Bowring edition did not vastly increase their numbers. In 1864 Richard Hildreth, an American lawyer and moralist, embarked on the strange project of translating back from French into English Dumont's very free version of some of Bentham's writings on the Principles of Legislation. Hildreth tells us in the preface to his translation that he was inspired to publish it because, in spite of their fame abroad, Bentham's works 'in England and America, though frequently spoken of, are little read'. This is still true; and a very great proportion of Bentham's published work has for long been relegated to an intellectual lumber room visited only by the historian. It is clear that the discouraging close print and double columns of the Bowring edition are not solely responsible for this. Even when the new and splendid edition to be published by the Athlone Press of the University of London becomes available, the reading of the largely unread Bentham will not prove easy. The difficulties are well known: so many of the major controversies to which his writings relate are dead or transformed; so many of the reforms demanded in the name of Utility have long been conceded; often only an historian with a detailed knowledge of the period could judge how far the Benthamite reforms which were not adopted would have been an improvement and what the total effect was of those reforms which were adopted. There is, moreover, along with the diverting wit and splendid invective, much eccentric and exasperating pedantry in Bentham's later style with its proliferation of invented 'Greek-sprung' technical terms and his exploration in infinite detail of every project.

Nonetheless, the legend of Bentham's unreadability is disturbing and it is worth attempting an amateur estimate of the amount of Bentham's published work which is, in fact, read at the present time.

* This essay first appeared in the *Proceedings of the British Academy* 48 (1962) and is reprinted here with some minor corrections by permission of the author, the British Academy and the Oxford University Press.

For most readers without a very specialized interest, Bentham's thought is represented by the *Fragment of Government* and the *Principles of Morals and Legislation*. These are easily accessible in modern editions, and are the only works of Bentham's which could be described as widely read and which at the present time enter regularly, though (*crede experto*) by no means in their entirety, into the academic teaching of political philosophy or politics or jurisprudence. The specialist in the philosophy of law—a small enough class in this country—reads the two brilliant works discovered by Mr. Charles Everett among the Bentham folios: *The Comment on the Commentaries*[2] and *The Limits of Jurisprudence Defined*.[3] Mr. C. K. Ogden's book, published in 1933 on Bentham's *Theory of Fictions* with its collection of passages from the essays on Logic, Ontology, and Universal Grammar, brought to the notice of philosophers, in most cases almost certainly for the first time, the fact that Bentham had anticipated by a century part of Bertrand Russell's doctrine on logical constructions and incomplete symbols. That doctrine, at the time of Mr. Ogden's publication, was looked upon by many English and American philosophers as the paradigm of philosophical method and the prime solvent of philosophical perplexities. Finally, Dr. Starks's recent three-volume anthology[4] of the economic writings, much of which had not been previously published, has done something to show to economists the range and power of Bentham's thought on monetary theory, investment, and employment. It is clear that there is cause to question Lord Keynes's judgement that 'Bentham was not an economist at all'.[5]

Quantitatively the works I have mentioned constitute a tiny fragment of the whole. They amount together to about 750,000 words. But the Bowring edition alone, if we exclude the last two volumes (which are occupied with correspondence and biography), must on a conservative estimate contain about 5 million words and it is by no means the whole of what will appear in the new edition now planned. How far does this matter? Do the few works which are commonly read and lectured upon or discussed in universities and elsewhere represent adequately all that is still of living speculative interest in the product of Bentham's mind? Is it true that the rest for all its bulk and diversity of subject-matter is only of historical interest? Constitutional Code, Education, Model Prison, Legislative Procedure, The Law of Evidence, Usury, Taxation, Declarations of Rights—is it true that all this is mere application and painful elaboration in detail of the few principles which can be adequately understood from the few works that are still constantly read? John Stuart Mill's essay may, I think, have done something to spread the impression that this must be so. For in his assessment of Bentham's qualities Mill asserts that the novelty and value of what he did 'lay not in his opinions but in his method' which Mill described as the 'method of detail'. My own view which I shall shortly attempt to substantiate is that this is a misleading dichotomy between opinions and methods. Methods sufficiently novel, as some of Bentham's were, cannot be mere innovations of method. They presuppose too fundamental a reorientation of the direction of inquiry, and too radical a shift in the conception of what is to be considered an acceptable answer. We are too often forced to the conclusion that Bentham has provided us with a new question, rather than merely a new answer, for his innovation to be considered matters of method alone.

Mill says that Bentham's novelty of method lay in his remorseless insistence on the criticism of existing law and institutions, and in his schemes of reform on 'treating wholes by breaking them down into parts, abstraction by resolving them into things and generalizations by distinguishing them into the individuals of which they are made up'. These are of course among the habits of thought and the modes of investigation of the scientist, and it may well be thought that when they are used in the application of the principles of Utility to such subjects as the Panopticon prison, or the reform of the Poor Law or the Court of Chancery, nothing of lasting speculative importance is likely to emerge. Haphazard experimentation with what I shall call (of course inaccurately) the unread Bentham, is apt to confirm this impression. A *sors Benthamiana* made with the finger at random is likely to bring to light a passage prescribing, perhaps, the precise shape and size of the beds or the form of central heating to be used in prisons, or the clothes or even the bedding to be used in workhouses. The following passage on the paupers' bedding perhaps conveys the flavour sufficiently well:

Beds stuffed with straw: one side covered with the cheapest linen or hempen cloth for summer; the other with coarse woollen cloth for winter. Stretching the under sheet on hooks, pins or buttons will save the quantity usually added for tucking in. In cold weather that the woollen may be in contact with the body the sheet might be omitted. A rug and two blankets and an upper sheet to be of no greater width than the cell and to be tacked on to one of the blankets. . . . Straw, the more frequently changed the better particularly in warm months. To the extent of the quantity wanted for littering cattle, the change will cost nothing, and beyond that quantity the expense will only be the difference between the value of the straw as straw and the value of it as manure.[6]

It is perhaps difficult when immersed in this—or indeed sunk in it—to remember that this is a philosopher writing; but two things should prevent our forgetting it. The first is that embedded even in this kind of detail there are bold and provocative reaffirmations of

the general principles which gain in clarity and in a sense reveal more
of their meaning when applied to small things. Thus only eight pages
before this disquisition on bedding there is a discussion of 'the only
shape which genuine and efficient humanity [in dealing with the
indigent poor] can take'.[7] As in the state so in the poor house 'the
duty-and-interest-juncture-principle' is to be applied so that throughout it shall be in the interests of the managers to look after those in
their care. The salaries of the governor is to be reduced for every
woman who dies in childbirth and to vary with the number of
juvenile inmates who survive from year to year. Extra premiums and
bounties are to be awarded for less than average mortality. Why so?
Because, says Bentham,

> every system of management which has disinterestedness pretended or real
> for its foundation is rotten at the root, susceptible of a momentary pros-
> perity at the outset but sure to perish in the long run. That principle of
> action is most to be depended upon whose influence is most powerful,
> most constant, most uniform, most lasting and most general among
> mankind. Personal interest is that principle and a system of economy built
> on any other foundation is built upon a quicksand.[8]

A study of the duty-and-interest-juncture-principle thus applied by
Bentham as early as 1797 to the microcosm of the poor-house would
correct many errors in the interpretation of Bentham's radicalism.
It would kill the common theory that to the objection that on his
principles there was no reason why the legislator should make such
laws as would secure the greatest happiness of the greatest number,
Bentham could only reply by making the assumption that the
legislator was a person who *happened* to find his own happiness in
promoting that of others.[9]

But, secondly, the extraordinary combination in Bentham of a
fly's-eye view of practical detail with boldness or even rashness in
generalization, especially about human nature, is of more than
psychological interest. It was part of the intellectual tactics if not the
strategy of the campaign for reform. It was said by Bentham's critics
that he believed mistakenly that if he could articulate to the last
detail the application of a general theory, he believed that this
showed the theory to be sound.[10] This interesting criticism is, I
think, false; what is, however, true is that he thought the criticism of
existing institutions unaccompanied by demonstrably practical
alternatives was worthless; and he believed this not only because
criticism, like everything else, was to be judged by its Utility, but
because hatred of anarchy and disorder was as strong a passion with
him as hatred of blind custom and conservatism. For all his vehe-
mence against the oppressors of his day and their abettors the

judges and lawyers, his advice was 'To obey punctually; to censure freely'[11] until a sober calculation in terms of utility showed a clear profit in disobedience. But to criticize and destroy *without* a clear conception of what was to follow was, for Bentham, the mark of the anarchical spirit, and the now tiresome blueprints with their forests of detail did more than manifest Bentham's strange temperament. They were intended to be a demonstration that a middle path between conservatism and anarchy was possible, and this was itself to destroy the neurotic fear of innovation which was one of the major obstacles to reform.

II

Still the question remains: What sort of speculative interest remains now to be extracted from the vast unread areas of Bentham? Will better acquaintance with them widen the scope of the discussion of his ideas which has for very many years been confined to a very few topics expounded in relatively few of Bentham's pages. For the topics have been few as well as the pages. In this century little of Bentham's thought has been regularly expounded, discussed, and criticized apart from the philosophical and psychological doctrines of utility which concern the relation of pain and pleasure to desire and action on the one hand, and to morality and the criticism of social institutions on the other. So it is, I think fair to say, that Bentham has become almost exclusively a text (often indeed displaced by Mill's *Essay on Utilitarianism*) for the debate of a few questions regarded of prime importance in the teaching of moral philosophy. Is all desire for pleasure or the avoidance of pain? Is it possible to compare the pleasures and pains of different persons? Is moral arithmetic, that is a calculus of pleasures and pains, intelligible and if intelligible is it applicable to all or only some types of moral issues or questions of legislative choice? Can Justice be accommodated within an analysis of all moral ideas in terms of Utility as merely the most efficient means of distributing pain or pleasure? Or can one accommodate it and other apparently recalcitrant moral notions with the aid of the refinement—or device—known as 'restricted utilitarianism' at which Bentham himself at least hinted[12] and which treats Utility not as the criterion of particular actions but of general rules and social institutions?

All these are of course immensely important questions in philosophy and with major changes in the general tone and temper of the philosophy of mind such as have taken place in the past thirty years, new life has been given to them. Thus, for example, in the light of the

new understanding of the concept of pleasure which has been gained
largely from a more detailed and philosophically more sensitive
scrutiny of the vast diversity of the *idioms* of pleasure it seems no
longer possible to treat pleasure, as Bentham for the most part does,
as always the name of an identifiable sensation[13] having the modali-
ties of intensity and duration and the other 'dimensions' which
he attributes to it. Nor is it possible to differentiate between the
different kinds of pleasure as Bentham appears to do, that is by distinguishing the different *causes* which produce the identifiable sensation of pleasure. It is of course true that we take pleasure in eating or
drinking; that we enjoy a walk; that we are pleased with a child's
progress, or by someone's good fortune, or at the news of an inheri-
tance, or of Hitler's defeat. These are examples of what Bentham
describes as the pleasures of sense, of property, of expectation, and
so on. But nothing but an obstinate loyalty to the philosophy of
mind of the eighteenth century could make us say that these are all
cases where a sensation of pleasure occurs and is produced by so
many different causes. What we *do* mean by referring to these as
cases of pleasure has, no doubt, not yet been exhaustively or even
sufficiently explained. But the outlines at least of a new and more
realistic analysis are clear. The elements previously treated as mere
empirical evidence of a separately identifiable sensation of pleasure
have now been introduced into the analysis of pleasure.[14] The wish
for prolongation of the activity or experience enjoyed; the resistance
to interruption; the absorbed or rapt attention; the absence of some
further end beyond the activity enjoyed—these are surely conceptually and not merely empirically linked with pleasure, and this
revision in analysis must call for a restatement of the propositions of
psychological hedonism and so for a fresh criticism of them. For the
proposition that all desire is for pleasure (or the avoidance of pain)
has now lost its simple outline which depended on treating pleasure
as always some sensation caused by our activities: and it was this
which made the idea appear easily intelligible even if it was empirically false.

Similarly, the idea of a calculus of pleasures and pains must be re-
interpreted in the light of a different and, I should say, better understanding of the concepts of pain and pleasure, if only because it
seems clear that they do not have the logical symmetry which
Bentham ascribes to them. But it is by no means clear that Bentham
will, on all points, be the loser by this process of reinterpretation; on
some points the wheel will perhaps be seen to come full circle. Thus
thirty years ago both philosophers and economists of repute said and
indeed wrote that it was logically impossible, not merely difficult, in
fact to compare one man's pleasure or satisfaction with another's.[15]

On this view, assertions that a starving man gets more satisfaction than a rich man from a loaf of bread or an extra £1 could never rank as a statement of fact though this status *was* allowed to an individual's comparisons between his own satisfactions as when he says that he got more pleasure from his breakfast than from his lunch. On this theory, dominant thirty years ago and perhaps still flourishing in some quarters, interpersonal comparisons of the intensity of pleasures or satisfactions were nothing but disguised value judgments of a non-utilitarian kind. They expressed the moral or conventional judgments that it was better to give the loaf to the starving man than to the rich man, better, not because it gave more pleasure or satisfaction or happiness but simply because it was 'in itself' better. This sceptical doctrine which would equally deny the status of factual statement to the assertion that one man was more angry or more frightened than another is now exceedingly difficult to sustain, whatever other objections there may be to Bentham's moral arithmetic. For it seems to depend on two dogmas: the first was that the intensity of pleasure is the intensity of a pure sensation; the second was that while the intensity of such sensations could be experienced by and so known to the subject, it could never be known or even inferred with reasonable certainty by others. Both these ideas seem now mistaken, and the second only to be acceptable as part of a total scepticism about the very existence of 'other persons' minds and feelings' which those who held that interpersonal comparisons were value judgments certainly did not intend to espouse. It may well be that for the purposes of an economic metric there were, and are, many good reasons for shifting from talk of satisfactions to 'indifference curves' or 'revealed preferences'. Such comparisons as we can make between different persons' pleasures are no doubt often too crude for the economist's purposes and may be useless to him unless we can not only compare the intensity of different persons' pleasures but *measure* the differences and say by how much one exceeds the other. Nonetheless, the old epistemological arguments against Bentham's doctrine seem wrong. His doctrine needs to be weighed again with the new weights provided by a different understanding of his fundamental concepts of pain and pleasure and the logical relation between them and their manifestations.

III

So though, as I have claimed, the proportion of Bentham's writings that are still texts for discussion is a tiny one, their importance is still very great and their vitality seems to be inextinguishable. I doubt, however, that on these central traditional Benthamite themes very much new light will be thrown as more of his work becomes physically more readable and in fact more read. It is rather a question of deciding what we shall say on these old themes when we look at them afresh through the framework of a new philosophy. I am, however, sure that there are buried amid the detail of the less-read works, new topics which ought to be added to the discussion and I shall devote the rest of this lecture to some examples of these which are pertinent to the disciplines of law and philosophy on which alone I have any right to speak.

I have already said that Bentham was as much inspired by hatred of anarchy and revolution as he was by hatred of the apologist for the established order and the worship, as he called it, of 'dead men's bones'. Now Bentham thought in a wholly original way of these two sets of adversaries blocking the path of rational criticism and reform. This is hardly represented in the few texts of his which are regularly discussed. For he thought of them as both equipped with poisoned weapons[16] for blinding men to their real interests and making them, on the one hand, submissive to tyranny and the oppression of the many by the few and, on the other, prone to insurrection and violence. These poisoned weapons were, in a sense, intellectual ones and are vastly heterogeneous. Some of them were old and false saws or fallacious maxims repeated so often and handed down so long that they have acquired a spurious patina of sanctity. Bentham thought that they stood in the path of the rational criticism of law and social institutions, just as the maxims of scholastic philosophy, wrongly held to be both universally applicable and self-evidently true, stood in the way of progress in the natural sciences:[17] as if, to take a modern example, Darwin's evolutionary theory with its supporting evidence had been met with some hoary causal maxim of the Middle Ages such as 'The less cannot produce the greater' ('Minus nequit gignere plus').

A great many of these stale shibboleths of reaction are collected, criticized, and exploded in Bentham's vastly entertaining *Book of Fallacies* which was conceived by him as an assault on the rhetoric of despotism. The general neglect of this work in the teaching of political theory seems to me strange;[18] for it is as readable and entertaining as it is instructive and it is full of contemporary relevance. Here are dissected The Chinese Argument or the argument from the Wisdom of Our Ancestors; The Hobgoblin Argument or 'No Innovation'; the argument called the Official Malefactors Screen with its slogan, still used, 'Attack us and you Attack all Government'. Here, too, is 'Non Causa pro Causa', by which the cause of progress and obstacles to it are confounded: as when the influence of the Crown and the presence of Bishops in the House of Lords are

represented as the cause of good government, or the education provided at Oxford and Cambridge as the causes of the spread of useful
national learning. Yet for all their importance fallacies of this sort
were not the most dangerous poisoned weapons in the armoury of
reaction nor did their identification and exposure call for the most
original of Bentham's talents. For these fallacies, however beguiling,
were largely of the nature of false statements of fact. Many of them
are indeed pseudo-truisms and their exposure consisted very largely
in rubbing people's noses in the earth of plain fact and plain language
about plain fact. Why speak of learning from the wisdom of our
ancestors rather than their folly? 'It is from the folly not the wisdom
of our ancestors that we have so much to learn.'[19] After all, the best
informed class of our wise ancestors were grossly ignorant on many
subjects compared with the lowest literate class of the people in
modern times.[20] How many of the laity in the House of Lords in the
time of Henry the Eighth could even read? 'But even supposing
them all in the fullest possession of that useful art, political science
being the science in question, what instruction on the subject could
they meet with at that time of day?'[21] So Bentham urges what are
called old times—the wisdom of old times—ought to be called
'young' or 'early' times; for to give the name old to earlier and less-
experienced generations is not less foolish than to give the name of
old man to an infant in its cradle.[22] So in the very name 'old times',
says Bentham, 'there is virtually involved a false and deceptious
proposition'.[23] As the last point shows, Bentham passes easily from
a criticism of fact to a critique of language, and *The Book of Fallacies*
has much to say under the headings of 'question-begging appellatives',[24] 'passion-kindling appellatives',[25] and 'impostor terms'[26]
concerning the use, in political and moral argument, of what is now
called emotive language and persuasive definition.

But behind these sources of deception Bentham saw others more
insidious and less easy to identify which arose quite naturally from
the very forms of human communication and reasoning. Language
was, he thought, an ambiguous instrument in the sense that though
possession of it raised men above the beasts (for not only communication but thought itself depended on it), yet its complex forms
contained possibilities of both confusion and deception which had
been exploited consciously or unconsciously by reactionary and
revolutionary alike. Bentham's writings on language and on logic
are among the most unsatisfactory of the Bowring texts, and a
recension of them by an understanding editor is certainly overdue.
Yet the main lines of his doctrines are clear. In the first place he
insists on the practical utility of these studies and says they are subordinate branches of the study of Human Happiness.[27] Logic had

not come to an end with Aristotle and the scholastics are blamed by Bentham both for conceiving of the subject in too narrow[28] a way and for failing to make clear what was the utility which they claimed for it.[29] In insisting on its utility, Bentham was not making an automatic gesture to his own principles. He really did think that the possibility of sane judgment in politics, and indeed in the conduct of life, depended on an awareness of the snares latent in the very texture of human discourse, the clarification of which was the province of logic.

I do not mean that his logical writings are only of value as so many blows against reaction and revolution. Besides the theory of logical constructions or 'fictions' there are many things of great speculative importance. Among these I should count his insistence on the pregnant truth 'that nothing less than the import of an entire proposition is sufficient for the giving full expression to any the most simple thought'[30] with its important corollary that the meaning of single words are the result of 'abstraction and analysis' from sentential or propositional forms. This idea—that sentences not words are the unit of meaning—was not to appear again in philosophy for fifty years. It was then asserted by Frege[31] and stressed in Wittgenstein's *Tractatus Logico-Philosophicus*.[32] Bentham's main innovations as a philosopher are based on this insight; for he believed that the relation of language and so of thought to the world is radically misunderstood if we conceive of sentences as compounded out of words which simply name or stand for elements of reality and thus as having meaning independently of sentential forms. Philosophy—and not only philosophy—has been perennially beset by the false idea that whenever a word has a meaning there must be some existent thing related to it in some simple uniform way appropriate to the simple uniform atoms of language. Unfortunately Bentham makes this seminal point in the context of a characteristically sketchy genetic theory. He rightly contrasts his own doctrine with the Aristotelian doctrine of terms and ridicules the idea which he thinks is implicit in it: the idea that at some stage in the history of mankind 'some ingenious persons, finding these terms endowed each of them somehow or other with a signification of its own, at a subsequent time took them in hand and formed them into propositions'.[33]

How much of the course of later philosophy would have been altered had Bentham been interested enough in his own doctrine to expound it carefully and at length, or even if his few observations had been read by philosophers no one can say. Certainly no modern philosopher familiar with the metaphysical and logical perplexities which from Plato to Lord Russell were generated by the assumption that words have references or meaning apart from sentential forms, would fail to recognize the importance of Bentham's denial that this is so. But the fate of these philosophical discoveries (for such they were) of Bentham's, was the same as the fate of his best thoughts on economic analysis and policy which anticipated modern views of the power of the State to raise the level of employment and investment. In both cases, ideas now accepted as true and important lay ignored for a century. Some of them were buried unpublished in the cellars of University College; others were published but scarcely less effectively entombed in the print of the Bowring edition.

Sometimes Bentham writes about logic in his very wide sense with an eye very closely on political argument and on the strategy for educating men into a proper awareness of its snares and pitfalls. Thus he believed that, in general, tyranny and oppression in politics were possible only where claims to infallibility of judgment were presumptuously made and stupidly conceded. It was necessary to oppose to these arrogant claims the truth that all human judgment, 'opinion', or 'persuasion' is fallible. This truth, says Bentham, 'whether for the exclusion of obstinate error, or for the exclusion of arrogance, overbearingness, obstinacy and violence [to which he added in a later passage "bigotry"][34] ought never to be out of mind'.[35] John Stuart Mill rightly identified this as a very important element in Bentham's teaching, and his own vindication of freedom of thought and opinion in his essay *On Liberty* is an elaboration of this same theme; for his central argument is that just because individual human judgments are fallible, freedom of thought and discussion are indispensable. But Mill does not attempt to explain why the claim to infallibility, so often made in defence of authority or the *status quo*, is false. Bentham did attempt to do this but I think failed. He thought that the falsity of all such claims to infallibility was a consequence of some simple truths about the character of human judgments; but here I think his limitations as a philosopher begin to appear. For his doctrine is the surely false one that 'of no matter of fact external to, of no matter other than that which passes in a man's own mind can any immediate communication be made by language'. He adds (using a dangerously ambiguous phrase) 'That to which expression is given, that of which communication is made is always the man's opinion nor anything more.'[36] So, according to Bentham, most of our ordinary statements of fact are elliptical and even the simplest is complex in a way not suspected by Aristotle. If, to take Bentham's example, I say that Eurybiades struck Themistocles, all I really assert and all I can assert is: 'It is my opinion that Eurybiades struck Themistocles. This is what I can be sure of and it is all that, in relation to the supposed matter of fact, it is in my power to be assured of.'[37]

This way of disposing of claims to infallibility must be mistaken. No doubt there is an intimate and important connection between the statement (call if *p*) made by a speaker (call him *X*) on a given occasion, and the statement that *X* believed *p*. The natural way of expressing this connection is that *in* saying *p*, *X implied* that he believed it. Of course the sense of a *person* implying something by stating something needs to be clarified and distinguished from the logical relation between two statements where one entails the other. That is, we must distinguish what is implied by *what* a man says from what is implied by *his saying* it. This is perhaps not easy to do; though it is a distinction as important in the law of evidence as it is in philosophy and logic. The analysis of this relationship shows it to be of a general kind in which Bentham himself in his writings on logic and language was much interested. For it seems clear that the intimate connection between *X* saying *p* and his believing it, and the strangeness of saying '*p* but I do not believe *p*', depend on the fact that one of the purposes for which human beings make statements is to invite or induce others to believe them by showing that the speaker believes them too. It may even be true that human discourse could not function as it does unless there is a generally, though not universally, respected convention that we do not say what we do not believe. But none of this supports the theory that the simplest statement is logically complex, so that in asserting *p* we are asserting that we believe *p*. Well-known paradoxes follow from such a theory.[38] So I fear Bentham's demonstration of the fallibility of human judgments fails. Some independent analysis is required of what it is to form and hold a belief or, as Bentham calls it, an 'opinion' or 'a persuasion about matters of fact'.

I have considered this unsuccessful doctrine of Bentham's not particularly to show his limitations, but rather to show that what looks like a Philistine insistence that all studies, logic and metaphysics included, must be shown to contribute to human happiness, was in fact no such thing. For the practical ends to be served were conceived by him in no small-minded way. It was no less than that of making men conscious of the seeds of deception and confusion buried in the very texture of human thought, and so to arm them against those who would use deception and confusion to cheat them of their happiness.

IV

So much for the intellectual armament of one set of adversaries. When Bentham turned from the logical and linguistic defences of blind custom and oppressive authority to his other adversaries—the forces of revolution and anarchy—he thought their principal appeal lay in their exploitation of the idea of an individual right. Here was the centre of the fallacies of Anarchy which tempted men to insurrection and violence by playing upon the very terminology of the law. To dispel the dangerous confusions which, as he thought, had grown or been woven round the idea of an individual's rights, he drew heavily on his doctrine of logical fictions, but his views are not merely an application of that doctrine but also of a less-explicit restrictive doctrine concerning the notion of a *reason* for an action or for feeling. His complete views on the idea of rights, legal and moral, have to be collected from a number of different texts; as widely different in subject-matter and date as the *Essays on Anarchical Fallacies*,[39] the *General View of A Complete Code of Laws*,[40] the *Pannomial Fragments*,[41] *The Limits of Jurisprudence Defined*,[42] *The Essay on Supply without Burden*,[43] and the writings on Ontology[44] and Logic.[45] It seems to me that Bentham really was afraid not merely of intemperate invocations of the doctrine of Natural Rights in opposition to established laws, but sensed that the idea of rights would always excite a peculiarly strong suspicion that the doctrine of utility was not an adequate expression of men's moral ideas and political ideals. There is, I think, something strident or even feverish in Bentham's treatment of rights which betrays this nervousness.

Bentham used his doctrine of logical fictions to dissipate the idea that words like 'duty', 'obligation', and 'right' were names of mysterious entities awaiting men's discovery and incorporation in man-made laws or social rules. Because names of logical fictions had been confused with names of real entities and had been thought to have the same simple relation with reality 'they have raised', says Bentham, 'those thick vapours which have intercepted the light. Their origin has been unknown; they have been lost in abstractions. These words have been the foundation of reasoning as if they had been external entities which did not derive their birth from the law but which on the contrary had given birth to it.'[46] Words like 'duty', 'obligation', 'right' did indeed, according to Bentham, require the special methods of analysis which he invented for logical fictions as a substitute for the straightforward form of definition by genus and species which he held inapplicable to them. Yet, though complex in this way, statements about men's rights or duties were reducible by proper methods to statements of plain unmysterious fact. We cannot say what the words 'obligation' or 'right' name or stand for because, says Bentham, they name nothing; but we can say what statements employing these words mean. 'Obligation', indeed, was Bentham's pet example of a logical fiction and he often uses[47] as a paradigm of his methods his demonstration that to say that a man has an obligation, legal or moral, is to say that he is likely, in the event of his doing or failing to do an action, to incur the 'sanction' of official punishment or popular disapproval.

My immediate concern here, however, is with the idea of a right which Bentham considered to be 'a kind of secondary fictitious entity resulting out of a duty'[48] and in the analysis of it he certainly made some strides. The notion of an individual's right to do something or to be treated in a certain way as distinct from the notion of the right thing to do has proved most elusive even in jurisprudence where only legal rights are at stake. Part of the difficulty is that the idea is not univocal either in law or morals. There are several distinct, though not unrelated, applications of the idea of a right and theorists have often become obsessed with one of them to the exclusion of the others. Hobbes, for example, is almost wholly preoccupied with the important sense in which to ascribe a right to a person is to say no more than that he is neither bound to do or not to do a specific action, or (as Bentham puts it) a sense in which a right 'exists from the absence of obligation'.[49] But of course we do not mean merely this when we say that a person has a right to be paid £10 under a contract or a right to exclude others from his garden. These are cases where the right springs, as Bentham says, not from the absence of a duty but from the presence of a duty upon someone else. Here, Bentham says, what we mean in saying that a person has a right is that he stands to benefit by the performance of a duty[50]; so that all duties necessarily have correlative rights except those 'barren' duties or 'ascetic' obligations which come into existence when, as only too often, the lawmaker flouts the requirements of utility altogether and creates duties which benefit no one.[51] So much for legal rights. As for natural rights or any rights except legal rights these are not logical fictions. To talk of them is nonsense. To assert their existence is like talking of 'a species of cold heat, a sort of dry moisture, a kind of resplendent darkness'.[52] Most often men speak of such rights when bent on having their way without giving a reason for it. Such talk is 'the effusion of a hard heart operating on a cloudy mind'.[53] At its most respectable the assertion that a natural or non-legal right exists is a confusing and usually confused way of asserting that there are good reasons why men should have certain legal rights.[54] Even this is respectable only where the good reasons are those of Utility. Most often the proffered reason is Natural Law and then all is confusion; for, argues Bentham, a reason for a right is not a right (any more than hunger is food) and Natural Law is not a law.[55]

Bentham's analysis of legal rights and the accompanying *reductio ad absurdum* of the idea of non-legal rights seems to me to be mistaken. But his mistakes are illuminating. They were inherited by Mill who struggled against them with only partial success, and I do not think that the later part of Mill's *Utilitarianism* where he has much to say about both rights and duties is comprehensible until we understand the difficulties to which Bentham's analysis gives rise. These difficulties spring indeed from certain fundamental features of Bentham's thought, which lie beneath the surface in many different parts of his works. They need to be brought to the surface and carefully examined. Here I can only indicate in outline the form which I think criticism should take.

Bentham's first error seems to me to be his assertion that in ascribing a legal right to an individual we are simply saying that he is a person who is likely to benefit by the performance of a correlative legal duty incumbent on another person. This view would have as its consequence that all laws, including criminal laws, which imposed duties that were capable of benefiting anyone would confer correlative rights.[56] It would follow that laws requiring military service or payment of income tax would confer legal rights on those who stood to benefit; and similarly a contract between two persons for the benefit of a third party would confer legal rights on him even if he could not himself enforce the contract. In fact, neither lawyers nor laymen treat rules of law which impose beneficial duties as always conferring rights. When they do think and speak of laws as conferring rights it is because as well as imposing duties such laws also provide, in a distinctively distributive way, for the individual who has the right. He is not merely one of an aggregate or class who are likely to benefit from the performance of some legal duty; for the idea of a right, even a legal right, is an essentially *distributive* one. According to the strict usage of most modern English jurists[57] only the rules of civil law such as torts, trusts, or contracts confer rights. Here the person who has a right is something more than a possible beneficiary of duty; he is the person who may, at his option, demand the execution of the duty or waive it. He has, in effect, a limited sovereignty over the person who has the duty and it is neither necessary nor sufficient (though it is usually true) that he will also benefit from the performance of it.

It is, however, also true that a somewhat wider usage of the expression 'a right' is common among non-lawyers and especially among writers on political theory who might not hesitate to say, for example, that when the *criminal* law forbids murder and assault it thereby secures to individuals a right to security of the person, even though he is in no position to waive a duty imposed by the criminal law. But even in this wider usage the person said to have the right is not viewed merely as a member of a class who as a class may be indiscriminately benefited by the performance of a duty. The duty not to kill or wound or assault is unlike a duty of military service; for breach of the former duty necessarily involves the infliction of harm upon a specific or (in Bentham's language) 'assignable' individual, whereas breach of the latter duty does not but at the most merely makes it likely that the community as a whole will be less secure.[58] Thus even this extension beyond the stricter legal meaning of the idea of a right, to include *some* cases where the relevant rule and duty is one of *criminal* law, preserves still some element of the distributive character of the idea.

Thus this analysis even of a legal right fails because it neglects the peculiar provision for individuals considered distributively made by laws which confer rights. But Bentham's *reductio ad absurdum* of non legal rights also fails because it too neglects, though in a different way, the essentially distributive chracter of the idea of a right. While disapproving of all talk of non-legal rights he allows, as I have said, that it sometimes has a meaning, viz. when it is simply an obscure way of asserting that there are good utilitarian reasons for creating a legal right with its corresponding duty. But here it is important to stress that though we may often insist that certain legal rights should be created simply because we believe society in the aggregate will on the whole be better off if this is done, this is not what is meant by the assertion that someone has a moral right.

A simple example may serve to show what we do mean. At the end of the last war it was decided, because of the needs of the economy, to give coal-miners the right of an early release from the forces. This was widely approved, but no one who thought they should be given this right of early release on this ground of general utility expressed his approval by saying that the coalminers on these grounds had a moral right to early release. For that statement would imply that there was a quite different sort of reason for giving them this right; such as that the miners had served longer than others, or more arduously, or had special needs. I do not wish to say these references to deserts and needs *exhaust* the class of reasons which are logically appropriate supports for the ascription of moral rights, but they illustrate the general character which such reasons must have. They must refer to the present properties or past actions of the individuals who are said to have moral rights as in themselves sufficient grounds for treating them in a certain way independently of the beneficial consequences to society of doing so.

It is perhaps plain from this example why Bentham could not, without serious modification of his fundamental principles, accommodate this aspect of non-legal rights and would have felt bound to dismiss it as nonsense. For it involves treating something as a reason for action which could not, according to Bentham, *ever* be a reason. It involves looking upon something such as the individual's deserts or past services as a reason in itself for now doing something for him rather than for someone else. Thus to invoke the past as in itself a determinant of the present distribution of social benefits (or burdens) was, in Bentham's eyes, mere *ipse dixitism*—a form of intellectual bad faith which uses the language of reason to express personal 'antipathy or sympathy', mere irrational sentiment.

It is the principle of antipathy which leads us to speak of offences as *deserving* punishment. It is the corresponding principle of sympathy which leads us to speak of certain actions as *meriting* reward. This word *merit* can only lead to passion and error. It is *effects* good or bad which we ought alone to consider.[59]

This restriction on what can count as a reason dictates the character of much that Bentham has to say on responsibility, on reward, and on moral and legal obligation as well as on rights. It may also account for omissions of which Mill complained such as that of conscience from the Tables of the Springs of Action: for conscience essentially involves accepting past wrongdoing as in itself a reason for remorse and making reparation. It is indeed plain that if we were to accept Bentham's doctrine we should have to discard many concepts besides that of moral or non-legal rights; and we may interpret Bentham not as analysing but as inviting us to discard all such concepts and to substitute others more consistent with the idea of reason implicit in his general philosophy. In either case I think we have here a subject which, for two different reasons, is of considerable contemporary importance. First, the philosophical criticism of Bentham would gain in freshness and precision if it shifted from the now traditional questions to consider the extent to which his philosophy can accommodate these concepts which constitute so much of the framework of any morality. Secondly, there are many contemporary voices calling for a revision on Benthamite lines (though not exclusively for Benthamite reasons) of these concepts. Among these instances of Benthamism revived are some modern attempts to dissolve the problem of free will and to eliminate or dispense with the idea of responsibility (in some at least of the senses of that Protean word) in the treatment of offenders against the criminal law.[60]

Here I can only briefly indicate the impact of Bentham's thought on these important concepts. It is clearest perhaps in his account of the mental conditions of responsibility. According to conventional thought a very fundamental principle of justice is embodied in the doctrine that a man who has done what, so far as outward conduct is concerned, the law forbids, should not be liable to punishment or blame, if at the time of his act he was insane, a young child, or did not know that he was doing what the law forbids, or was under duress, or could not control his bodily movements. This is the doctrine, accepted in all civilized legal systems, that makes what English lawyers call *mens rea* a necessary condition of liability for serious crime. Bentham accepts this doctrine but consistently with his general principles turns its face to the future away from the past. We are to observe such restrictions on the use of punishment not because there is any intrinsic objection to punishing a man who at the time of the crime lacked 'a vicious will' or lacked the 'free use of his will' but because his punishment will be 'inefficacious'. But Bentham does not show why such punishment *must* be useless.[61]

Bentham's analysis of obligation legal and moral similarly looks to the future away from the past, and it is this feature which, I think, renders it defective as an analysis of our actual moral and legal discourse of obligations. Stripped of its interesting complications, due to Bentham's employment of the methods of analysis which he held necessary for logical fictions ('archetypation', 'phraseoplerosis', and 'paraphrasis'),[62] the essentials of his doctrine is that to say that a man is under an obligation to do some action is to say that in the event of failure to do it he is likely to suffer: in the legal case at the hands of officials and, in the moral case, from the manifestations of general 'ill will' by the community or by his associates.[63] So, in this analysis a central place is assigned to the probability or predictability of 'sanctions', i.e. future suffering in the event of non-compliance. There is no doubt an important general connection between the probability of sanctions or of social pressure and obligation; yet the connection is not so close that the statement that someone is under an obligation is a mere assessment of the chance of suffering in the event of disobedience; for the relation between past disobedience and later suffering is not a mere *de facto* relationship of usual concomitance. This is shown by the fact that whereas in any particular case the statement that someone has an obligation to do some action may be easily combined with the assertion that he is in fact (for any of a variety of reasons) unlikely to suffer for neglecting it, it cannot be combined with the statement that his neglect of it is no *reason* why he should suffer. This is so because there is analytically involved in statements, even of legal obligation, acceptance of the idea that past action or failure to act is a reason or justification in terms of legal rules for the infliction of 'sanctions'. Where the sanctions are predictable, this is a derivative consequence of the fact that the connection between disobedience and sanctions is looked upon in this non-predictive justificatory way.

Among the concepts which adhesion to this aspect of Bentham's thought would force us to discard or at least revise is gratitude. Here Bentham who thought and wrote much about the connected idea of reward made his position particularly clear. According to our present concept of gratitude, if we are correctly said to feel gratitude and show gratitude for past benefits it must be the case that we acknowledge past services as a reason in themselves for present feeling or action towards our benefactor. We should no longer be said to be or to feel grateful or to be applying our present concept of gratitude if our reasons for returning the past service was that we should thereby encourage our benefactor or others to repeat or extend their beneficence. Saying 'Thank you' is not just a device for getting more—even for others. Bentham in thinking out when there should be *legal* rights to remuneration for past voluntary services insists that the services alone could never be reason for a reward. Only if the practice of reward is likely to lead to beneficial consequences could there be any reason for reward. 'Reward for past services is an instrument for creating future services.'[64] As a theory of the principles on which the law should compel payment for past services this is no doubt all very good sense; but as a deduction from a philosophical doctrine concerning the idea of a reason for acting it raises disputable issues of vast importance.

What is to be said for and against accepting the restrictive concept of reason, implicit and sometimes explicit, in these parts of Bentham's work? It seems impossible to claim that this is the actual concept of reason which we already have. Yet, at certain points in his attacks on the abuse of sympathy and antipathy or *ipse dixitism*, Bentham attempts to show that it is. His arguments are chiefly developed in connection with the case of contracts or agreement where he condemns those who have failed to see that a past promise is 'no reason in itself', or in itself no 'justifying base' for an obligation. If a promise or agreement constituted a reason in itself it would always be binding but, says Bentham, it is universally agreed that certain contracts of 'pernicious tendency' should not be binding and all legal systems treat them as void. It is therefore the useful tendency of the agreement that renders it valid.[65] This argument seems to me fallacious, or at least inconclusive, though again the legal policy derived from it is very good sense. At the most such argument shows that Utility is a paramount reason which in certain cases of conflict may override other reasons. The argument shows these other reasons to be subordinate to Utility but does not show that they are derived from it.

John Stuart Mill followed very closely Bentham's analyses of obligations and rights and in chapters III and V of his Utilitarianism sought to avoid some of the consequences. He added the 'internal sanction' of conscience to Bentham's list of the sanctions which are 'constitutive' of obligations, and he sought to make the analysis of a moral or non legal right acceptable by insisting on the 'extraordinarily important and impressive kind of utility' on which the assertion of such rights may rest. I may be wrong in thinking that these expedients do not avoid the difficulties inherent in Bentham's restrictive doctrine of reason, but until the ramifications of this doctrine throughout both the work of Bentham and Mill have been fully considered and discussed I do not think we shall have an adequate critique of the Utilitarian philosophy.

These then are some of the topics which I think should be added to the exposition and critical discussion of Bentham. I have no doubt that an economist or political theorist could make at least as good a selection as I have made as a philosopher and a lawyer. But there are some tasks which cannot be adequately performed by one man without the co-operation of others. I hope I have made abundantly clear my conviction that of such necessarily co-operative tasks lecturing on the unread Bentham is one.

NOTES

1. *Dissertations and Discussions*, vol. i, 330–392. 'Bentham' first published in the *London and Westminster Review*, 1838.
2. Oxford: Clarendon Press, 1928.
3. Columbia University Press, 1935. The full version of this work was published in 1970 under the title of *Laws in General* as one of the volumes in the Collected Works of Jeremy Bentham (University of London: The Athlone Press).
4. Allen and Unwin for the Royal Economic Society (London, 1952).
5. *The End of Laissez-Faire*, 19.
6. *Outline of Pauper Management Improved* (Bowring, vol. viii, 389) first published in Young's *Annals of Agriculture*, 1797.
7. Op. cit., 381.
8. Ibid.
9. Some ambiguity in the expression 'legislator' (as between the framer of an ideal Benthamite Constitution and those possessing legislative authority in actual governments) may have befogged the issue. See A. J. Ayer in *Jeremy Bentham and the Law* (London, 1948), 213, where Bentham is said to have made this assumption about the 'lawgiver' or 'legislator'. Professor Ayer cites in support the Introduction to the *Constitutional Code* (Bowring, vol. ix, 7) but here Bentham merely says that the only reason why he himself desires that form of government to be adopted, which would bring about the greatest happiness of the greatest number, is that this would be 'in the highest degree contributory to my own greatest happiness'. He does not assume that this is true of the rulers of any society; their interest must be *made* to coincide with the universal interest by the institution of representative democracy and the other applications of the 'duty-and-interest-juncture-principle' enjoined in Bentham's Constitutional Code.

10. Leslie Stephen, *The English Utilitarians*, vol. i, 283.
11. *A Fragment on Government*, Preface, para. 16. Bowring, vol. i, 230.
12. e.g. in his explanation of the binding force of alienations of property and contracts. See *Principles of Civil Code*, Bowring, vol. i, 332.
13. Interpretations of Bentham's concept of pleasure have sometimes been given which divorce it from sensation or even enjoyment. Thus Burton in his Introduction to the Bowring edition (vol. i, 22 et seq.) claimed that 'the term nearest to being synonymous with pleasure [in Bentham] is volition. What it pleases a man to do is simply what he wills to do.' Though this resembles some modern analyses of pleasure there are formidable objections to it as an interpretation of Bentham: (1) Bentham frequently refers to pleasures as sensations, e.g. in the *Principles of Morals and Legislation*, chap. iv, ss. 5 and 6, and most strikingly the manuscripts published as Appendixes 4 and 5 in Baumgardt's *Bentham and the Ethics of Today* (Princeton U.P., 1952) especially 556, 557 and 577. (2) Bentham gave fifty-eight synonyms for pleasure including in them 'enjoyment' but not 'volition', 'choice' or 'preference' or any cognate idea (see *Table of the Springs of Action*, Bowring, vol. i, 205). The idea of pleasure is said to 'apply itself' to the will and to have as its 'effects' or 'consequences' *velleity, volition*, and *action* (op. cit., 209). (3) For Bentham pleasure and pain are 'real entities' whereas *all* other psychological entities including volition are 'fictions' (op. cit., 211, and Bowring, vol. viii, 207–8). Pleasure and pain are said to be 'susceptible of existence' without the rest and 'as often as they come unlooked for do actually come into existence' without them (Bowring, vol. i, 211).
    Notwithstanding these objections it is certainly arguable that Bentham did not think of the connection between voluntary action and pleasure as merely contingent. But if he did not, it seems likely that he thought 'volition' definable in terms of pleasure and pain rather than vice versa.
14. See T. Penelhum, 'The Logic of Pleasure', *Philosophy and Phenomenological Research*, 1957, 488; G. Ryle and W. B. Gallie, 'Pleasure', *Proceedings of the Aristotelian Society* (Suppl. vol. 28), 1954, 135; B. A. Williams and E. Bedford, 'Pleasure and Belief', ibid. (Suppl. vol. 33), 1959, 57.
15. Robbins, *The Nature and Significance of Economic Science* (London, 1937), 138 et seq.
16. *The Book of Fallacies*, Bowring, vol. ii, 486.
17. *A Fragment on Government*, Preface, para. 24, n. 2.
18. It was published as a paperback in 1962 (Harper Torch-books, New York).
19. *The Book of Fallacies*, Bowring, vol. ii, 401.
20. Op. cit., 400.
21. Ibid.
22. Op. cit., 398–399.
23. Op. cit., 398.
24. Op. cit., 436.
25. Op. cit., 438.
26. Ibid.
27. *Essay on Logic*, Bowring, vol. viii, 221–222, 240–241.
28. Op. cit., 220, 232.
29. Op. cit., 232–234.
30. *Essay on Language*, Bowring, vol. viii, 322.
31. 'Nur im Zusammenhange eines Satzes bedeuten die Wörter etwas', *Die Grundlagen der Arithmetik* (Breslau, 1884), 73.
32. London, 1933. Propositions 3.3 and 3.3:4.
33. Bowring, vol. viii, 322.
34. Op. cit., 321 n.

35. Op. cit., 300 n.
36. Bowring, vol. viii, 321.
37. Ibid.
38. It would follow that two speakers would not be contradicting each other if one of them said 'This is red' and the other 'No; it is not'; they would simply be comparing autobiographical notes about their beliefs. Also if the theory were correct the truth of the statement 'I do not believe this is red' would entail 'this is not red'.
39. Bowring, vol. ii, 500–505.
40. Ibid., vol. iii, 158–160, 181–186.
41. Ibid., vol. iii, 217–221.
42. (Everett ed.), 55, 85, 316–318.
43. Jeremy Bentham's *Economic Writings* (ed. Stark), vol. i, 332–337.
44. Bowring, vol. viii, 206.
45. Op. cit., 245–248.
46. Bowring, vol. iii, 160.
47. e.g. Bowring, vol. iii, 180 and vol. viii, 247–248.
48. *Of Laws in General*, 294.
49. Bowring, vol. iii, 181.
50. Op. cit., 220.
51. Op. cit., 181 and 221ff.
52. Jeremy Bentham's *Economic Writings* (ed. Stark), vol. i, 335.
53. Ibid.
54. Jeremy Bentham's *Economic Writings* (ed. Stark), vol. i, 335, and Bowring, vol. ii, 501.
55. Bowring, vol. ii, 501, vol. iii, 221.
56. Bentham expressly says that this is the case. 'All those words *rights obligations services offences* which necessarily enter into the civil laws are equally to be found in the penal laws. But from considering the same objects in two points of view they have come to be spoken of by two different sets of terms. *Obligations rights services* such are the terms employed in the civil code; *injunction, prohibition, offence*—such are the terms of the penal code.' Bowring, vol. iii, 160.
57. For Austin only those duties of the criminal law which corresponded to offences against determinate persons had correlative rights. All other duties of the criminal law were 'absolute duties'. For Bentham the only duties without correlative rights were self-regarding duties and those, the performance of which could benefit none (see Austin, Lectures on Jurisprudence, Lecture XVIII, 5th ed. 405–406) and Bentham, *Of Laws in General* 58, 294, and Principles of Morals and Legislation, chap. XVI, para. 25N).
58. Bentham distinguishes between offences against assignable individuals. But he nowhere restricts correlative rights to the former class. See *Principles of Morals and Legislation*, chap. xvi, ss. 2–10; Bowring, vol. i, 97–98.
59. *Theory of Legislation* (trans. Hildreth, 2nd ed., London, 1867), 76. This quotation is wrongly referred to Bowring, vol. i, 383, 391, by Halévy in *The Growth of Philosophical Radicalism*, 55. According to C. K. Ogden the chapter ('False methods of Reasoning on the subject of Legislation') from which this quotation is taken is not to be found in the Bowring edition, though the original manuscripts of it are preserved in the University College Collection (Nos. 29 and 32). See *The Theory of Legislation*, ed. C. K. Ogden (London, 1931), xxxviii.
60. See Barbara Wootton, *Social Science and Social Pathology* (London, 1959), chaps. viii and xi, and 'Diminished Responsibility', *Law Quarterly Review* (1960), 224.

61. *Principles of Morals and Legislation*, chap. xv, Bowring, vol. i, 84–85 and 844. See for criticism of this argument my 'Prolegomenon to the Principles of Punishment', *Proceedings of the Aristotelian Society* (vol. 60), 1959, s. 4.
62. *Essay on Logic*, Bowring, vol. viii, 246–248.
63. Op. cit., 247.
64. *Principles of Civil Code*, Bowring, vol. i, 340.
65. *Principles of Civil Code*, Bowring, vol. i, 341. Cf. *Rationale of Reward*, chap. vi, Bowring, vol. ii, 203.

Chapter 5

Bentham's Justification of the Principle of Utility*

Bhikhu Parekh

How ultimate moral principles can be justified is a question that has exercised the minds of nearly all moral philosophers across the centuries, and utilitarians were no exception. Nearly every utilitarian moral philosopher from Paley to Sidgwick has asked how the principle of utility could be shown to be the only proper standard of moral judgment. In this paper I intend to single out Bentham's attempt to justify the principle of utility for detailed examination.

I

Bentham formulates the principle of utility in a number of different ways. Since he believes, for reasons we shall discuss later, that pleasure alone is good, he is clear that morality consists in the pursuit of happiness. But when it comes to specifying whose happiness, he oscillates a great deal. Sometimes when he takes man to be an essentially selfish being[1] he suggests that an individual cannot be expected to judge moral actions by any standard other than his own greatest happiness. But he realizes that if pleasure alone is good, an individual's own happiness cannot be morally more important than anyone else's; therefore at other times he formulates the principle of utility as one that requires moral actions to be judged by their tendency to affect the happiness of 'the community at large'.[2] Since men in other parts of the world too feel pleasure and pain, Bentham feels he cannot consistently stop at the political frontier of a community, and therefore at other times he takes the principle of utility to require that a moral action should be judged by its tendency to affect the happiness of all mankind.[3] But even this cannot be the end of the story since animals too are capable of feeling pleasure and pain. Thus he formulates the principle of utility in cosmic terms and argues that the 'influence of a man's conduct on the happiness of the whole race of sentiment beings must be taken into account before it can with propriety be termed virtuous or vicious, simply and without addition'.[4]

When formulated so widely the principle of utility makes demands that Bentham knows are impossible to meet. It requires a moral agent to ask himself continually how best he can maximize the total

---

* I am grateful to my friends Professors Preston King and Jim Moore for commenting on an earlier draft of this paper.

quantity of happiness in the universe. It implies, for example, that when a man is deliberating whether or not to visit a friend in hospital, or to take his wife out for dinner, he should ask himself if he cannot increase the overall quantity of happiness by, say, writing letters to the victims of a Peruvian earthquake or Pakistani floods, or by taking his neighbour's dog for a walk, or by going from house to house raising money for Oxfam. As the possibilities of increasing happiness are myriad, and as no individual can be expected to know about or be motivated by them all, Bentham knows that if his standard is not to founder on the rock of practicability, he must draw a line somewhere. For the most part therefore he formulates the principle of utility as a 'principle which approves or disapproves of every action whatsoever according to the tendency which it appears to have to augment or diminish the happiness of the party whose interest is in question'. The last phrase 'the party whose interest is in question' is crucial.

Although Bentham does not spell it out in any detail, he seems to want to say that every action takes place within a definite context, and that it is this context that delimits the class of men whose interests constitute the moral agent's primary concern. As different individuals occupy different positions in society,[5] the range of persons whose interests are affected by their actions naturally varies. An ordinary man in ordinary circumstances undertakes actions that affect a relatively small number of people, and therefore can only be expected to take account of the interests of these men. Thus in deciding whether or not to visit a friend in hospital, I do not need to think of the starving millions in the third world or of countless old age pensioners I could cheer up, but only of those likely to be affected by whatever decision I take in this particular case and context. If I had promised to look after my neighbour's children who would be upset if I were to leave them alone and whose misery might cause a great deal of pain to their paralysed mother, I should weigh up the total pain likely to be caused to all these individuals against the amount of pleasure my visit might give to my wife, and decide accordingly.

A public officer or a government is in a very different position. The government is the custodian of the interests of the community as a whole and its actions affect all its members. Its context of action, and therefore its moral constituency, is much wider than that of a private individual. It should therefore promote the happiness of the entire community. In matters concerning foreign policy or war or international trade, its decisions affect the happiness of men in other countries whose interest it should also therefore take into account. Although Bentham is not entirely clear on this he seems to believe that in such cases the government should not give priority to the interests of its own community but should pursue a policy that maximizes the happiness of all involved.[6]

Bentham seems to want to place philosophers, intellectuals and other 'enlightened' men in a special, third, category.[7] As men who have developed universal benevolence, who are not 'seduced' by personal interests or are blinded by sectional 'prejudices', and whose knowledge and wisdom are of universal value, he thinks they can be expected to have a 'real zeal for the service of mankind' and to take sustained interest in the happiness of the entire species. They could and should be expected to expose the rule of 'sinister' interests in other countries, and propose ways and means by which these societies can evolve a form of life capable of maximizing their members' happiness. Bentham looked upon himself as a universal man, as a man who saw all men as his 'fellow-citizens' and to whom the happiness of every man in every part of the world was as dear as his own. And he devoted his life to sending messages and memoranda to almost every country that in his view needed his services. He even advocated an international seminar where enlightened men of different countries could meet, discuss their problems, and work out codes suited to their societies.[8]

Whether a man is a private individual or a public officer or a philosopher, the moral standard governing his action is the same: the pursuit of the greatest happiness of the parties whose interest is in question. What differs is its application, which varies according to the social position of the moral agent and the range of persons affected by his actions. As Bentham's principle of utility is intended to accommodate this diversity of application, it is a mistake to define it as requiring the pursuit of the greatest happiness of the community as a whole, since this is not generally an obligation on a private individual. It is no less a mistake to define it as requiring the pursuit of the greatest happiness in general, since only a philosopher seems to have such an abstract obligation. Bentham's own formulation of the principle of utility as one that enjoins the pursuit of the happiness of those *whose interest is in question* is reasonably unambiguous and best expresses what he has in mind. While it does not eliminate many of the difficulties involved in the principle of utility, it at least delimits its range of application.

Although this formulation of the principle of utility is reasonably unambiguous and clear Bentham seems to have thought that it was not, and therefore he sometimes uses the more involved formula, the greatest happiness of the greatest number.[9] He believed that as the second part of the formula only spelt out the implications of the first, it presented his principle of utility much more clearly than otherwise. However, he came to see later that this was not so. In his unpublished essay on utilitarianism written around June, 1829 he admits that although the greatest happiness of the greatest number formula has 'on the surface' the qualities of 'clearness and correctness', it has 'at bottom the opposite qualities'.[10] Taking the example of a community of four thousand and one men among whom the stock of happiness is more or less equally divided, he argues that if the means of happiness, say the property, of two thousand of them was to be distributed 'anyhow' among the remaining two thousand and one, the amount of unhappiness caused to the minority would so outweigh the happiness issuing to the majority that, while such a move would increase the happiness of the greatest number, it would diminish[11] the total quantity of happiness. Bentham makes his point even more succinctly by imagining what would happen if the two thousand men were distributed as slaves among the rest. While increasing the happiness of the greatest number, would it lead to the greatest happiness in general? 'The question answers itself.' For 'reasons altogether incontestable', Bentham therefore decides to drop the 'appendage' of the greatest number, and the principle of utility as he wants it to be understood centres solely around the aggregative notion of the greatest happiness.

Bentham's principle of utility then lays down that moral actions should be judged by their ability to promote the greatest happiness of the parties affected. In the following sections I shall examine how Bentham shows it to be the only right and proper moral standard.

II

Ideally, says Bentham, a moral principle, like any other proposition, should be accepted only if it can be proved, that is, established conclusively and beyond doubt. A proposition in his view can be proved[12] either empirically by appealing to relevant sense-experience, or deductively by deriving it from a more general proposition. Neither mode of proof, however, is possible in the case of a moral principle. There is no empirical observation that can confirm the principle that it is right to pursue general happiness; and as the principle of utility is the most basic of all moral principles, by definition there is no other more basic proposition from which it can be deduced. Bentham concludes that the principle of utility cannot be 'proved'.[13]

Seeing that it cannot be proved, he sometimes veers to the subjectivist extreme. At times he suggests that since every moral theory must ultimately depend on some general principle that it cannot establish and whose validity it must take for granted, his own moral theory takes the principle of utility as its 'postulatum'.[14] But he is not entirely happy with this position and sometimes inclines to a straightforward emotivist view.[15] 'When I say the greatest happiness of the whole community ought to be the end or object of pursuit . . ., what is it that I express? This and no more, namely that it is my wish, my desire, to see it taken for such. . . .' The principle of utility, in other words, is no more than a statement of Bentham's 'wish', 'feeling', so that if his reader finds a similar wish 'in his breast', Bentham's writings have a message and relevance for him; otherwise it is a 'useless trouble' for him to read them. At other times[16] Bentham gives his wish a hedonistic orientation and argues that as he personally finds pleasure in increasing others' pleasure he is recommending a principle whose adoption would increase general happiness. At other times Bentham takes an intuitionist[17] line and takes it to be self-evident that happiness is good and the greatest happiness the highest good. If some men do not see its self-evident truth, he suggests, that can only be because their minds are clouded by 'prejudices' planted by misguided moralists, or because they are 'sinister' men interested in pursuing their own happiness at the expense of others.

Although Bentham toys with the postulationist, emotivist and intuitionist position, he is clearly not happy with any of them. They are all ultimately subjectivist and provide no check on what postulate a man chooses or what wishes he holds dear. As a political reformer, further, he needs a principle that no 'rational' man could refuse to accept, and that could demonstrate conclusively what institutions or practices are evil and in need of change. Bentham shared Mill's view that ethical subjectivism suited the defenders of the status quo, but never radical reformers. Bentham also feels that unless he can establish the principle of utility on objective grounds, his moral and political science would rest on a shaky foundation.

Realizing that scientific and mathematical models of proof are inapplicable to moral discussion, and that subjectivism is unsatisfactory and unsuitable for his purpose, Bentham looks around for a model that could offer a way out of the impasse. As befits an ex-lawyer and a jurist, he turns to law. Just as a lawyer proves his client's case not in a scientific or mathematical manner but by establishing it beyond reasonable doubt by showing its strength and exposing the weakness of his opponent's case, Bentham evidently thinks that, a moral philosopher too can establish his ultimate principle beyond any reasonable doubt by showing, positively, how it is basically correct and by demonstrating, negatively, how its 'rivals' or 'opponents' are wrong. Bentham does not seem to be conscious of applying the legal model, but the general structure of his argument and his language and assumptions[18] clearly indicate that his justification of the principle of utility is modelled after the lawyer's defence of his client. Accordingly he divides his justification of it into two stages: he first makes out a positive case for the principle of utility and then subjects all other principles to detailed criticism with a view to exposing their inconsistencies and contradictions.

III

Morality, Bentham argues, consists in the pursuit of good and avoidance of evil. As morality is the *pursuit* of good and the avoidance of evil, good and evil by definition are pre-moral notions. There are no goods called *moral* goods; there are only goods whose *pursuit* constitutes morality.[19]   In other words the terms moral and immoral can only be used to describe human pursuits, and not their ends or objectives.[20] We must therefore first define good and evil before we can determine what moral conduct consists in. By good, Bentham says, we mean that which we like or enjoy, and by evil that which we loathe or dislike. As the only thing a man can possibly like or dislike is an experience, a sensation, it is only a sensation that can properly be referred to as good or bad. Morality therefore is a pursuit of enjoyable, and an avoidance of disagreeable, sensations. Now the sensations which men enjoy vary from individual to individual: they find different activities pleasant and unpleasant. If therefore we can find out why men enjoy or loathe these activities, and ascertain what sensations they naturally, by the very constitution of their nature, find enjoyable or disagreeable, we would arrive at a conception of what is really, naturally, ultimately, good or evil. What we need to do therefore is to undertake a systematic analysis of human nature. To put the point differently, every moral theory in Bentham's view ultimately rests on a theory of man.

Bentham knows that any such attempt to 'base' a moral theory on a theory of man is an exceedingly complicated enterprise. A moral theory cannot require man to do what he is constitutionally incapable of doing; it must therefore accept him as he is. But if it only demands what he anyway does naturally, it would lack prescriptive power and would not in any sense be a moral theory at all. In other words, it must only demand what man can do, but at the same time it must demand more than what he is generally in the habit of doing.

Bentham's theory of man is too well-known to need elaboration. Man for him is a creature who, by the very necessity of his nature, desires pleasures and loathes pain. As Bentham puts it in a famous paragraph:

Nature has placed mankind under the governance of two sovereign masters, pain and pleasure. It is for them alone to point out what we ought to do, as well as to determine what we shall do. On the one hand the standard of right and wrong, on the other chain of causes and effects, are fastened to their throne. They govern us in all we do, in all we say, in all we think: every effort we can make to throw off our subjection, will serve but to demonstrate and confirm it. In words a man may pretend to abjure their empire: but in reality he will remain subject to it all the while.[21]

There can be no action without a cause, and what causes human action is a motive. As the pursuit of pleasure (and the avoidance of pain) is the only motive a man can be guided by, all human actions are and cannot but be caused by the desire for pleasure. As Bentham puts it, 'take away all pleasure and all pain, and you have no desire', and when there is no desire, there is no motive, and no will.[22] As J. S. Mill was to put it later,[23] 'to desire anything, except in proportion as the idea of it is pleasant, is a physical and metaphysical impossibility'. 'To be happy or *not to be at all*: such is the option which Nature has given to every human being,[24] Bentham remarks.

As pleasure and pain are the ultimate constituents of human nature, all human desires, motives, moral values are reducible to them. They are 'the roots—the main pillars or *foundations* of all the rest, the matter of which all the rest are composed'[25]; 'without any of the rest, these (pleasure and pain) are susceptible of existence', but without them, 'no one of all those others ever had, or ever could have had, existence'.[26] If we take any human desire and analyse it into its basic components, we shall see, says Bentham, that it is at bottom a desire for pleasure. A politician seeks office because he finds pleasure in exercising power; a businessman seeks wealth because he finds pleasure in owning and spending money; a martyr dies for his cause because he finds more pleasure in it than in anything else. Again, take any of the moral virtues like temperance and justice or moral vices like cruelty. What makes them virtues, Bentham argues, is the fact they promote human happiness. Cruelty is bad because it causes pain; temperance is a virtue because it avoids the pains of excesses, and justice is a desirable quality because it 'prevents the pain of disappointment'. Or take, again, the ideas of duty and obligation. A man discharges a legal obligation because he fears the punishment that would otherwise follow, and he fulfils a moral duty because he loathes the pains of social disapproval and those arising from 'pangs' of conscience. On the basis of these and other examples Bentham concludes that unless they are traced to pleasure and pain, moral, psychological and political entities have 'no fixed, no real import'[27] and are 'so many empty sounds'.

Having shown that by the very constitution of his nature man desires nothing but pleasure, Bentham thinks he has no difficulty in showing why pleasure is good. By good he says we mean that which we enjoy or like. By his very nature, Bentham argues, man likes pleasure; therefore pleasure is *a good*. As Bentham thinks he has shown how all good things are pursued only because of their hedonistic content, he concludes that pleasure is *the good*, the only good there is. He goes even further. Good for him means whatever we enjoy; but this is also how pleasure itself is defined, pleasure being the sensation we enjoy. Thus pleasure and good are conceptually identical and are two different ways of describing the same thing. Pleasure, in other words, is not just *a* good, or *the* good, but *goodness itself*. To say that *X* is good but not pleasant, or that *Y* is pleasant though not good, is in Bentham's view to make a self-contradictory statement, and to betray ignorance of the meaning of the terms 'good' and 'pleasant'. To avoid misunderstanding of Bentham's position it must be repeated that in describing pleasure as good he is not using the term 'good' in a moral but in a pre-moral or natural sense. As we saw earlier, Bentham believes that moral good can be defined only after 'good' itself has first been defined in natural or non-moral or 'pathological' terms.

As pleasure alone is good, Bentham argues that it is only rational to have as much of it as possible. To pursue less of it when more is available, or to forego opportunities of pursuing it, is not only irrational but also immoral.[28] It is true that certain pleasures are 'impure' and bring pain in their trail. It is also true that some pleasures are very intense and desensitize their recipients to other pleasures, thus diminishing their overall happiness over a period of time. While this means that pleasures should be pursued in moderation, moderation is not to be practised as intrinsically valuable (as Aristotle had argued) but only as a means to an eventual maximum, as part of a larger strategy of maximizing the total quantity of happiness. In other words, while the immoderate pursuit of *a* pleasure can be irrational, pleasure itself must be pursued to the highest possible degree.

Further, as pleasure alone is good, it is good irrespective of whether it is your pleasure or mine. A moral man therefore ought to aim at the greatest happiness in general, irrespective of whether it is he himself or someone else who is its recipient. One unit of *X*'s happiness is equal to one unit of *Y*'s happiness, and there is no reason why he should prefer himself to *Y*. Similarly if an action of his gives him two units and *Y* three units of happiness, it is irrational of him to prefer himself to *Y*. As pleasure and pain alone are morally relevant, individual men are morally irrelevant by definition, except as representing so many units of pleasure and pain. Since morality is essentially a matter of the arithmetic of pleasures and pains, it is irrational, indeed immoral, to consider individual men as separate factors in moral deliberation.

Let us briefly recapitulate the way Bentham relates his moral theory to his theory of human nature. His view of man is that he finds pleasure enjoyable and therefore good. Since pleasure is good, and it is man's nature to pursue it, Bentham accepts it as an end of moral action. In this basic sense Bentham's moral theory is grounded in his theory of man. It is not, however, man's natural tendency to pursue the greatest happiness in general. Often he pursues his own happiness at the expense of others, and at times he does not pursue even his own happiness in a way that secures the greatest quantity of it. Bentham's moral theory, on the other hand, lays down that since pleasure is good, the only *rational* thing for an individual to do is to pursue it to the maximum, and to pursue it irrespective of whether it is his or anyone else's. In this twofold sense of emancipating the pursuit of happiness from its egoistic basis, and insisting that the pleasure sought must be the maximum possible, Bentham's moral theory goes beyond what men generally do. It draws the end of morality, viz. happiness, from human nature; but gives it a direction (happiness not only for oneself but for all) and a quantitative aspect (maximum possible happiness), both of which are contributions made by human reason. For Bentham, in other words, moral theory is ultimately nothing more than a coherent rational reconstitution of man's natural desires. That is, morality is only rationalized or rationally reconstituted (human) nature. As Bentham himself puts it, hedonism is the 'foundation' on which the structure of utilitarianism 'the fabric of felicity', is built 'by the hands of reason'.[29]

IV

Having made out a case for the principle of utility, Bentham argues that if it is correct then all other principles that differ from it— all its 'rivals' as Bentham calls them—'must necessarily be wrong'.[30] If he can show that this is so, Bentham thinks he would have provided an additional reason for accepting the principle of utility. Now the principle of utility as he has outlined it maintains two basic theses. First, a moral action ought to be judged by its consequences. And second, consequences ought to be judged in terms of pleasure. Its 'rivals' therefore fall into two categories. They either maintain that an action ought not to be judged by its consequences but by something else, which Bentham thinks can only be the 'internal' subjective 'feelings' of the moral agent; or they might accept that a moral action should be judged by its consequences, but insist that consequences should be evaluated not in terms of pleasure but pain. These two rival moral theories Bentham refers to as the principle of sympathy and antipathy and the principle of asceticism respectively.

He defines the principle of sympathy and antipathy (which he sometimes also calls 'the principle of caprice', the 'arbitrary principle' and 'ipsedixitism') as a principle 'which approves or disapproves of certain actions not on account of their tending to augment the happiness . . . of the party whose interest is in question, but merely because a man finds himself disposed to approve or disapprove of them: holding up that approbation or disapprobation as a sufficient reason for itself, and disclaiming the necessity of looking out for any extrinsic ground'.[31] It is a principle that in Bentham's view appeals to individual sentiments and produces no other ground for a decision than that the moral agent thinks or feels so. Any moral theory that does not appeal to consequences is in his view forced to adopt such a subjectivist view, as he thinks is the case with all traditional moral theories like natural law, common sense, moral sense, equity, right reason and fitness of things.[32] For example, the moral sense of different individuals differs, thus leaving room for interpretation that must inevitably remain subjective. Similarly the law of right reason or nature, Bentham argues, is only a pretentious way of clothing the speaker's personal likes and dislikes in the language of general principles. When a man talks of right reason, it is not right reason *per se*, because there is no such thing, but only the reason that *he* considers right that is being held up as an authority. And similarly as there are no principles written in the universe or in human heart, natural law, 'an obscure phantom', in effect refers to nothing more than the moral feelings of the individual moral agent. The appeal to common sense is particularly pernicious as no man likes to appear to be without it, and therefore any principle that does not accord with his feelings is automatically ruled out as not in accord with common sense.

Bentham rejects the principle of sympathy and antipathy on a number of grounds. As a 'despotical' principle that makes the feelings of a single individual the arbiter of what is good and bad, it provides no means of deciding what is to be done when feelings of different individuals conflict. As subjective feelings are made the sole standards of judgment, discussion and debate are not possible; each individual states his feelings on a matter under discussion, asserts his approval or disapproval, and that is the end of the matter. As Bentham puts it, 'Let the common sense of one of them command what the moral sense of another leaves indifferent or forbids . . ., or let the like conflict have place between two philosophers of the common sense. When each of them has delivered the response of his oracle . . . all argument should . . . be at an end'.[33] As they do not share a common universe of discourse, they lack common general criteria in terms of which to formulate and resolve their differences. They might perhaps agree to resolve their differences by vote. But that is not easy, since someone's moral sense or common sense might disapprove of such a procedure. And even if they all did agree, someone might insist that his moral sense dictates unanimity as the only acceptable procedure in certain types of decisions. In other words, the principle of sympathy makes organized social life impossible. Bentham angrily remarks that it is such an absurd principle that its 'progenitor' must be a 'genius of nonsense'.[34]

In politics the principle has further dangerous consequences. It leaves the ruler free to behave as his subjective feelings dictate. James the First burnt two Arians because he took a strong dislike to their views, and he almost banned the consumption of tobacco because he disapproved of it. The principle of sympathy offers us no ground on which to criticize him. Further, this principle is a recipe for social decay. It accepts individual preferences as given, as natural, and credits them with an infallibility they do not merit. It does not inquire, and even declares impossible any attempt to inquire, into how an individual came to have the subjective feelings he has,[35] whether they were planted from outside by 'sinister' interests and/or misguided religions, and whether and how they can be replaced. As the principle of sympathy thus forecloses the possibility of reforming the individual and society, it is essentially an enemy of progress and human well-being.

The principle of sympathy is open to other objections as well. Subjective feelings do not generally form a coherent whole; and as they tend to pull in different directions, individual judgment tends to lack consistency.[36] A man might approve of a practice today, but if his feelings change, he would disapprove of it the next day. When human behaviour lacks predictability and regularity, no social life is possible. Again, as feelings are more easily aroused by immediate events and experiences than by remote but perhaps more important events, a near and clear evil tends to get attention while a remote but more dangerous evil arouses no concern at all. Such a society lives from day to day and is unable to cope with major crises or to execute radical reforms. Finally, Bentham thinks the principle of sympathy breeds intolerance. As each individual feels that his subjective feelings are right and infallible, and he has no means of resolving his differences with others, he is more likely than not to be intolerant of disagreement, and wish to suppress it.

Having disposed of the principle of sympathy to his satisfaction, Bentham turns to the principle of asceticism. By the principle of asceticism, which Bentham believes is held by some philosophers, mainly Stoics, and by Quakers, Dumplers, Moravians and 'other religionists', he means a principle 'which, like the principle of utility, approves or disapproves of any action according to the tendency which it appears to have to augment or diminish the happiness of the party whose interest is in question; but in an inverse manner: approving or disapproving of actions in so far as they diminish his happiness; disapproving of them in as far as they tend to augment it'.[37] Bentham finds it such an absurd principle that he cannot see how any sane man could ever subscribe to it.

As he is convinced that man is essentially a pleasure-seeking animal, Bentham believes that when men appear to pursue pain, they must really be motivated by the hope of eventual pleasure, whether on earth or in heaven. He takes a few facetious examples to show that this in fact is the case. When Christian and religious ascetics engage in harsh practices and inflict pain on themselves, this is because they believe that it will please God and secure them divine merit. When non-religious ascetics endure pain, their motivation is not very different either. Even though Stoics, for example, claimed to despise pleasure, they were, in fact, opposed only to physical or 'so-called' gross and sensual pleasure. And this was so because they thought that only thus could they obtain spiritual happiness. Referring to Peregrinus Proteus who burnt himself alive, Bentham remarks that all available evidence points to the fact he was really guided by the pleasure of reputation which 'had shut the doors (of his mind) not only against all future contingent pleasures but against the pain of burning'.[38] As Bentham feels he has shown that ascetics are ultimately motivated by pleasure, he concludes that the principle of asceticism is 'at bottom but the principle of utility misapplied'.

He also notices other weaknesses in the principle of asceticism. It is incapable of consistent universal application. If everyone acted on it, the species would become extinct in a day.[39] A principle that spells universal death can hardly be accepted as a moral principle. It is also worth noting, says Bentham, that while its adherents believe pain to be good, they do not advocate inflicting pain on others, which is strange and inconsistent, since if pain was good, one should inflict it not only on oneself but also on others. In other words, when it comes to social relationships, the adherents of the principle of asceticism are forced to fall back on the principle of utility.

V

Bentham's case for the principle of utility considered above is open to a number of objections and must be judged unsatisfactory.[40]

Following our order of exposition I shall first examine Bentham's positive arguments in support of his principle, and then his critique of its rivals. I shall then comment very briefly on the propriety of the legal model that underlies his justification of it. Needless to say, I am not interested in evaluating the principle of utility in general but only the way Bentham justifies it.

As we saw earlier Bentham's positive case for the principle of utility rests on two basic theses: the first, psychological hedonism, asserts that pleasure and pain are the ultimate principles of human action; and the second, ethical hedonism, asserts that pleasure alone is good, and pain alone evil. Neither thesis is convincing.

Although pleasure and pain are central to his theses, Bentham never analyses their nature and relationship. He refers to them as sensations without realizing that this is true only in those cases where pleasure can be abstracted from an activity and enjoyed in itself. Urmson's[41] example of smelling roses because one enjoys the pleasant sensation of smell would seem to belong to this category. There are, however, other more common and important cases where, as Bradley puts it, 'not a pleasure but something pleasant is what we experience',[42] so that pleasure is not a sensation but a tone, a quality, an 'aspect' of a sensation. Again, Bentham believes mistakenly that all hedonic sensations or aspects of sensations can be exhaustively classified into those of pleasure and pain. There are states of mind, for example, a feeling of indifference to the consequences of one's action, that cannot properly be described as states of pleasure or pain. Also, pleasure, like pain, is a sensation of a certain minimal intensity. And therefore before this intensity is reached, it is not a sensation of pleasure or pain at all. There are, for example, sensations of discomfort like the tickling of the sole of the foot or a slightly sore throat that have not yet become sensations of pain. This raises some acute conceptual problems and some have felt that they could only describe these sensations as cases of 'nonpainful "pain"'[43] a 'pain' that has not yet reached a threshold of pain.[44] Bentham is also wrong in assuming that pleasure and pain are opposites. There are unpleasant sensations, a pricking sensation for example, that are not painful. And similarly there are painful sensations, pressing a wound for example, that need not be unpleasant.

Neither is it true that man is naturally and necessarily averse to pain. It is not an uncommon experience to search an aching tooth with one's tongue and deliberately to aggravate the pain.[45] Or take the example of a masochist. It might be that he endures pain because he gets pleasure out of it, or rather that he suffers one *type* of pain because he likes another type of pleasure that grows out of it.[46] But this need not necessarily be so. It is not impossible to imagine a masochist who suffers pain, shows all the signs indicating distress, and yet offers no evidence of enjoyment. It would be wrong to assert in the absence of any identifiable signs that he *must* unconsciously be enjoying his pain in some mysterious depths of his being.[47] In that the term 'masochist' refers to a man who *enjoys* or *likes* pain, who suffers pain *because* he gets pleasure out of it, we need another term to describe a person who suffers pain not because he likes it but simply because he *wants* to, and who gets no pleasure whatever from his pain.

If pleasure and pain are not opposites, and if the absence of pleasure does not mean pain, and the absence of pain pleasure, it becomes extremely important to decide whether man is motivated by the desire for pleasure or by the desire to avoid pain. Bentham hedges on this crucial question.[48] Sometimes he says that man is motivated both by the desire for pleasure and aversion to pain. But this is clearly unsatisfactory, since we need to know how the two are related. Which is more basic—the desire for pleasure or aversion to pain? What happens when they conflict? Can one be explained in terms of the other? Can one say, for example, that pleasure 'is wholly caused by pain' and that it is only a 'consciousness or freedom from . . . pain'?[49] Does man loathe pain *because* he desires pleasure? Or does he desire pleasure *because* he loathes pain? If the desire for pleasure is more basic, it gives rise to an activist and adventurous view of man and to a moral theory that makes pursuit of pleasure its central end. If aversion to pain is more basic, a rather timid and cautious view of man emerges, and the moral emphasis would tend to be on eliminating pain rather than on conferring pleasure, on negative rather than positive utilitarianism. The difference between the two views is, of course, one of degree, but this degree is of considerable significance. Unlike Locke and James Mill who held that aversion to pain was more basic and therefore explained human action in terms of the desire to remove 'uneasiness', Bentham generally tends to take the more buoyant and optimistic view that the desire for pleasure is more basic.[50] Since, strictly speaking, a hedonist is one who regards the pursuit of pleasure, and not merely the absence of pain, as the spring of human action, Bentham is a hedonist in a way that Locke and James Mill are not. If this sounds too drastic a conceptual contrast, one might say that while Locke and James Mill are negative hedonists, Bentham is a positive hedonist.

Bentham's hedonism requires him to argue that since man desires pleasure, all his desires are desires for pleasure and that it is the hope of eventual pleasure that motivates all human actions. As T. H. Green observed, Bentham is required to say that a desire is excited by

the anticipation of its own satisfaction.[51] While this view can account
for those activities where there is a conscious pursuit of pleasure, it
does not account for many others. When I am thirsty, I desire a
drink. I desire it because I want to remove the 'pain' of thirst. This
would seem to be a perfectly satisfactory explanation of why I want
a drink and is in accord with common experience. But Bentham
cannot be satisfied with this explanation. He needs to say that I
desire a drink because I desire the pleasure that would issue when I
have quenched my thirst. In other words, I must have a conception
of future pleasure before I can desire to drink. Now this is a mistake.
In the first place, we are not conscious of hoping for such a pleasure
when we desire a drink, but only of the actual pain we wish to relieve.
Second, it confuses what Bradley called 'a pleasant thought' with 'a
thought of pleasure'.[52] When thirsty I find my drink pleasant, but it
is not the case that I am desiring it in order to get the pleasure of a
thirst quenched. As I desire a drink it is the drink and not pleasure
that is the *object* of my desire. The thought of the drink is pleasant,
but there is no reason to postulate the pleasure of a satisfied thirst
as a separate thought. This point comes out most clearly in the case
of a martyr. His commitment to his cause excites and pleases him and
carries him through his act of self-sacrifice. But he makes this
sacrifice because he values his cause, and not because he is pursuing
the pleasure that it would give him. If pleasure was his only concern,
he could have obtained it in a variety of other ways. Bentham's
theory cannot explain why he chose this act rather than any other.

The concern to establish psychological hedonism, to see the desire
for pleasure in every human action, leads Bentham to some strange
conclusions. Empirically it is an observable fact that all human
activities have specific objectives: to write an article, to see a friend,
to help a stranger cross a road, to outwit a colleague, to drink a glass
of water. And it is these specific objectives that determine the sorts of
action men undertake.

Since this is so, the question that a hedonist has to answer is how
specific objectives of human actions are related to the general desire
for pleasure. Bentham maintains that the specific objectives are
means to, and are caused by, the desire for pleasure, and men pursue
them because they think the attainment of these objectives will give
them pleasure. Now Bentham is clearly correct up to a point, since
it is an observable fact that men do pursue objectives that in their
view would give them pleasure. The difficulty, however, arises when
we consider actions where this is not so obvious. There are habitual
actions that are done almost mechanically with no conscious motivation. There are actions which begin as means to pleasure but
gradually become ends in themselves. Moore's critique of Mill's

discussion of the love of money throws some pertinent light on this point.[53] Or take other fairly common experiences. I might spend hours trying to solve a cross-word puzzle. I could give it up and pursue another more pleasant activity, and yet I might persevere. Clearly it is difficult to see what pleasure could be motivating me. There are elements of self-respect and pride involved, but as Mill pointed out, these are outside Bentham's conceptual framework. Bentham might say that unknown to me, I am unconsciously prompted by a desire for pleasure. While it is certainly possible for men to be prompted by motives of which they are not conscious, we must surely have some means of checking if the motives attributed actually prompted the men concerned, otherwise the argument becomes a mere assertion. We are therefore right to ask Bentham to offer us a criterion by which we can establish that a man does actually seek pleasure in all he does; and clearly this criterion will have to be other than the obvious fact that he actually undertakes the action in question. But Bentham offers no such criterion. He does not specify what characteristics of an action should be taken to signify that it is motivated by pleasure. Consequently he cannot show that my persevering with the cross-word puzzle is actually motivated by pleasure, and not, for example, by an unconscious fear of God or by an unconscious desire to torture myself for having once dreamt of killing my father. Bentham's view that I am seeking pleasure in some unspecified way, and his more general hedonistic thesis from which this view springs, are therefore mere assertions, metaphysical dogmas in the worst sense of the term.

Bentham's difficulties arise from his mistaken attempt to dissociate pleasure from concrete human activities and to turn it into an abstraction to which they are seen as mere means. As we saw earlier all human desires are specific and determinate and pursue concrete objectives. Barring a few activities where we desire pleasure itself we generally desire concrete objects; and it is because we desire them that their achievement satisfies us and gives us pleasure. If we did not desire them and took no interest in them our efforts to attain them and our eventual attainment of them would leave us indifferent and not be a source of pleasure. In other words, in almost all human activities desire precedes pleasure and not the other way round as Bentham maintains. Further we desire X or desire it more than Y because we are or aspire to be certain sorts of persons. Human desires, in other words, cannot be abstracted from the character, the way of life, of the desiring person. As considerations of morality unavoidably enter into the determination of a way of life, a well-considered theory of desire presupposes a wider theory of character, and therefore of morality. Since a moral theory logically *precedes* a theory of desire it cannot be derived from it as Bentham maintains.

As for Bentham's ethical hedonism we have already hinted at some of its difficulties. He claims that ethical hedonism is the only principle capable of accounting for our ordinary moral judgments. This is not true. Rawls has shown how our notions of fairness and justice cannot be explained by the principle of utility. On Benthamite grounds a mother distributing sweets among her children should give more to the envious child. But this violates our notions of fairness. Again, the principle of justice requires that reward should be proportionate to desert; but it is difficult to see how Bentham can accept this if the less deserving persons were likely to feel enormous pain at being left out.[54] Again, Bentham analyses the concept of legal obligation in terms of likely punishment, and yet the whole point of having a legal obligation is that one accepts the law-making authority as legitimate and recognizes a duty to obey it. It is because one accepts it as legitimate in the first instance that one acknowledges its right to punish. It is, that is to say, the concept of punishment that needs to be explained in terms of the concept of obligation and not the other way round. Similarly, my failure to do my duty causes me pangs of conscience because I have come to believe that I ought always to do my duty. That is, it is not the 'pain' of conscience that explains my sense of duty, but it is my general sense of duty that explains why I should have this pain at all.

Again, feelings of anguish, remorse, guilt or sinfulness, for example, cannot be understood at all if seen merely as so many quantities of pain. They are different in *kind* from other types of painful feelings like having indigestion or losing a purse. They imply an ideal, a conception of perfection, from which one believes one has fallen or which one has failed to reach. Their essence, what makes them the types of feeling they are, is not the bare and incidental fact of pain but an awareness of the distance between one's ideals and actual conduct. Abstracted from such an ideal they simply do not make any sense. In reducing different types of moral feelings to so many units of abstract and undifferentiated pleasure or pain, Bentham destroys their character, their identity, their uniqueness. It is hardly to be expected that a theory reducing quality to quantity can come anywhere near to giving a proper account of unique and qualitatively different human activities and feelings.

Far from accounting for ordinary moral judgments as Bentham claims, his moral theory flouts them at every important point. Since pleasure alone is good, it can only be distinguished as greater or less, but never as higher or lower, and yet it is precisely upon this latter distinction that ordinary moral consciousness insists. Again, if pleasure alone is good, however perverse, every pleasure *qua* pleasure is good. As Bentham himself puts it, the pleasure of vengeance 'considered abstractly is, like every other pleasure, only good in itself'.[55] This means that if a murderer finds pleasure in his act, his guilt is to that degree *reduced*. Or if a man enjoys torturing another the evil of his act is to that extent *mitigated*. To state the point is to see how wildly it differs from our ordinary moral judgments, since we generally believe that if a man inflicts pain on another that is bad enough; but if he enjoys it, his act is worse, not better as Bentham asserts.

There is another major difficulty with Bentham's ethical hedonism. As we saw earlier, Bentham defines pleasure as a sensation we enjoy. But he also defines good as that which we enjoy or like. Thus to say that pleasure is good to say that a sensation we enjoy having is a sensation we enjoy having, that pleasure is pleasant, a bare tautology. Bentham, in other words, does not give any reason at all why pleasure should be considered good. He simply asserts it as true by definition. In order to establish ethical hedonism satisfactorily he would have to separate the two concepts of pleasure and good and define both independently. Thus he could redefine pleasure in other terms than the presumed fact that it is a sensation we enjoy having. Or he could redefine good in some other way than that it is what we like or enjoy. But Bentham's general philosophical framework makes it impossible for him to do either. Given his physicalist tendency to reduce all moral ideas to physical sensations, and given his concern to define good in a non-moral and natural sense, it is difficult to see how he could define good in any other way than that it is something likeable, enjoyable. It is therefore only the concept of pleasure that he could redefine. But then it is difficult to see how else it could be defined than as an enjoyable sensation or an enjoyable aspect of a sensation.

As both psychological and ethical hedonism on which Bentham's principle of utility is based are untenable, Bentham's positive case for his principle must be rejected as unsatisfactory. As for his criticisms of its rivals, they are not very convincing either. While Bentham's criticisms of the principle of sympathy and antipathy do make some shrewd points, they remain ultimately unsatisfactory. Following his crude 'bipartitionist' method that divides everything into two, Bentham divides all moral theories into those that appeal to something he calls external and to something he calls internal. As the latter is made so broad a category that almost all non-utilitarian theories are lumped into it, they are all grossly oversimplified and their differences are ignored. Theories of moral sense, natural law, right reason, common sense and natural equity, for example, differ as widely from each other as they do from Bentham's principle of utility. Moral sense theory in one of its versions appeals to individual feelings, while the natural law theory in its most common Stoic-Christian variety appeals to objective moral principles. Again, the natural law doctrine of Hobbes, for example, claims to elucidate universal principles from an analysis of human nature, which is exactly what Bentham says he is doing, and is no more subjective than Bentham's own principle of utility. Bentham's whole discussion of the principle of sympathy and antipathy is based on a confused and ultimately untenable distinction between 'internal' and 'external', and an equally muddled identification of the external with the objective and the internal with the subjective. Clarke's fitness of things, Cudworth's eternal and immutable principles, and Locke's right reason are external principles in the sense of being 'outside' the individual moral agent and independent of his caprice. Bentham, of course, is right in saying that these principles have to be identified and interpreted and that this involves a subjective, perhaps even an arbitrary element. But this is true of every moral theory, including Bentham's own which is not based on human nature as such, but on human nature as *Bentham* understands and interprets it. Bentham's moral theory, further, cannot claim to appeal to an 'external' principle. Even if the appeal to consequences was accepted as an appeal to something external (which, as we shall see, it cannot be), Bentham's concern to judge consequences in terms of the uniquely subjective feelings of pleasure and pain makes his principle of utility as subjective as the principle of sympathy. As Bentham mistakenly equates an appeal to consequences with an appeal to an external principle, he misses out a crucial dimension of moral life. An act of murder, for example, produces an external consequence in the sense that it deprives a man of his life. But this is not its only consequence. It also affects the murderer, by, for example, breaking down his inhibitions against the use of violence or by strengthening his hatred of civil authority. As these changes are produced by the act in question, they are a part of its total consequences. But because Bentham is interested only in emphasizing 'external' consequences, they simply fall out of his conceptual sieve.[56]

Even though the concept of consequences is so crucial to Bentham's moral theory and to his criticism of the principle of sympathy and antipathy, he never clearly explains what he means by it. He imagines rather naïvely that an act produces consequences almost exactly as a stone breaks a head. A more appropriate analogy would seem to be that of a stone producing a series of ripples that are clearly identifiable up to a point but gradually fade away, making it impossible to decide where ripples end and calm waters begin. A moral act occurs

within the context of an ongoing and fluid pattern of human inter-
action and produces a number of changes, however marginal, that
are not clearly identifiable. It affects a number of people in a number
of different ways, requiring them to adjust to its impact in their own
unique manner. How precisely it will affect them, how their pattern
of life will be disturbed by it, how long they will take before they
have fully adjusted to it are questions impossible to answer with the
degree of precision Bentham's utilitarian moral theory requires. Not
only are the consequences of an act not clearly identifiable; it is not
even possible to determine where an act begins and ends. Does it
begin when I start making appropriate physical movements? Or
when I will it? Or when I conceive the idea of it? But will and
desire are not *sui generis*, and arise from a complex of other desires
from which they cannot easily be abstracted or separated. Bentham
does not notice that the identity of an act, and of its consequences, is
never clear cut and self-evident but largely a matter of drawing a
boundary that appears reasonable to a community of moral agents
within a given context. Because of its inherent subjectivity and con-
ventionality, the concept of consequences lacks the kind and degree
of objectivity that Bentham ascribes to it.

As for Bentham's criticism of the principle of asceticism, it is
extremely crude. While he is right that on occasions men do court
pain with a view to getting eventual pleasure, or that there are
ascetics like some Indian sadhus or Simeon stylites who torture
themselves in order to earn popular admiration or divine pleasure,
he has no conception of the real meaning of the principle of asceticism or of its importance for its adherents. He sets up ascetics as
inhuman monsters and ridicules them but never comes to grips with
their basic beliefs. The fundamental concern of the ascetic is not to
court pain for its own sake as Bentham imagines but, as the New
Testament puts it, 'Herein do I exercise myself to have a conscience
void of offence towards God and towards men'. An ascetic has no
'horror of pleasures' as Bentham argues, but aims at a state of consciousness that is above pleasure and pain altogether, that is not
seduced by pleasures and afraid of pains. For a variety of reasons,
right or wrong, an ascetic believes that he should live a life of total
self-sufficiency of which complete independence of external influences is a necessary precondition and expression. Or if an ascetic
is religiously motivated, as he generally is, he believes that he 'owes'
it to God to make himself 'a beautiful soul' and so discipline his
body, mind and soul that they can become pliable instruments of
His will. It is difficult to see what secret pleasures the ascetic as we
have described him is aiming at, and in what sense he is to be
considered a crypto-utilitarian.

Even assuming for the sake of argument that Bentham's criticism has some validity for certain versions of the principle of asceticism, it still remains open to a number of objections. He attacks it on the ground that if consistently applied it generates enormous amounts of pain and misery. But an adherent of the principle of asceticism would easily rejoin that since pain is good, this is precisely what he wants. That is to say, unless pain is already accepted as bad, unless one has already accepted the principle of utility, Bentham's criticism has no relevance.

Again, Bentham makes much of the fact that while adherents of the principle of asceticism consider pain good, they are reluctant to inflict it on others. But this is not true, as Calvin's Geneva and the practices of some Christian and Hindu sects show. However, even if it was true, it only means that ascetics reject asceticism as a *political* principle, not that they reject it as a *moral* principle capable of regulating their personal life. What Bentham is doing, in other words, is to criticize the principle of asceticism as a *political* principle in order to discredit it as a *moral* principle. This manœuvre makes sense only on the assumption that personal and political life should both be regulated by the same principle. But there is no reason why this should be so, and in any case Bentham does not give any.

Bentham, we cannot but conclude, has failed to make out a case for the principle of utility. While his failure is due to a number of factors, such as his dogmatic naturalism, abstract hedonism, and a mistaken theory of human action, there is one that is of particular methodological interest. We observed earlier how Bentham executes his task of justifying the principle of utility on the model of a lawyer. But as the activity of a lawyer is very different from that of a moral philosopher, it provides a highly unsatisfactory model for the latter to emulate. A lawyer is partisan, a man committed to a cause. And he is partisan because given the nature of his activity he cannot be otherwise. He works within a dualistic framework: his client on one side, his opponent on the other. And his task is clear: to show that his client is right and his opponent wrong. His professional morality too is therefore clear: it is a morality of attack and defence. He has a definite brief. He is hired to fight, to devote all his intellectual energy to defending his client and attacking his adversary.

The activity of a moral philosopher is almost entirely different. While a lawyer's task is to determine whether or not an empirical event did occur or occurred in a way contended by one party, there is no such empirical truth that a moral philosopher is concerned to identify. Unlike a lawyer, his world is not delimited and simplified by the clear existence of two sides. There are almost as many different moral systems as there are organized societies, and it is rare even in a well-organized society for all its members to subscribe to a single moral point of view. Since a highly varied and variegated moral life cannot be defined in terms of one single ideal, but only a set of ideals which can be combined in different ways—all good, though not equally good—no moral system has a monopoly of truth. This is not relativism, but pluralism, a view that like relativism insists on the variety of good, but unlike it permits a dialogue among different moral systems, and does not foreclose the possibility of developing a higher more comprehensive moral perspective. As each moral system emphasizes a dimension of moral life that others ignore or under-emphasize none of them can be dismissed as false. They are all 'true' in different degrees. They are therefore not rivals as Bentham calls them but partners capable of conversing and learning from each other. A well-considered moral philosophy would not dismiss other theories out of hand but would try to elucidate their truth and falsity, their insights and deficiencies. In other words, moral philosophy, like any other branch of philosophy, needs sharper and subtler tools than those of a lawyer. A moral philosopher who works out a favourite moral theory and insists that all others should conform to it or be banished is proceeding wrongly. He has not learnt the basic rules, indeed, the essential morality of his craft.

NOTES

1. *Works*, ed. Bowring, vol. IX, 5f.
2. *A fragment on Government And An Introduction to the principles of Morals and Legislation*, ed. Wilfried Harrison (Basil Blackwell Oxford, 1960), 127 (chap. I, para. 9) and 147 (chap. III, para. 1). (hereafter referred to as *Principles*). See also Works, vol. X., 511 and 585.
3. II, 537f. See also 'Sympathy to Mankind' in *Table of the Springs of Action*, vol. I.
4. *Rationale of Punishment* (London, 1830), 126, and Box 14, p. 310.
5. *Principles*, 2, where in both paragraphs 2 and 3 it is clearly stated that the party whose interest is in question may be a private individual or the community as a whole.
6. II, 536ff.
7. For a detailed discussion of this point, see the *Introduction*, VIIIff.
8. MSS. (British Museum), 33551, 17.
9. In his *Principles of Morals & Legislation* first printed in 1780 but not published until 1789, Bentham, never uses this formula, and almost always talks of the 'greatest happiness'.
10. MSS. UCL, Box 14, pp. 384–6.
11. Ibid.
12. *Principles*, 128; and VII, 81 and VIII, 110 and 164.
13. *Principles*, 128 (chap. 1, paras. 11, 12, 13).
14. *Limits of Jurisprudence Defined*, 115f.
15. IX, 47.
16. Ibid. Also, MSS, UCL, Box 15, p. 57 and Box 36, p. 82.

17. *Principles*, 128f.
18. *Principles*, 132f. See also the use of the legalistic terms like 'adversary', 'partisan', 'party', 'advocate', 'defence' and 'case for' and 'case against' in chaps. I and II. See also how he divides all possible positions on a question into two, one of which is right and the other wrong.
19. I, 206; VII, 36; III, 212ff. Also *Theory of Legislation*, Tr. R. Hildreth (London, Second Edition, 1871), 3.
20. '*Moral good* is . . . *pathological* good in so far as *human will* is considered as instrumental in the production of it: in so far as anything else is made of it, either the *word* is without meaning, or the thing is without *value*. And so in regard to evil.' I, 206. By the term pathological Bentham means anything referring to a sensation, and he generally uses the term interchangeably with physical or natural. '. . . all physical good is moral,' Box 14, p. 24.
21. *Principles*, 125.
22. Vol. VIII, 280.
23. *Utilitarianism*, Everyman edition, 36.
24. Quoted in Mary Mack, *Jeremy Bentham, An Odyssey of Ideas* (Heinemann, 1962), 213. Italics added.
25. Vol. I, 211.
26. Ibid.
27. Vol. III, 286.
28. Deontology, vol. I, 165.
29. *Principles*, 125. Italics added. For a very clear statement of the relationship between reason and nature, see *Deontology*, vol. I, 156.
30. *Principles*, 132.
31. Ibid., 139.
32. Ibid., 140f.
33. VI. 239.
34. MSS., UCL. Box 14, Folder 45, 33.
35. *Principles*, 141f.
36. Ibid., 143.
37. *Principles*, 132/3.
38. Ibid., 136.
39. Ibid.
40. For a sympathetic critique of Bentham, see A. J. Ayer, The Principle of Utility in *Jeremy Bentham and the Law*, ed. George W. Keeton and Georg Schwarzenberger (Stevens and Sons, London, 1948).
41. Aristotle on Pleasure in *Aristotle*, ed. J. M. E. Moravesik (Anchor Books, 1967), 329.
42. *Mind*, vol. XIII, 1882, 2.
43. G. H. Bichop, *Physiological Review*, 26 (1946), 98.
44. Roger Trigg, *Pain & Emotion* (Clarendon Press, Oxford, 1970), 143ff. Trigg rightly points out that the notion of 'non-painful "pain"' makes sense only if it is assumed that pain must be unpleasant. I am not sure that his introduction of the concept of 'pain-quality' avoids the difficulty. What is needed is a more general concept like discomfort or unpleasantness of which pain can be seen as one form.
45. Ibid., 151.
46. Hospers, *Human Conduct* (London, 1963), 113.
47. Trigg, op. cit., 153.
48. 'Pleasure is in *itself* a good; nay, even setting aside immunity from pain, the only good.' *Principles*, 218. Bentham seems to suggest here that immunity from pain is not to be equated with pleasure. See also *Works*, vol. III, 214f.

49. Benjamin Franklin, *A Dissertation on Liberty and Necessity, Pleasure and Pain* (New York, Columbia University Press, 1930), 16f.
50. Criticizing Locke's view Bentham remarks that not uneasiness but a hope of future pleasure is the motive behind human actions. *Deontology*, vol. I, 81.
51. T. H. Green, *Prolegomena to Ethics* (Clarendon Press, Oxford, 1844), 175.
52. For a further discussion of Bradley's distinction, see G. E. Moore, *Principia Ethica* (Cambridge University Press, 1960), 70.
53. *Principia Ethica*, op. cit., 72.
54. I have argued this point in some detail in my Bentham's Theory of Equality, *Political Studies*, vol. XVIII, no. 4, Dec. 1970, 494.
55. I, 383.
56. See, for example, *Deontology*, vol. II, 97f. for some very odd remarks.

Chapter 6

Bentham's Ideal Republic*

Thomas P. Peardon

Seldom read today, Bentham's *Constitutional Code* (1820–1832),[1] nevertheless ranks among the most significant political treatises of the last century. It contains an extended statement of the ideas of Philosophic Radicalism on the eve of their partial victory in the Reform Bill of 1832. It must be nearly, it may be actually, the last work of any important figure of the eighteenth-century Enlightenment. At the same time it is one of the first works in which through the fog of doctrinaire radicalism there can be seen fairly clearly the characteristic features of the contemporary state with its extreme centralization, its myrmidonian corps of bureaucrats, its elaborate administrative apparatus, and its miscellaneous services to the public. There are few books of a century ago in which the contemporary political scientist, provided he can overcome initial hurdles of style and manner, ought to feel more at home, if only because he will find there the twentieth-century student's interest in institutions and the emphasis on administration that plays so large a part in the study of government today.

The *Constitutional Code* may be regarded as Bentham's view of the best possible commonwealth—a Utilitarian Utopia. Like all Utopias it was the product of disappointment with the here and now. It is well known that Bentham turned to systematic consideration of constitutional questions only after repeated failure to persuade the rulers of England to accept his legal reforms and especially his Panopticon scheme for a model prison. His early confidence that 'the people in power . . . only wanted to know what was good in order to embrace it'[2] gave way to a conviction that fundamental constitutional changes were prerequisite to other improvements. By 1808 or thereabouts he had come to regard the English system of government as essentially bad, unfit to be copied in other lands, and 'in a state of constant deterioration.'[3] The intricate mechanism that had evoked the reverential tributes of Blackstone and Burke seemed to Bentham a detestable structure 'composed of the conjunct action of force, intimidation, corruption, and delusion'.[4]

This conclusion had important consequences. It caused Bentham to assume the intellectual leadership of the movement for parlia-

* Reprinted from *Canadian Journal of Economic and Political Science*, vol. XVII, No. 2, May, 1951.

mentary reform in the last quarter-century of his life, and at the same
time it stirred him to closer analysis of the means—the sanctions,
promises, myths, symbols and slogans—by which a few are enabled
to command and the many are induced to obey even when government is corrupt and oppressive. But Bentham could never be content
with mere analysis. Once he had been brought to concern himself
seriously with political questions, it was inevitable that his incurably
constructive mind should busy itself with devising the institutions of
a well-governed state. Especially so, since the Pannomion which it
was his life-work to prepare would not be complete without provision
for a constitutional code.

In 1821 the 'General and Extraordinary Cortes of Portugal'
accepted Bentham's offer to prepare an 'all comprehensive' code of
laws for that unhappy country. By the next year he was offering to
codify for any liberal state.[5] A year later his outlook had grown sufficiently ecumenical for him to write *Leading Principles of a Constitutional Code for Any State*.[6] During all this period of proposal, too,
he was actually working at the code itself. In 1830 one volume was
published and on Bentham's death two years later the work as a
whole was left behind in an unfinished condition. The material was
put together by Richard Doane and appeared in 1843 as volume IX
of the Bowring edition of Bentham's *Works*. A worse place could
hardly have been chosen. Few men had been so badly served by their
literary executors as was Bentham. Bowring chose his editors badly,
gave them incompetent supervision, and crowned his sins by issuing
the finished product in eleven volumes of double-columned pages of
very fine print. It is one of the intellectual crimes of the nineteenth
century that so many of Bentham's books should lie entombed in the
dismal Bowring collection. Some of them have escaped the consequences of this sepulture by being re-edited as single works. But the
Constitutional Code has not yet met with this happy resurrection.
Nor is it likely soon to do so. It is too long and too full of those
eccentricities of style and presentation that marred Bentham's later
writings. It has suffered, too, from the fact that so many of its
proposals were realized in legislation under the stimulus of Bentham's
disciples. Yet in its own way it is certainly a classic and one that
ought to be more easily available to students.[7]

It seems worth while, therefore, to attempt a critical exposition and
appraisal of Bentham's great work. In doing so, it will be convenient
to divide the treatment into four parts, unequal both in length and
in importance: the statement of fundamental political principles; the
appraisal of the three classic forms of government; the analysis of
the process of misgovernment; the prescription of new institutions.
The last part is by far the longest and most important.

I

By the end of his life Bentham had crystallized his political philosophy into three principles which received their most succinct expressions in the *Code*.

The first of these, the 'greatest happiness principle,' declares what *ought* to be: 'The right and proper end of government in every political community, is the greatest happiness of all the individuals of which it is composed, say, in other words, the greatest happiness of the greatest number.'[8]

The second, 'the principle of self-preference' or 'the self-regarding principle,' declares what *is*: 'The *actual* end of government, is, in every political community, the greatest happiness of those, whether one or many, by whom the powers of government are exercised.'[9]

The two principles are stated so flatly as almost to obscure Bentham's real position.[10] That he does not really exclude social sympathy as an influence on shaping men's conduct may be seen from a later passage describing the factors that determine political allegiance.

Of action the sole efficient cause is interest, if interest be taken in its most enlarged sense: *i.e.* according to each man's perception of what, at the moment in question, is his most forcibly influencing interest: the interest determined by social sympathy and antipathy, as well as that which is of a purely self-regarding complexion, included.

Thus to the purpose of action, to the aristocratical section belong all such individuals who, by hope of factitious honour, power, or wealth, are dependent on the members of the aristocratical section: so to the democratical belong all those who, their self-regarding interest in any of these shapes notwithstanding, are listed on the democratical side by sympathy with the sufferings of those belonging to that section, or by antipathy to this or that portion of the aristocratical section: belonging in reality to a side to which they are opposed in appearance.[11]

Bentham was hopeful, too, that the influence of sympathy could be increased at the expense of self-regard by wisely contrived political arrangements. Even now, he further concedes, 'In a highly matured state of society, in here and there a highly cultivated and expanded mind, under the stimulus of some extraordinary excitement, a sacrifice of self-regarding interest to social interest, upon a national scale has not been without example' (61). But such a phenomenon is less frequent in occurrence than insanity. Taking man in the mass and over the long run, the legislator drawing up a code should disregard anything but the operation of a rather narrow self-interest, especially since, though individuals may occasionally sacrifice private interest to the universal good, groups of men will not do so. 'Every body of men is governed altogether by its conception of what is its interest, in the narrowest and most selfish sense of the word interest: never by any regard for the interest of the people' (102). It follows that government can be made to serve the greatest happiness only if institutions are so arranged that rulers in seeking their own felicity cannot avoid serving the cause of the greatest happiness of the greatest number at the same time. Hence the idea of the artificial identification of interests which is stated in the 'means-prescribing principle.'

The third of Bentham's political principles is called 'the means-prescribing or junction-of-interests prescribing principle':

If as above, so it be, that in the situation of a ruler, whatsoever that situation be, the conduct of no man can reasonably be expected to be governed by any interest that stands, at that same moment, in opposition to that which, in his conception, is his own individual interest, it follows, that for causing it to take the direction in which it will be subservient to the universal interest, the nature of the case affords no other method, than that which consists in the bringing of the particular interest of rulers into accordance with the universal interest. (6)

II

Having established the basic principles of politics, Bentham proceeds to appraise in their light the three classic forms of government. His wholly unfavourable criticism of monarchy is aimed especially at the limited form prevailing in England. It seemed to him absurd in the extreme that an indispensable part in legislation and an important share in executive and appointing power should reside in a functionary who owed his position to the chances of heredity. He held, too, that the life of a monarch deprives him of the chance of acquiring real knowledge of government. He is too busy, too insulated from contacts with the people, too dependent on a narrow circle of sycophantic advisers to acquire even that measure of competent judgment in political questions that resides in the average elector.[12]

This lack of intellectual aptitude is serious enough to condemn the institution. Worse yet is the monarch's lack of moral aptitude, that is, of an impulse or propensity to act in the general interest. A monarch, in Bentham's view, is too remote from the great mass of people to feel any association of their interests with his own. This same remoteness deprives him of knowledge of popular wants and sufferings, and, lacking that knowledge, he has no impulse either to satisfy the one or to relieve the other. He lacks both 'sympathy of affection' and 'sympathy of conception.'

Even the people are deteriorated in their political functioning by the existence of a monarchy. Where their ideas are not consciously controlled their judgment is led astray by the fulsome adulation surrounding royal words and acts. Thus public opinion, an essential factor in good government, is corrupted at its source.

With the wisdom of experience we know that an hereditary chief of state can render many services unrecognized by Bentham. More recently too, we have begun to appreciate the psychological value of monarchy. We know something of the need for unity and pageantry in government and realize that it is better to find unity in a dignified symbol than be compelled to seek it through a demagogic tyrant. Bentham, who saw so much, failed to see this. But his analysis of monarchy was no mere doctrinaire abstraction. The very points that Bentham was making a hundred years ago are repeated today by those who are concerned about the realities rather than the pretty fictions of politics.

The same objections that condemn monarchy in Bentham's mind apply also to aristocracy. Aristocrats are powerful, opulent, and titled. But it is axiomatic with Bentham that political competence and virtue tend to vary inversely with the possession of power, wealth, and 'factitious dignity'.

Thus only democracy can accomplish that artificial identification of interests made necessary by the contradiction between the Greatest Happiness and Self-Regarding Principles. The people, being the majority, will endeavour to choose representatives who will serve the interests of the greatest number. This being so, men who seek election at the hands of the people will endeavour to win popular approval by serving the interests of the greatest number. Nor can it be argued that the popular choice will be badly made. In private affairs each man is best fitted to choose his own agents. So are the people best fitted to choose agents for common affairs. Even if we assume that the popular choice is not very good, at least there is no other system that is likely to produce better results. The people have the advantage over monarchs and aristocrats of at least desiring to choose agents who will serve majority rather than minority interests. With time and experience their knowledge and judgment will improve.

III

If non-democratic forms of government are so obviously contrary to the Greatest Happiness Principle, it becomes necessary to explain their persistence. What are the props and stays of misrule? Bentham's analysis of what we may call the process of misgovernment constitutes a pioneer essay in political psychology.[13] It is vitiated by the

Utilitarian proneness to think too much in terms of the rational pursuit of interests, but it shows clearly that Bentham was reaching forward to an appreciation of the place of non-rational factors in politics.

Four instruments enable the few to command the obedience of the many even where the greatest happiness is not the goal of government: corruption; delusion; fiction; factitious honour.

By Corruption, Bentham meant the whole process of moral deterioration by which men are induced to lower their standards in order to enjoy the rewards of the *status quo*. In part, he regarded it as a deliberate use of the instruments of power—money, office, honours. But he saw also that corruption need not take shape in any specific act nor originate with any specific individual who has sinister interests to serve. The very laws and institutions of a country, its 'system and frame' of government may be corruptive in their effect. And beyond the sphere of politics, all the other institutions of an inegalitarian society—aristocracy, religious establishments, endowed foundations—operate as a standing inducement to men to stifle conscience for the sake of position and profit.

Corruption touches especially the *élite*, the indispensable lieutenants of the ruling one or few. The necessary acquiescence of the people is secured by psychological devices to which Bentham gives the title 'delusion'. By the pageantry and trappings of monarchy, by impressive official raiments, by 'laudatory discourse' (or propaganda, as we would say) concerning rulers, the people's eyes are blinded. By the use of 'fictitious entities'—abstract terms such as Crown, Throne, Church, Altar, Law, Property, instead of concrete ones such as King, Churchman, Lawyers, the Rich—the imagination of men is tickled and rulers clothed in artificial respect and veneration. Everything co-operates to surround them with an air of false glamour—'a sort of clouded majesty'—through which they appear to the people supremely competent, benevolent, and even sacred. Criticism becomes a violation of good taste, of that 'decorum' which Bentham rightly recognized as one of the props of the English social and political system.

By substituting the principle of taste to the greatest happiness principle, taste is made the arbiter of excellence and depravity; and thus the great mass of the community is in the very sink of depravity. Witness the use that is made of the words *bad taste* and *disgusting*. Bad taste pours down contempt; disgusting is a superlative above flagitious, it is a *quasi* conjugate of *taste* and *bad taste*. Those of the democratical section, in so far as they adopt such expressions, act in support of the hostile section against themselves. For the rich and powerful will always be the arbiters of taste: what is an object of disgust to them will, to those who follow this principle.

be an object of disgust likewise. But that the poor, labouring and non-labouring, all those who cannot afford a clean shirt every day, and a suit, of clothes every two or three months, are, to the men of the first circle objects of disgust is altogether beyond dispute. (46)

By means of the devices of delusion, public opinion, which ought to be the great corrective of the misrule, becomes instead an aggravation. The channels through which the people get their information and opinions are controlled in the interest of a few. They have prejudices rather than true opinion.

Fiction and factitious honour are really forms of corruption and delusion, though treated separately. Bentham had a keen appreciation of the importance of fiction in general.[14] But he regarded fiction in law and government as merely action upon an assertion acknowledged to be false, an admission of conscious misgovernment, and inevitably demoralizing in its effect on all concerned. It takes some historical sense to appreciate the value of fiction in law and politics, and Bentham was notoriously blind to history. He is more penetrating in his remarks on 'factitious honour'. By this contemptuous term he sums up titles of rank and all the other honorific trappings that mark an aristocratic society. Such distinctions are delusive in effect because they are artificial and a fraud upon the people. They command for a favoured few tokens of respect they have not really earned and would not otherwise receive. They are also peculiarly and perniciously corruptive in effect since the prospect of a title will often win the support of those whom money cannot buy. Bentham proposes to substitute an elaborate system of 'natural honour' whereby meritorious public servants would be rewarded by public recognition and registration of judicially proven services.

IV

On these foundations of political principle and political psychology Bentham erected the structure of his ideal state. From three-quarters to four-fifths of the *Constitutional Code* is devoted to the presentation of specific institutional proposals along with explanatory matter. Under each topic in the Code the clauses are labelled Enactive, Ratiocinative, Expositive, Instructional, and Exemplificational. Clauses labelled under the first three heads were meant to be inserted in the formal constitution of any country adopting the Benthamite system—the enactive for obvious reasons, the expositive as necessary to a right interpretation, and the ratiocinative as helping people to understand the reasons underlying their constitution and why it was a good one. The instructional and exemplificational might be eliminated from the actual constitution since they were intended merely to give assistance to the constitution drafters rather than to become rules of action. This elaborate classification may be ignored by one who is reading the Code merely as a document in the history of thought.

The Legislature. Bentham's structure of good government rests upon three main pillars. The first is a fully sovereign parliament:

The Supreme Legislature is omnicompetent. Coextensive with the territory of the state is its local field of service; coextensive with the field of human action is its logical field of service. To its power, there are no limits. In place of limits, it has checks. These checks are applied, by the securities provided for good conduct on the part of the several members, individually operated upon. . . .

Only by unalterable physical impotence, is the Supreme Legislature prevented from being its own executive, or from being the sole Legislature . . . in case of non-performance, or unapt performance, or well-grounded apprehension of either, to the exercise of no function of the Executive or Sub-legislative authority can the Supreme Legislature be incompetent. Unfaithfulness, yes: but to the Supreme Legislature, neither can usurpation nor encroachment be imputed. (160)

Bentham's unqualified assertion of parliamentary sovereignty, of which the *Constitutional Code* was not the first expression, marked a stage in the development of English radicalism. Fearful of the corroding effects of power, the eighteenth-century constitutionalists had sought to restrain authority by devices familiar to Americans—constitutions overriding ordinary laws, bills of rights, separation of powers. Bentham shared their fear of power. All power is evil, he says, and 'by every addition made to power, addition is made to evil' (350). Like his libertarian predecessors, too, he declares government acceptable only as the lesser evil. But his supreme value is utility, not liberty. To secure the greatest happiness he is willing to waive the niggling concern over the powers of government that has so often paralysed liberal thought. He saw that the powers of government, if government is to be effective, must not be minimized; that the problem is to establish a government that is controlled but powerful. He taught the important lesson that a properly constituted and efficiently organized sovereign legislature could be a powerful instrument by which to secure reform. It was a lesson the English never forgot.

By a properly constituted legislature, Bentham meant one elected annually and directly by the people, voting by secret ballot in equal election districts. He would exclude from the suffrage only four classes of persons: females; minors; those who had not passed a reading test; 'passengers'. The exclusion of women he opposes on principle but accepts on the expedient ground that the prejudice against giving them the vote was too general and too intense to make the proposal practicable at the time.[15] To avoid expense, delay, corruption, and frustration of the popular will, the legislature must be unicameral. To sharpen responsibility and avoid corruption, the members must be subject both to legal responsibility for their acts and to recall.

It is, however, on the subject of the efficient organization of the legislature that Bentham is most suggestive. Writing at the dawn of one of the great ages of legislative fertility, he envisages his parliament as a continuously functioning body, constantly engaged in devising laws that would bring government into ever closer harmony with the Greatest Happiness Principle. Sittings were to be held regularly six days a week and, in case of need, on the seventh as well. Elaborate precautions were to be taken to ensure attendance. The member must sign a book on arriving and the time of his entry was to be noted therein. To leave he must secure the permission of the president. He was to be paid only for the days he attended, except for vacation days. Even when absent through illness he was not to be paid for days missed. Unexcused absence, moreover, meant that the seat was vacated and a new election ordered. These provisions seem less rigorous when one recalls that for every office (including membership in the Legislature) Bentham permitted the use of a deputy for the performance of almost all functions.[16] Probably they would be less irksome to most members than the requirement that a 'Table of Fallacies' be hung in a conspicuous place as a guide to speakers and hearers.

Bentham was sensible of the need for provision to secure continuity in spite of annual parliaments. Business unfinished at the end of one parliament need not be introduced at the beginning in the next. Each Legislature before expiring was to elect a Continuation Committee whose members were to seek to persuade the next Legislature to finish the projects left over by its predecessor. Membership in this Committee would be open both to members of the existing Legislature and to those of the existing Continuation Committee. 'Thus may any person serve as a Continuation Committee-man for any number of successive years' (170). As such he would receive the same pay as a regular member and, though denied the vote, have full right of initiation and speech on any matter.

An efficient legislature must have in it not only that element of continuity provided by the Committee just described. There must also be adequate information at the disposal of members and an element of *expertise* in the drafting of laws. To provide the first, Bentham would confer more powers on legislative committees and commissions of inquiry than was bestowed by existing arrangements in England. The second would be secured by the establishment of a Legislation Minister.

The functions of the Legislation Minister fall into several classes. His first duty was to act as general assistant to the Legislature. He was to watch over and seek to improve by his suggestions the rules and tactics of that body. With some exceptions, all proposed legislation would go to him before being introduced on the floor in order that he might report on its form and suggest improvements in drafting. He might even declare a measure incapable of being harmonized with the rest of the code of laws in the time available. The initiator, assuming him to be a member, might still bring the measure before the house, but presumably the minister's criticism would make its passage difficult.

From another angle too the Legislation Minister would play an important role in the making of laws. It is an interesting feature of Bentham's Code that the judiciary could suggest amendments in existing law. Such proposals were to be sent to the minister and by him given adequate and immediate publicity. If no objection was expressed by any member or by any judge within seven days the measure would become law. Even private citizens could send legislative proposals to the minister although those emanating from this source would apparently require formal action by the house. Bentham thought that by combining a very broad right of initiation with supervisory power in the hands of the Legislation Minister, liberty and order would be combined in law-making. At the same time, he pictured the office of this functionary as a school where young men might be trained in the business of law-making for the public good as traditionally they had been trained in private offices for the ordinary practice of law.

The administrative structure. The second pillar of Bentham's state was an elaborate administrative machine. At its head would be a Prime Minister, an official who resembled in some respects the American President. Thus although he was to be elected by the Legislature he could neither sit in that body nor even speak there except by special invitation. His term was to be four years. To provide a sufficient number of experienced candidates at every election, it was provided that the Prime Minister would be ineligible for reelection unless there existed a certain number (Bentham suggests two or three) of former prime ministers from whom choice might be made.

The Prime Minister would appoint all other ministers except the Justice Minister. Subject to removal, they would hold office for life. In addition to the usual departments (Army, Navy, Foreign Relations, Trade, Finance) Bentham proposes others for Elections. Preventive Service, Interior Communications, Indigence Relief,

Education, Domain, and Health. At the same time he was well aware of the possibility of a more functional grouping and suggests as possible combinations: (1) Army, Navy, and Preventive Service; (2) Interior Communications and Domain; (3) Indigence Relief and Education; (4) Trade and Finance. Whatever the division, however, there must always be a single individual at the head and finally responsible. This emphasis on the absolute necessity of individual responsibility was a cardinal administrative principle with Bentham. 'A *board* . . . is a *screen*.'[17]

Taken collectively, the ministers would be more like the American than the English analogue, yet not very close to either. They were all (except the Justice Minister) to be subordinate to the Prime Minister, they would act as individuals rather than as a body and were not to be collectively responsible. Nothing could be further from a cabinet in the English sense. Without being members of the Legislature, ministers were required to attend in person or through deputy, in order to answer questions. They could also take part in debate and even propose legislation. They could not, however, vote.

It should be noted also that the ministers were to be experts, not amateurs such as English ministers are supposed to be. The list of talents appropriate to each department makes this clear (273). Bentham's Health Minister would be trained in medicine, his Interior Communication Minister would be an engineer, and his Finance Minister would know what those 'damned dots' meant.

The duties of the ministers in charge of Preventive Service, Indigence Relief, Education, and Health suggest how far Bentham reached ahead of his time towards the social service state of today. The Preventive Service Minister was to take measures not only against such calamities as collapse of buildings, earthquakes, floods, and fire, but also against dangerous working conditions, bad public health, and contagious disease. The Education Minister would be in charge of all government activities in this field, he would preside at most examinations for the public service (to be discussed later), supervise local or private educational enterprises (including an official inspection in person or by deputy at least once a year), and arrange for training the surplus poor for colonization abroad.

The duties of the Health Minister would be even more manifold. He was not only to have charge of government hospitals, lazarettos, and laboratories, but to inspect, keep records of, and suggest improvements in all institutions for the preservation of the national health, including those maintained by local agencies, corporate bodies, and individuals. Subject to appeal to the courts, he could cause to be destroyed or rendered inapplicable for medical use any medicines that had become unfit for such use. By order of the Prime

Minister, he could be placed in charge of securing a supply of water for any town. He was to collect from local sources full and regular vital and weather statistics. And, finally, he was to keep a watchful eye on the doctors to see that they formed no special combinations likely to injure public health by regulating fees, attendance on patients, and similar matters in their own rather than the general interest.

The remaining ministers need little comment. The Election Minister would supervise local as well as national elections. The Interior Communications Minister combined the functions of a Minister of Transport and the Postmaster-General. Among the Foreign Minister's tasks in Bentham's ideal republic was to be that of reporting upon the non-observance of treaties by his own state, upon wrongs committed by citizens of his own nationality against the governments or individuals of other states, and upon occasions where his own government had taken advantage of the weakness or distress of any foreign régime.

Subordinate to the Supreme Legislature and the central departments would be the agencies of local government. For the chaos of local authorities that prevailed in his day Bentham would substitute a clear and rational arrangement based on the national election districts. Each such district would be the territory of a Sublegislature. Beneath these would be 'subdistricts,' from each of which would come one delegate to the Sublegislature. A third area, the 'Bissubdistrict' would be under a Local Headman. Further divisions of territory were to be made as seemed necessary, always with due attention both to 'simplicity and uniformity' as in post-revolutionary France and to 'natural expressiveness' as in England.

The primary purpose of the Sublegislatures was to assist in 'giving execution and effect to all Government arrangements, when and in so far as called upon to do so by the Legislature' (640) or, subject to the legislature's overriding authority, by the Prime Minister or other ministers. The Supreme Legislature was to lay down rules according to which the proceedings of Sublegislatures were to be conducted. It could annul, reverse, or amend any ordinances or other decisions of the subordinate bodies and was to settle disputes between two or more of them. The supervisory role of the Legislation Minister in connection with this relationship between central and local agencies has already been noted. It will be recalled too that on the administrative side the work of the subordinate legislatures and of the subministers who served them was subject to inspection by the central departments.

It is not true to say, however, that Bentham meant the Sublegislatures to be mere agents of the central government. They derived their being directly from the people as did the Legislature itself. They were to serve as a seminary in which statesmen might be trained for larger responsibilities. Moreover, Bentham had a healthy respect for experiment in politics. He thought of the territories of the Sublegislatures as areas within which new schemes might be tried out and he was willing to allow a considerable measure of diversity in order to secure the benefits of such tests.

In so far as, in the exercise of these powers, any of the sublegislatures pursue rules different from those laid down in this Code, for the General Legislature, it will thus, at the instance of its own portion of the community, be making experiments in Legislation, wherefrom useful instruction may naturally be derived; and by the exercise of this faculty, the sentiment of free agency will be felt and nourished. If from improper exercise, serious danger in any shape to the community at large, should on any occasion be apprehended, the superordinate power of the Legislature will suffice for the averting it. (640n.)

There is a remarkable degree of freedom implied in this statement. Given a representative democracy, Bentham was perfectly willing to allow large scope for discretion.

The Local Headman in each 'Bis-subdistrict' was to be chosen by the electors for a one-year term from candidates who had given proof by examination of their aptitude for the position. He combined administrative and judicial functions. That is to say, he could do anything the Legislature or, subject to the will of the Legislature, the Prime Minister, any other minister, or the judge in his district called upon him to do. Bentham seems to have regarded him as a combined father confessor and maid of all work in his district. Thus, one of his specific functions was to seek to prevent litigation by using his good offices to reconcile family differences. He was to give useful information to the poor and helpless, aid the unemployed to find work, participate in expeditious settlement of disputes between travellers and local persons, and dispose of the bodies and effects of strangers who died in the neighbourhood. It is typical of Bentham's care for detail that he also empowered the Headman to cut down and remove trees and grass to prevent the spread of fire.

The Local Headman was to work in close association with the Local Registrar, a permanent official appointed by the Justice Minister. The Registrar was to record every act done by the Headman and to attach his opinion, which the Headman might observe or ignore as he saw fit. On the other hand, the Headman was to give his judgment on the course pursued by the Registrar. The effect on their relations can be imagined. Bentham's idea was that the permanent, experienced Registrar would act as the 'natural mentor' of the Headman, a purely temporary functionary. For an analogy, he refers to the relations between a City of London alderman, when acting as a Justice of the Peace, and his clerk.

Apart from his relations with the Headman, the Registrar's most important task was that of recording the statistics of deaths, marriages, births, arrivals at maturity, and insanity. For many years Bentham had been insisting on the desirability of such registration and his suggestions were later incorporated in great part in the act of 1836.

The importance given to a permanent official such as the Local Registrar caused Halévy to refer to Bentham's local government as 'half-elective and half-administrative'—almost a correct designation of the system that exists at the present time in England.[18] Even more significant was the provision for the subordination of local authorities to the central administration as well as the central legislature, and especially the implementation of this subordination by provision for regular inspection. Central legislative supremacy was as old as the sovereignty of parliament, but central administrative control was a novel idea, probably invented by Bentham himself. Its application revolutionized local government in England.[19]

Bentham was mortally afraid of collaboration in sinister design between the executive and the judiciary. Of all the ministers, only the Minister of Justice was to be chosen by the Legislature and not by the Prime Minister. Moreover, the official residences of the Prime Minister and Minister of Justice were to be placed as far apart as could conveniently be done and, a characteristically Benthamite touch, a trumpeter was to be assigned to each to precede him on all occasions of absence from home. There were to be no secret deals in the Utilitarian Utopia. Such arrangements show that Bentham was not as completely free from the doctrine of separation of powers as he liked to think.[20]

In his judicial system as in other aspects of his government, Bentham aimed at concentrated responsibility, control by public opinion, speedy and accessible justice, equality between rich and poor, and expertness and efficiency.

To secure concentration of responsibility, the Justice Minister was made as clearly head of that branch of administration as the Prime Minister in the remaining branches. Moreover in each court there would be only one judge. He alone would have the power to reach a decision and he alone would bear the responsibility for it when given.

This, of course, means that the judge would be freed from the restrictions of a jury. For a long time, Bentham had proposed to have no form of jury whatever. But by the time he had come to write the *Constitutional Code* the protests of friends and the desire to give institutional expression to the force of public opinion had caused him to devise the compromise form of 'Quasi-Jury'. [21]

The members of the Quasi-Jury would be divided into two classes: the Ordinary and the Select or Erudite. Each jury would have twice as many Ordinaries as Selects. The one would represent the majority of the people, the other be chosen from those with knowledge and ability. Thus both moral aptitude (a desire to realize the greatest happiness), which exists most strongly among ordinary people, and intellectual aptitude (knowledge and judgment) would be sure to be found in every Quasi-Jury.

The Quasi-Jury would be allowed to listen to evidence, read documents, inspect exhibits, ask questions, and make comments during the course of a trial. It might propose modifications in the judge's decision and these would be entered in the official record. But the judge would not have to accept the jury's recommendations except in certain cases where it demanded an appeal to a higher judge. Greater powers were not necessary, in Bentham's opinion, in order to enable the Quasi-Jury to exercise its two primary functions of enabling public opinion to express itself in the judicial process and at the same time instructing the people in the functioning of justice.

Public opinion was to express itself, however, not only through the Quasi-Jury, but also through the spectators at a trial. These Bentham refers to as the 'Judicial Inspectors', a committee of the 'Public Opinion Tribunal'. So important were they in his opinion that he suggested legislation to compel the attendance of a minimum number of citizens at every trial. Their mere presence would guarantee publicity and assure that some attention would be paid to the Greatest Happiness Principle. Their intervention was to be made more effective by the right, at the discretion of the judge, to inspect, interrogate, and comment during the course of the proceeding.

Several provisions were intended to make justice equally accessible to all classes. An Eleemosynary Advocate would be attached to each court. In addition, the poor could draw upon an Equal Justice Fund made up from state and private contributions. In some instances the costs of litigation were to be graduated in proportion to the wealth of the litigants.

Justice must be swift. Therefore at least one judge was to be available every hour on every day of the year. Typical of Bentham's ungovernable care for details is the provision that the judge on night duty may sleep unless and until business arise. He is to sleep in a bed with his feet towards the entrance. On each side and at the foot of the bed rise boards across which may be slid another board equipped with paper and other materials. 'To exercise his function, the Judge has but to sit up in bed' (541–542 and note).

To secure a satisfactory personnel, finally, judges were to be appointed by the Justice Minister from persons who had given proof of fitness by examination and a period of apprenticeship. Professional lawyers would be ineligible for judicial posts, for which, says Bentham, they are as little fit as a procuress is qualified to be mistress of a girls' school. This he maintains in spite of the fact that professional lawyers in the state he proposes would receive a very different training from any that has prevailed hitherto. After passing the general civil service examination, to which reference will be made below,[22] they were to serve four years of probation either in the 'Judicial Inspectors Gallery' or equally divided between such attendance in courts and practice as an Eleemosynary Advocate. This suggests that the poor were not to get the most competent legal advice after all.

'On architecture good Government has more dependence than men have hitherto seemed to be aware of' (165). One of Bentham's basic rules in this matter was that the proper placing of offices will aid communication between those that ought to work together and can at the same time be used to prevent or hinder 'unseen and unheard communications' between those, e.g. the administrative and judiciary, that ought to remain separate. The Legislation Minister he would place in the legislative building. To house the other ministers he considers various shapes of building—crescent, circular, polygonal, and oval—finally giving preference to the crescent shape as the best for ventilation. He proposes that the Prime Minister be placed in a central position and that all ministerial offices be connected with the Prime Minister and with each other by 'conversation tubes', a device which Bentham had experimented with to determine its value in government and which was apparently already in use in certain public offices (326–327, 452). Bentham suggests also arrangements for sending documents from office to office in boxes pulled by ropes; and gives the most elaborate directions as to the proper construction of buildings so that citizens who call on officials may be sure of easy, orderly, and secret access. He was also greatly interested in the acoustics of legislatures and court rooms.

Administrative personnel. No one has been more insistent than Bentham on the necessity of securing the best possible personnel in government. Fitness for government requires the possession of three types of aptitude: moral, intellectual, and active. Moral aptitude is defined as 'the being in an adequate degree actuated and guided by the desire of securing to the greatest number in question, at all times, the greatest quantity, or say the maximum, of happiness' (97). Intellectual aptitude means the possession of the necessary knowledge and judgment. It is not perfectly clear just what Bentham means by active aptitude, but it seems to be the possession of such qualities as industry, efficiency, punctuality, interest in the job, and perhaps energy and health—everything that makes a man able to do his task efficiently provided he possesses character and intelligence to begin with. How shall we guarantee that rulers shall possess these qualities or, at least, that they shall be hindered in 'sinister design' when they do not possess them?

It should be noted that, as has been pointed out previously, Bentham placed some, though very little, reliance on the existence of a vein of social sympathy in the human makeup and on the fact that the ruler has some slight share in the universal interest. Chiefly, however, he places his reliance in several expedients of artificial construction. There is, in the first place, the existence of a representative democracy with manhood suffrage, popular recall of officials, an omnicompetent, unicameral legislature, and annual parliaments. In the second place, and equally important, is the constant rule of public opinion, with adequate institutional provision for its effective working.[23] His third device is liability to court action for official conduct. In the fourth place, he stresses the importance of administrative arrangements to protect the citizen against the oppression of officials. For example, he suggests appeals to superior officials, the public display of rules of official conduct, adequate publicity for all relations between officials and non-officials, the keeping of adequate records, and the use of complaint books in which citizens may enter their grievances. Fifthly, he mentions, as a counter-force to misrule, the traditional security of an armed militia (50–52, 58, 609).

Most of these provisions were common enough among certain schools of thought, but Bentham was a pioneer in the attention he paid to the problem of the training, recruitment, and remuneration of administrative personnel. To assure a trained personnel, he proposes a system of schools in which potential candidates for the public service could be educated. To these schools a limited government aid might be given. The limits to this aid are curiously fixed and are an interesting illustration of those quirks of judgment that appear in Bentham's schemes. He objects to any aid to students in the form of lodgings or food on the ground that in any area where a school would exist there would always be found a sufficient number of pupils whose parents were capable of supporting them in these items. But he is willing that the government should make an allowance for clothing, not so much for the sake of needy students as to protect the sensibilities of the well-to-do! 'As to *clothing*, if any Government allowance is made, it will be in the view of preventing the comparatively opulent from being excluded from the benefit of the instruction, by disgust produced from the spectacle of deficiency or uncleanliness, on the part of the comparatively indigent.' (278) The schools thus established, while intended primarily for instructing men to be public officials, would serve also in Bentham's plan for national instruction in general and would tend to produce citizens better able to judge the operations of government.

The actual recruitment of officials was to be done in three stages. The first would be the preparation of an eligible list by means of a public examination following due advertisement of vacant posts. Examinations were to be given by a board consisting of (1) the ministers under the presidency of the Justice Minister or the Education Minister (Bentham names sometimes one, sometimes the other), and (2) a Quasi-Jury made up of those who had instructed the various candidates in preparation for the examination. Examinations were to be public throughout. Candidates were to be permitted to submit evidence of their preparation and competence for posts and this was to be followed by questioning, apparently oral, not only by the examiners, but also by rival candidates. At the conclusion of the tests, which would vary with the positions to be filled, the judges would rank the candidates in order of merit in a published list called the 'Ranking-table'. They would also make inquiry into the moral aptitude of aspirants and enter the results in a 'Candidates' Character Book'. But this inquiry was to be restricted to those moral qualities that affect fitness for public service. Purely private matters like sex behaviour were specifically excluded.

Thus far Bentham was applying rather rigidly what has come to be called the merit system. That he should anticipate its application long before the birth of the English Civil Service is a remarkable example of his prophetic genius for political invention. But the public examination constitutes only the first of three stages in Bentham's system of recruitment. The second is more surprising to twentieth-century students. It can only be understood in the light of Bentham's peculiar ideas about remuneration.

Bentham had a strong, even exaggerated, sense of the importance of prestige in public office. He sees the rewards for service as consisting of four main elements: money, power, reputation, and dignity or honour (232, 288, etc.). The non-monetary rewards in his opinion may be so effective that men will be willing to serve gratuitously or even to pay for a post. In such case, to pay a salary in that office is to do a public wrong, to waste public money. Moreover, the greater a man's relish for an office, the great his aptitude is likely to be and therefore the man who is willing to pay for a post is probably eminently qualified to fill it. He is also more likely in Bentham's opinion to possess the requisite moral qualifications since he has less incentive than others to engage in depredation. Of course, such argumentation is quite inconsistent with Bentham's analysis elsewhere of the political effects of opulence. It doubtless arose from his passion for economy and justified him in a variety of expedients aimed at cutting down the monetary value of public employment. He refuses, for example, to entertain the idea of increases in salary for length of service except in the case of military personnel. He could see no more reason for increasing pay on account of length of service than for paying higher prices to shopkeepers thirty years in business than to those ten years in business. On the basis of a similar analogy, he rejects retirement pensions.

Bentham proposes to use honour as a substitute for or supplement to money rewards by instituting what he calls an 'Extraordinary Service' or 'Public Merit' Register. In this book might be inscribed the names of those who, after proper judicial inspection, were found to have rendered some unusual service to the public. A court decree was to state the nature and proof of such service. This device Bentham calls 'natural honour augmented'.

Having established by examination a list of those with the appropriate aptitude, Bentham would institute a 'Pecuniary Competition', a form of auction among those whose rank on the 'Locable List' had previously been ascertained by the tests just mentioned. 'Competition is no less applicable to the price of labour than to the price of goods; to one sort of labour than to another; to labour in the service of the public than to labour in the service of an individual' (266). The rule that follows is both clear and absurd. If any competent man will pay for the privilege of performing the functions of an office, give it to him first. Other things being equal, let him who will pay highest have it first. If no competent man will pay, give it to one who will serve gratis. If there are none who will serve gratis, let the office go to the man who will work for the smallest pay.

By combining competitive examinations with 'pecuniary competition' Bentham thought that he could apply the basic rule: 'Aptitude maximized; expense minimized.' Perhaps so, but he would also have given a monopoly of office to the wealthy.

It was, of course, an equally important administrative tenet with Bentham that for every act there must be some clearly responsible individual. In deference to this principle he had consistently rejected all boards, commissions, or other hydra-headed entities. To leave the actual selection of functionaries to an examining body (which would be the result if a list of names in order of merit must be followed in making appointments) or to the impersonal operation of 'pecuniary competition' would violate this principle. Therefore, actual appointment to office, the third stage in recruitment, must always rest with an individual minister or other superior official. He need not pay absolute deference to the results of the examination or pecuniary competition. He might pass over men on the examination lists in favour of someone who would serve for less pay. Or he might give great weight to a man's experience as a 'Depute' or subordinate in his office. But he is always clearly responsible for the decision he reaches and must give public reasons for it. The normal result, Bentham thought, would be an exact following of the examination ranking, pecuniary competition operating only as between equal candidates.

The three principles corresponding to the three stages of recruitment were named by Bentham the 'public examination', 'pecuniary competition', and 'responsible location' principles. They were to be applied especially in the selection of permanent officials such as ministers, judges, and officers in the Army and Navy and their subordinates, with such modifications from office to office as the necessities of the case dictated. It is striking, too, that Bentham seems to have thought that in the long run legislators would be chosen only from those who had passed a general civil service examination and been placed on the 'General Locable List'. What a house-cleaning that device would produce in most capitals!

One could extract from Bentham's *Code* a fairly complete treatise on public administration. Its range would comprise such major aspects as the province of administration and the relation of administration to other branches of government, the training, selection, remuneration, organization, and discipline of personnel, the establishment of responsibility, and the relations between central and local agencies. And it would contain in addition a wealth of suggestions on the proper care of records, inter-departmental communications, the relations between officials and the public, securities for adequate publicity concerning public activities, the architecture of public buildings, and many other subjects. Bentham would move freely in an age of schools of public administration, legislative drafting bureaux, budget surveys, and statistical analyses. After all, he invented or suggested most of them more than a hundred years ago.

Public Opinion. An omnicompetent legislature and a complicated, permanent, scientifically organized administrative machine would spell tyranny were they not subordinated to an ever vigilant and, in the political sense, ultimately sovereign public. The people are the third pillar of Bentham's state. They do not, it is true, rule directly. The essence of a political society being found in the division of the community into those who rule and those who obey, direct democracy is an impossibility, not a form of government at all. But the people are to Bentham more than merely the source of government or the sleeping sovereigns of Locke's Commonwealth. One of the 'authorities' in his state, on a plane with the Legislative, the Operative, and the Judicative, is the Constitutive, that is, the electorate. Once a year they choose the supreme legislative and at all times they may recall ('dislocate'), directly or indirectly, their members and other officials. Upon the possession and exercise of this political power by the people Bentham places great emphasis.

He placed even more emphasis, however, upon the popular control of government through the 'moral sanction' of Public Opinion. By public opinion Bentham meant the opinion of: 'all those by whose obedience, the power of the monarch be he who he may, or of the rulers, be they who they may, is constituted. Let this opinion take a certain turn, the habit of obedience ceases on the one part, and with it, all power on the other' (51). Under this definition, clearly, public opinion operates in every kind of government. Its importance may be greatest in an absolute monarchy because there other popular sanctions are missing. It is never restricted to the electorate, but includes also the views of non-voting citizens such as women and children and even those of aliens who have an active interest in a question at issue.

So great was the importance attached by Bentham to public opinion that he believed its free operation in a despotism would be all that was necessary to secure reform. This confidence in the 'moral sanction' preceded by many years his conversion to Radicalism. In particular it helps explain the importance he attributed to publicity in his views of procedure, evidence, and judicial organization which were arrived at many years before the *Code*.[24]

Bentham thought of Public Opinion as being more than merely a force playing upon government. It was to him, as to all realistic students of government, a part of the machinery and process itself. In the first place, he draws an interesting analogy between Public Opinion and the Common Law:

Public Opinion may be considered as a system of law, emanating from the body of the people. If there be no individually assignable form of words in and by which it stands expressed, it is but upon a par in this particular with that rule of action which, emanating as it does from lawyers, official and professional, and not sanctioned by the Legislative authority, otherwise than by tacit sufferance, is in England designated by the appellation *Common Law*. (158)

In the seond place, Bentham thinks of Public Opinion as having its own institutional channels of operation which are really part of the machinery of government. He speaks constantly of the 'Public Opinion Tribunal' as one of the most important of his political institutions:

The members of the public-opinion tribunal in a community, are the members of that same community, the whole number of them, considered in respect of their capacity of taking cognizance of each other's conduct, sitting in judgment on it, and causing their judgments in the several cases to be made known. In the English House of Commons, in the formation of a committee of the members for this or that particular purpose, an order that now and then is seen to have place is, that all who come to the committee, shall have voices. The members of the public-opinion tribunal, are to the members of the community at large, what the members of the House of Commons' committee thus formed, are to the members of the house. (41)

Among such informal public opinion committees are juries, the audiences at sessions of courts and legislatures, at public meetings, and even at plays, all persons having business at administrative offices, and all those who write, speak, or reflect on acts and words of public officials (157–158). The most important single channel of public opinion is, however, the press. For this reason, restrictions on the press and on its right to criticize governors are the most heinous of all offences against good rule, the clearest indication of an inclination towards tyranny. Less important ways by which opinion may be given a leverage on officialdom include the posting in every office of placards containing rules and warnings regarding official conduct and the requirement of solemn public engagements to rule in accord with proper maxims of statecraft.

The role of the Public Opinion Tribunal is to gather information about the conduct of government, suggest improvements, censor the acts of rulers, and, finally, execute its judgments by the public expression of approval or disapproval in words or acts. Bentham was insistent that criticism of public officials must not be weakened by considerations of 'good taste' or 'decorum' or too great fear of unjust accusation. 'The military functionary is paid for being shot at. The civil functionary is paid for being spoken and written at. The soldier, who will not face musquetry, is one sort of coward. The civilian, who will not endure obloquy, is another. Better he be defamed, though it be ever so unjustly, than that, by a breach of official duty, any sinister profit sought should be reaped' (159). Not a bad motto to have in public places.

If the Public Opinion Tribunal is to fulfil its role, there must be a clear and concentrated responsibility for every act of government. This means, in Bentham's opinion, as we have already said, that appointments and ultimate administrative decisions must always rest in the hands of an individual. It means, in the second place, that, with unavoidable exceptions,[25] full publicity must attend every act of the sittings of legislatures and courts and that the duties of officials must be clearly revealed to the ordinary citizen.[26] It means, thirdly, that elaborate care must be taken to make government as clear and simple as possible. Even when the simplicity is obtained, Bentham saw well enough, the business of government, especially of legislation, is more complicated than one would like who wishes the people to understand and rule intelligently.

The successful functioning of public opinion requires, finally, that accurate and adequate records be kept in every department and that access to information be made as easy as possible.

Bentham was one of the first persons to see the supreme importance of the problem of information in government in order both that government be efficient and that responsibility to the people be real. He gives a very detailed discussion of the 'statistic' and 'recordative' duties of the different ministers even to the point of describing the various types of books (inventories, journals, loss books, etc.) that ought to be kept and of giving minute specifications of the matter that ought to appear in each and the proper manner of entry.[27] He demands that full and regular reports be made by every department to the Legislature and Prime Minister and that regular publication, in printed or other form, be given to important documents. With what delight Bentham would have gazed on the noble procession of publications that now march year by year from His Majesty's Stationery Office!

Since Hume, at least, it had been a commonplace of political speculation that all government rests on opinion. But where Hume had contented himself with brilliant suggestiveness, Bentham with his characteristic thoroughness sought to work out systematically the significance of public opinion for government, and like the political scientist today he treated it in terms of institutions and to some extent of psychology rather than of philosophy alone.

NOTES

1. *The Works of Jeremy Bentham, Published under the Superintendence of His Executor, John Bowring* (11 vols., Edinburgh, 1828–43), IX, *Constitutional Code*. This will be referred to hereafter as *Code*.
2. Bentham, *Works*, X, 66.
3. *Code*, 407.
4. Ibid., 9.
5. *Codification Proposal, Addressed by Jeremy Bentham to All Nations Professing Liberal Opinions*, 1822. *Works*, IV, 535–594.
6. *Works*, II, 267–274.
7. General treatises on the development of political thought seldom pay much attention to the *Code*. Exceptions are Robert von Mohl's *Die Geschichte und Literatur der Staatswissenschaften* (Erlangen, 1858), III, 623–627, and Geza Engelmann's *Political Philosophy from Plato to Jeremy Bentham* (New York, 1927), 329–383. In the latter work, the digest of Bentham's ideas by Engel-

mann and the introduction thereto by Oscar Jaszi are based on the *Code*, especially Book I.

8. *Code*, 5.

9. Ibid., 5. This is the political expression of a psychological principle of self-preference, defined by Bentham as 'that propensity of human nature, by which, on the occasion of every act he exercises, every human being is led to pursue that line of conduct which according to his view of the case, taken by him at the moment, will be in the highest degree contributory to his own greatest happiness, whatsoever be the effect of it, in relation to the happiness of other similar beings, any or all of them taken together.'

10. Concerning Bentham's attitude towards human nature, Bowring said: 'Of human nature, Bentham had an exalted opinion. He once told me he had known many men who held honours and riches cheap, in comparison with the delight of doing useful service to their race.' *Works*, XI, 77.

11. *Code*, 46. References to the *Code* will be given hereafter in the text.

12. Tom Paine had made the same point more succinctly in *Common Sense*: 'There is something exceedingly ridiculous in the composition of monarchy; it first excludes a man from the means of information, yet empowers him to act in cases where the highest judgment is required. The state of a King shuts him from the World, yet the business of a King requires him to know it thoroughly. . . .' *The Political Writings of Thomas Paine* (Boston, 1870), I, 22–23.

13. Compare Jaszi in Egelmann, *Political Philosophy*, 336, 337.

14. He is said to have anticipated Vaihinger's *Philosophy of As-If*. C. K. Ogden, *Bentham's Theory of Fictions* (New York, 1932), xxxi–xxxii.

15. Bentham was, of course, a strong believer in women's rights. He thought that education should be fully open to them and he favoured female doctors. He argued strongly in favour of the principle of woman suffrage, basing his case partly on their right to an equal share in the general happiness, partly on their right to compensation for physical weakness and suffering, partly on the probability that legislators would pay more attention to women's rights (or, rather, wrongs) if women voted, partly on experience (successful female monarchs). He would not, however, admit women to the legislature or executive because 'the reciprocal seduction that would ensue in the case of a mixture of sexes . . . would lead to nothing but confusion and ridicule.' *Code*, 106.

16. The same suggestion was made recently by Sir Richard Acland of the Common Wealth Party: 'I most earnestly recommend the suggestion that each member, after his election, shall be allowed to choose a deputy—or Parliamentary Private Secretary—whose views, in his judgment, correspond as closely as possible with his own. These two should work as a team. And either but not both of them should have the right to speak and vote in all sessions of the House or its committees.' Sir Richard Acland, *What It Will Be Like in the New Britain* (London, 1942), 170.

17. *Works*, V, 17, quoted by E. Halévy, *The Growth of Philosophic Radicalism* (New York, 1928), 398.

18. Elie Halévy, *The Growth of Philosophic Radicalism*, 431.

19. Redlich and F. W. Hirst, *Local Government in England* (London, 1903), I, 95–96, quoted by A. V. Dicey, *Lectures on the Relation between Law and Opinion in England during the Nineteenth Century* (London, 1920), 307, note 1.

20. E. Halévy, *The Growth of Philosophic Radicalism*, 408.

21. 'It was probably in order to yield to Dumont's entreaties, and to reconcile his personal conviction with the demands of the surrounding liberalism, that Bentham conceived in 1823 the formula of the quasi-jury.' Ibid., 401.

22. See below, pp. 198–199.
23. On public opinion, see below, pp. 200–203.
24. Halévy, *The Growth of Philosophic Radicalism*, 411.
25. Secrecy was permissible in certain phases of the work of the Army, Navy, Preventive Service, Health, Foreign Relations, and Judiciary Departments. Bentham also favoured the secret ballot.
26. For further remarks on Bentham and the problem of publicity, see C. J. Friedrich, *Constitutional Government and Politics* (New York, 1937), 417ff.
27. *Code*, 232–253. This section extends to some 20,000 words. Among the many interesting suggestions is that of a manifold system of writing so that documents would exist in several exact duplicates.

Chapter 7

Bentham on Sovereignty*

H. L. A. Hart

Readers of Austin's still influential *Province of Jurisprudence Determined* and of his now somewhat neglected *Lectures on Jurisprudence or the Philosophy of Positive Law* cannot fail to notice the marks of Bentham's powerful influence on the development of Austin's thought. In both these works Austin makes a number of respectful references [1] to Bentham, sometimes avowing his 'habitual veneration' for him; and it is clear that he regarded Bentham as his master in jurisprudence, even though he quite frequently ventured not only to differ from but to criticize his master with some asperity.[2] The truth is, however, that Bentham is not only Austin's master in the sense that Austin has learnt from him; he was also a far more profound and original thinker, and a much greater philosopher of law. Bentham's conception of analytical jurisprudence and his legal theory was richer, subtler and more sensitive to the variety and wayward complexities of legal phenomena than Austin's monolithic and easily teachable doctrine. Sometimes, as in his discussion of sovereignty, with which this article is concerned, Bentham's perception of the complexity of the subject made him not only less dogmatic in his conclusions than Austin, but perhaps also more obscure and less consistent. But the obscurities and inconsistencies of great minds are frequently more illuminating than the clarities and consistencies of lesser ones.

Bentham's stature as an analytical jurist of great power and originality has long been obscured; this is partly because some of his most important and profound contributions to jurisprudence are to be found scattered through the enormous range of his writings on other subjects, but it is chiefly because the greatest of his writings on jurisprudence and the philosophy of law, written in 1782, remained unpublished and buried in the cellars of University College, London, until 1945. In that year, Professor Charles Everett, of the Department of English of Columbia University, published most of this unknown work under the title of 'The Limits of Jurisprudence Defined',[3] having correctly identified it as the hitherto unpublished continuation of Bentham's best known work, the *Introduction to the Principles of Morals and Legislation*. Professor Everett's edition was not a

* This essay first appeared in *The Irish Jurist*, vol. II, Part 2, Winter 1967 and is reprinted here with some minor corrections by permission of the author and the editor of *The Irish Jurist*.

large one and it has long been out of print, but a corrected and expanded version of it has now been published under the title *Of Laws
in General* (which was the title Bentham chose for it in 1782) as one
of the first volumes of the vast new edition of all Bentham's work
published by the Athlone Press of the University of London under
the sponsorship of the Bentham Publications Committee. A full
account of this remarkable but very complex work could well be the
subject of several articles, for in it there are some anticipations not
only of certain themes of twentieth century jurisprudence but also of
some sophisticated forms of modern logic. In this article I shall draw
on two passages from this work in order to exhibit Bentham's views
on sovereignty.

II

Austin esteemed Bentham's doctrines on sovereignty very highly.
Indeed, in defending Hobbe's account of the legally illimitable nature
of 'sovereign power' Austin says 'I know of no other writer ex-
cepting our great contemporary, Jeremy Bentham, who has uttered
so many truths at once new and important concerning the necessary
structure of supreme political government'.[4] It is true that at one
point[5] Austin criticized Bentham for making, as Austin thought, a
careless mistake in 'forgetting to notice' that among the defining
characteristics of a sovereign there was an essential negative characteristic that the sovereign (as well as being habitually obeyed by the
bulk of the community) 'must not be habitually obedient to any
other certain individual or body'. I discuss this criticism later, but
here I wish to draw attention to the fact that Austin either did not
know, or for some inexplicable reason thought it unnecessary to
mention, that Bentham's doctrine of sovereignty differed from his
own in certain far more important respects. For, apart from the
negative characteristic already mentioned, two other attributes which
Austin regarded as essential attributes of sovereignty were not so
regarded by Bentham.

Austin agreed with Bentham in regarding all positive law as the
command, express or tacit, of a sovereign, but Austin, it will be
remembered, insisted both that the sovereign power to create law by
issuing commands was 'incapable of legal limitation' and that in any
political society the sovereign is *one* individual or *one* body of
individuals. The meaning of these two stipulations can best be
grasped by considering the possibilities they exclude. The first stipulation excludes the possibility that there may be some law which the
sovereign could not legally make: if he is sovereign he cannot lack
legal competence to make any conceivable law; his making of it

cannot be an illegal act; and it cannot be void or invalid. The second stipulation is more complicated than appears at first sight, for it excludes two different possibilities: (i) that there might in any given political society be more than one sovereign person or bodies each with legally unlimited sovereign power, and also (ii) that the sovereign power might be divided or distributed among separate independent persons or bodies, each separately competent to legislate in relation to different spheres of conduct or different sectors of the population or territory, and each within that sphere not subject to any legal limitation. So the two stipulations taken together exclude the following three things: (i) legal limitation of sovereign power; (ii) division of sovereign power; and (iii) plurality of sovereigns each having full sovereign power.

Of the three things which I have distinguished as excluded by Austin's definition of sovereign power, the first two, legal illimitability and indivisibility are of course the most important; for it is Austin's insistence on these two attributes of sovereign power which makes it impossible for him to give an undistorted account of those legal systems where a rigid constitution imposes restrictions on the legislative power of its supreme legislature, or divides legislative power between a central federal legislature and a legislature of constituent states or provinces. In such cases there is no legally unlimited or undivided sovereignty to be found, and many of Austin's critics, including myself, have been concerned to show that Austin never succeeded in squaring his doctrine of illimitable and undivided sovereignty with the legal phenomena presented by the constitution of the United States and other rigid constitutions.[6] But the third possibility noted above and excluded by Austin's doctrine, that there might be more than one sovereign in a single political society each vested with unlimited legislative power has scarcely been discussed in the literature. No doubt this is because the idea of a constitution providing for two or more omnicompetent or sovereign legislatures seems too absurd to entertain, unlike the legal limitations and divisions of supreme legislative power which are prominent features of many modern constitutions. But a plurality of sovereigns is not logically impossible. And David Hume, in one of the most perceptive of his essays entitled 'Of Some Remarkable Customs', drew attention to the fact that in the Roman Republic two independent legislative bodies the *comitia centuriata* and the *comitia tributa* each possessed full and absolute authority 'to establish two distinct legislatures, each of which possesses full and absolute authority within itself, and stands in no need of the other's assistance in order to give validity to its acts; this may appear beforehand altogether impracticable as long as men are actuated by the passions of ambition, emulation and avarice, which have hitherto been their chief governing principles . . . but there is no need for searching long in order to prove the reality of the foregoing supposition; for this was actually the case with the Roman Republic.' Bentham may have noted this passage in Hume's essay. For on one of the occasions when he expressed himself doubtful about the necessity of there being one absolute sovereign in each political society, he cited, among other examples, the Roman Commonwealth as a counter-example.[7]

III

Bentham's views on the possibility of limitation and division of the supreme legislative power have to be collected from passages and often from footnotes in his *A Fragment of Government, an Introduction to the Principles of Morals and Legislation* and *Of Laws in General*. He first approached the topic in Chapter I of the Fragment in the course of an attempt to disperse what he calls 'the mist' which Blackstone's ambiguously worded discussion of the origins of government had caused to settle on the notions of 'government', 'society' and 'state of nature'. To clear the air Bentham puts forward firm definitions of these terms and defines political society as follows: 'When a number of persons (whom we may style subjects) are supposed to be in the habit of paying obedience to a person or assemblage of persons of a known and certain description (whom we may call governor or governors) such persons altogether (subjects and governors) are said to be in a state of political society.'[8] In the following paragraph and an elaborate footnote to it he explains further, among many other terms, 'authority', 'superior' and 'habit of obedience'. It is important to observe, as Austin did, that in this passage Bentham does not say that the governor must satisfy the negative condition of not habitually obeying any other determinate individual or body. But this is not, as Austin thought, a mistake on Bentham's part, for in this passage Bentham is not concerned, as Austin later was, to tell us either what constitutes a single independent political society or the supreme or sovereign power within it. Instead Bentham is here concerned to state the general characteristics of political union, i.e. what it is for men to be in a state of political society as distinct from a state of nature. This is elucidated by reference to the notion of habitual obedience to a governor or superior and it is immaterial for Bentham's purpose at this stage whether the governor is subordinate or supreme. He is not, therefore, in this passage[9] concerned with the characteristics of sovereignty or supreme power.

In chapter IV of the Fragment, however, 'the supreme governor', 'the supreme power' and the 'authority of the supreme body' are certainly the subjects of discussion, and here Bentham faces the question whether the supreme power may be limited, or as he puts it have 'assignable bounds'. On this question Bentham appears at first sight to adopt firmly the general doctrine that with one exception 'the authority of the supreme body cannot . . . be said to have any assignable, any certain bounds.'[10] But readers of his most interesting discussion of this subject must be warned that although the exception is made tolerably clear the general doctrine is not; for Bentham seems to oscillate between thinking it impossible and thinking it merely dangerous or inexpedient to limit the supreme legislature. Readers must also be warned that they will not find in Bentham's discussion any clear cut distinction between de facto limitations of power and legal limitations of legislative authority.

The exception which Bentham allows is the case where the supreme governor's authority is limited by what Bentham terms 'an express convention'.[11] This is the case where one independent state submits on terms to the government of another, or where a number of independent states by agreement unite in a federal union and set up a federal legislature with limited authority over the constituent states. Bentham reproves Blackstone for his acceptance of the general doctrine unqualified by this important exception: it is wrong, Bentham held, to say, as Blackstone did, that in 'all forms of government there must be an authority which is absolute'. This, Bentham claims, 'would be saying that there is no such thing as government in the German Empire; nor in the Dutch provinces; nor in the Swiss Cantons; nor was of old in the Achaean League'.[12] Bentham repeats this point a little more tentatively in the only passage in the Introduction to the Principles of Morals and Legislation where he discusses sovereignty.[13] There, he tells us, that he would be afraid to have said that there must necessarily be an absolute power in the government of every society. 'In the United Provinces, in the Helvetic, or even in the Germanic body, where is that one assembly in which an absolute power over the whole resides? Where was there in the Roman Commonwealth? I would not undertake for certain to find an answer to all these questions.'

Bentham says tantalizingly little about the juridical status of the express convention which may limit the supreme legislature. He does not tell us whether it or the limitations it imposes are to be thought of as legal, but he does give some account of his reasons for allowing this form of limitation and not others. And his explanation shows that in his view the importance of an express convention in limiting the authority of a supreme legislature was derivative from the more fundamental fact of the subjects' limited habitual obedience. The express convention was important in Bentham's view only as a 'signal' showing the extent of the subjects' disposition to obey; it marked off those laws which the subjects were prepared to obey from those which they were not. Bentham, unlike Austin, always insisted that the habit or disposition to obey might be present with regard to one sort of act and absent with regard to another, and limited sovereignty is simply the correlative of a limited habit and disposition to obedience. 'For a body then which is in other respects supreme to be conceived as being with respect to certain sort of acts, limited, all that is necessary is that this sort of act be in its description distinguishable from every other.'

This explanation of limited sovereignty is simple even if it is, as I shall later attempt to show, an inadequate one. What complicates the story is Bentham's apparent yet not consistently maintained refusal to accept any other mode of limitation except express convention between formerly independent states. He insists, indeed, that except where there is an express convention, it is an abuse of language to speak of an act of supreme legislature as void or exceeding its authority, or to speak of a law which that legislature cannot make.[14] Yet it is also plain that Bentham contemplated the possibility that legal limitation on supreme legislative power might be secured by something like a system of judicial review. He allows that some meaning could be given to the otherwise meaningless statement that a law enacted by a supreme legislature was void if it were the case that the judges exercised a controlling power over the acts of the legislature. This 'mode of opposition' to the legislature 'passes' he says 'under the appellation of a legal one',[15] and Bentham apparently thought of it not as impossible but as generally dangerous, 'Give to the judges a power of annulling [a parliament's] acts and you transfer a portion of the supreme power from an assembly which the people will have had some share at least in choosing to a set of men in the choice of whom they have not the least imaginable share.'[16]

It is much to be regretted that Bentham did not explore further the limitation of supreme power by judicial control. Had he done so he might have been led to free himself from the constricting terminology of 'commands' and 'habits and disposition of obedience' limited or unlimited. This terminology was inadequate to express his insight that the varieties of possible constitutional arrangements could not be reconciled with the doctrine that in every constitution there must be an unlimited and indivisible sovereign power. In Chapter 2 of *Of Laws in General*[17] Bentham returned to the topic of limited sovereignty in two footnotes intended to qualify the definition in the text of a sovereign as a person or assemblage of persons to whose will a whole political community is supposed to be in the disposition to pay obedience. Here he puts forward in very emphatic terms his own view which he says 'may perhaps not be found very conformable to the most current notions' that sovereignty may be limited or unlimited and this depends solely on whether the subjects' disposition to obey 'which may admit of innumerable modifications', is limited or unlimited. 'The people may be disposed to obey the command of one man against the world in relation to one sort of act, those of another man in relation to another sort of act, else what are we to think of the constitutional laws of the Germanic body?' This in the terminology explained above would be a case of divided sovereignty. But Bentham also adds '[the people] may be disposed to obey a man if he commands a given sort of act: they may not be disposed to obey him if he forbids it and vice-versa'. This would be a case where the sovereignty was limited but not divided. In this work Bentham does not confine these possibilities of limited and divided sovereignty to cases where there has been an express convention. He does however stress that in all such cases 'one great difficulty is to draw the boundary line betwixt such classes of act as the sovereign may and such as he may not take to the objects of his law and to distinguish it by marks so clear as not to be in danger of mistaken'. But in this passage also Bentham is tantalizingly brief, and it must be confessed, obscure. For he says that the limited obedience which makes the limited sovereignty 'may (in point of practicability I mean) be settled by law, as well as by inward determination which bids defiance to the law'. But unfortunately he does not explain what sort of law would 'settle' such matters or how its existence could be reconciled with his general doctrine that all law is the command, express or tacit, of the sovereign.

On these two last questions light is thrown by Bentham's interesting discussion [18] of the question whether the supreme legislator can be bound by his own covenants. Can there be laws *in principem*? His view, which again has to be collected from a long note qualifying statements in the text, is that unless the sovereignty is divided between the supreme legislator and the Courts the obligation imposed by such covenants would not be 'political' (i.e. legal) but moral or religious. These can indeed be effective and account for such systems as the 'Germanic body' or the Act of Union with Scotland. But the division of sovereignty between supreme legislator and Courts is not logically impossible, and if the Courts had power 'to judge so as to coerce' the sovereign for breach of his covenants, this obligation would be 'political'. Again, Bentham thinks such a divided sovereignty would rest on a divided habit of obedience.

IV

That Bentham's explanation of limited or divided sovereignty in terms of limited disposition to obey is inadequate may be fairly simply demonstrated. Suppose that in a country where, as in the United Kingdom, there is no constitution restricting its legislative power the supreme legislature enacts for the first time laws relating to religion, e.g. requiring under penalty some attendance of some form of public worship on the part of all adults. The fact that some such laws were generally disobeyed and that those disobeying announced their firm intention to continue to disobey would surely not be enough to show that parliament had exceeded its powers and that those disobeying had committed no offence. Such a conclusion would obviously be absurd if the courts convicted those who disobeyed and the penalties were duly inflicted. If the courts refused to convict in such cases and the legislature maintained obdurately its attitude e.g. by enacting laws to punish the recalcitrant judiciary, and by enacting further laws requiring religious conformity, a division between the legislature and the courts would emerge. There would be a constitutional breakdown or lapse of the normal consensus between legislature and courts, and until it was resolved there would be a situation in which no firm statements about the powers of the legislature could be made. It might be that in course of time either the legislature or the courts would give way and a new consensus reached, or the old one restored. If the legislature gave way and recognized that it had no power to enact such laws we might say that a previously unrestricted legislature had been transformed into a restricted one. If the courts gave way we would say the legislature had retained its old unrestricted powers.

These above considerations show that limited obedience is not *sufficient* to make a limited legislature. The following consideration shows that limited obedience is not *necessary* for the existence of a limited legislature. Suppose that under a written constitution which hitherto has worked perfectly smoothly the supreme legislature has no power to enact laws on matters of religion. Suppose that this legislature, disregarding this restriction, enacts the laws described above and these are regularly obeyed by the mass of the population. This surely is not sufficient to show that the legislature had not exceeded its legal powers, and the laws in question were valid. It would be absurd to assert this if the courts refused to punish those who in fact disobeyed the new laws and contended that they were unconstitutional. Again, a split between legislature and courts might emerge if the legislature maintained its attitude and enacted laws to punish the recalcitrant judiciary. On the other hand the courts might in course of time come to treat the disputed religious laws as valid and punish those who disobeyed them. In this case there would be a new consensus and a new constitution in which legislative powers were no longer restricted.

In these two schematic examples it may be seen that the relevance of limited obedience to the question whether the supreme legislature is limited or not is far less direct than Bentham thought. Disobedience *may* show that a constitution is beginning to fall apart; obedience *may* be the first stage of a process leading gradually to the transformation of a constitution in which the supreme legislature is restricted to one where it is unrestricted. But legal limitations on legislative power and limited obedience are not simple correlatives, as Bentham seems to have thought. How precisely we should describe in juridical terms the constitutional consensus between legislature and courts, which is in fact presupposed in statements about the legal competence of a supreme legislature, is a matter of difficulty and controversy. Bentham at least deserves our thanks for showing us that the problem exists to be solved, and for resisting the oversimplifications of the doctrine of legally illimitable and indivisible sovereignty.

NOTES

1. See e.g. *The Province of Jurisprudence Determined* (ed. Hart: Library of Ideas, London, 1954), 16, 111ff, 163ff, 279ff.
2. Op. cit., 180, 191, 212; and *Lectures on Jurisprudence* (5th ed.), 692, 743, 765, 882.
3. Columbia U.P., New York, 1945.
4. *The Province*, 279.
5. Op. cit., 212.
6. See for my criticisms *The Concept of Law* (Oxford 1961), 72–76, 242–243.
7. *Infra.*
8. *A Fragment on Government*, chap. 1, para. 10.
9. Bentham never mentioned explicitly the negative condition of sovereignty or of an independent political society. But that he would have agreed with Austin on this point seems clear. See op. cit., chap. 1, para. 22–24.
10. Op. cit., chap. 4, para. 26.
11. Op. cit., chap. 4, paras. 23, 26, 34–36.
12. Ibid., para. 34.
13. Chap. XIV, paras, 17ff.
14. *Fragment*, chap. IV, paras. 26–27.
15. Ibid., para. 30.
16. Ibid., para. 32.
17. Pp. 18–20.
18. Op. cit., 64–65, 66–71.

Chapter 8

Bentham's Critique of Political Fallacies*

J. H. Burns

There is a kind of justice in the concentration of so much academic attention on the fallacies of Bentham's utilitarianism; for Bentham himself was unsparing in his condemnation of what he took to be the fallacies of others. Yet to concentrate on Bentham's defects as a creative or constructive thinker is, however just the censures, to miss one of the most valuable parts of his work. It was perhaps as a critic of ideas and arguments that Bentham most frequently succeeded, and a desirable correction of a certain disequilibrium in common assessments of his achievement may have set in with the reappearance two decades ago, in a modern and somewhat popularized version, of *The Book of Fallacies*.[1] But there is still little evidence that the Bentham known to most readers is other than the old Bentham, to be found in the early chapters of the *Introduction to the Principles of Morals and Legislation* and such parts of the *Fragment on Government* as the perhaps exasperated reader has got through. True, no one can read even this much without sensing Bentham's critical powers in the detection of fallacious reasoning; but despite Professor Larrabee's edition, the dialectical skill and pungency (and the fun) of *The Book of Fallacies* remain largely unknown. And apart from an over-quoted phrase about natural rights, Bentham's devastating attack on the Declaration of the Rights of Man and the Citizen is still more profoundly buried in the uninviting pages of the Bowring edition of his *Works*.

The main purpose of this paper is to look more closely at Bentham's critique of political fallacies and its place in his work as a whole, and to suggest some topics on which useful reflection may still be stimulated by reading Bentham, even if we cannot accept his account as final or exhaustive.

Concern for the exposure of fallacious reasoning in social and moral discourse is one of the unifying factors in Bentham's long and diverse career as a writer. The huge mass of his manuscripts bears repeated witness to this. Naturally this concern was more emphatic

---

* A revised version of a paper delivered (under the title 'Political Fallacies: Bentham's Analysis and Beyond') to the Political Studies Association of the United Kingdom in 1964. The works of Bentham chiefly cited are *The Book of Fallacies* (in *The Works of Jeremy Bentham, published under the superintendence of his executor, John Bowring*, Edinburgh, 1838–1843 [hereafter Bowring], ii, 375–487); and *Anarchical Fallacies* (Bowring, ii, 489–534).

and absorbing at some periods than at others; and the lack of apparent continuity between these phases may suggest that the unity referred to is rather spurious. Thus Bentham in his twenties, during the 1770's, seems mainly concerned with the fallacies of legal conservatism: the attack on Blackstone in the *Fragment* and in the (then unpublished) *Comment on the Commentaries*[2] illustrates this. Twenty years later, in his forties, he seems more concerned with the fallacies of revolutionary democracy: hence the attack on natural rights and cognate doctrines, later published as *Anarchical Fallacies*. After still another twenty or thirty years, as Bentham approached and passed the age of seventy, the emphasis seems again to have shifted decisively—this time to the fallacies of inert and reactionary political conservatism: the swingeing polemics of *The Book of Fallacies* reflect this concern.

Now it would be absurd to deny that these varying emphases do correspond to real changes in Bentham's thought and attitudes. It is the case that in the 1770's his attitude was largely a-political, his attack on the entrenched prejudices of the legal profession conceived as something independent of the political struggle of parties and factions. It is also the case that in the 1790's Bentham's now real and considerable political awareness was engaged largely in what may be termed the anti-Jacobin cause,[3] And finally, most obvious of all, it is evident that the Bentham of *The Book of Fallacies*, the vehemently committed suptuagenarian radical reformer, is a very different person from both the detached jurist of thirty and the alarmed Tory of fifty. Bentham himself was—sometimes at least—well aware of this: never more so nor more engagingly so than when he scribbled on an old sheet of manuscript the bewildered query, 'What can this be? Surely this was never my opinion!' Yet the fact of personal identity and continuity remains—all the more striking and important because of the care with which Bentham preserved his papers throughout his life and the frequency with which he returned to old material and reworked old themes. A closer inspection of the evidence may at least soften the sharp edges of the episodic picture sketched above.

First, then, the a-political character of Bentham's early years is by no means unqualified. The *Fragment on Government* itself, though concerned rather with what may be called constitutional jurisprudence than with politics, has evident political implications. But more important is the fact that Bentham was already applying the methods of critical analysis he had used against Blackstone to subjects more immediately involved in political controversy. His association with John Lind (1737–1781), an active propagandist on behalf of North's administration at the period of the American war, brought Bentham into marginal contact with the pamphleteering of the period. His share in shaping Lind's *Remarks on the Principal Acts of the Thirteenth Parliament of Great Britain*, recorded in Bowring's *Memoirs*,[4] shows him decisively committed against the claims of the American colonists. More significant still, however, is the contribution Bentham made in 1776 to Lind's *Answer to the Declaration of the American Congress*; for here is the first explicit evidence of his unhesitating rejection of the doctrine of natural rights:

This they 'hold to be' a 'truth self-evident'. At the same time to secure these rights they are satisfied that Government should be instituted. They see not . . . that nothing that was ever called government ever was or ever could be in any instance exercised save at the expense of one or other of those rights, that in as many instances as Government is ever exercised, some one or other of these pretended inalienable rights is alienated. . . . In these tenets they have out done the extravagance of all former fanatics.[5]

On the other hand, while most of the evidence we have confirms the impression that Bentham's political position, such as it was, tended at this period strongly towards conservatism, he was not unaware of fallacies on the conservative side too. In the legal profession and among the apologists for the established legal system he found many such fallacies; and there is at least fragmentary evidence that he recognized similar faults in conservative political reasoning. The mass of inchoate material prepared in the mid-1770's for Bentham's work on 'critical jurisprudence' includes a few passages on constitutional matters. One of these deals with the current theory of 'virtual representation' in the unreformed parliament:

It is plain that . . . this which has been called virtual representation can have nothing to do with representation. For either a man has a vote in the election of an Officer, or he has not. If he has, he is actually represented. If he has not, he is not represented at all. If representation has anything to do with election, then if any one man who has no vote to give in the election of an officer can be said to be represented by that Officer, any man whatever may. The King of Prussia, or the Grand Signior may be said to be virtually represented by a City Member.[6]

Yet it seems clear that, despite a short but not unimportant flirtation with democratic ideas during the first stages of the French Revolution, Bentham remained convinced that the 'sober and accurate apprehension of the import' of 'fundamental words', towards which so much of his intellectual effort was directed, has as one of its primary virtues that of being 'the only effectual antidote against the fascinations of political enthusiasm'.[7] By 1792 he was already recalling with satisfaction his attack on the rights of man sixteen years before;[8] by the middle of the decade he had developed his full-scale attack on the French Revolutionary version of the doctrine (the later *Anarchical Fallacies*); by the opening of the nineteenth century he was offering this onslaught to Cobbett under the title *Pestilential Nonsense Unmasked*, with the suggestion that, if unsuitable for Cobbett's own purposes, it might be passed to the editor of the *Anti-Jacobin*.[9]

As the new century advanced and the struggle to have Panopticon adopted by government did not, Bentham's mind turned to new forms of fallacy in politics. The manuscript evidence shows that what later became *The Book of Fallacies* existed in outline as early as 1806 or 1807 and in embryo even earlier. It is true that when Bentham conceived the notion of scrutinizing what he then called 'Parliamentary Fallacies', the direction of his attack was not, apparently, at variance with his essentially anti-Jacobin position: a fragment dated 1804 suggests that he was first concerned with the use of fallacy by the opposition Whigs led by Fox in their attack on Pitt's ministry.[10] But as the papers accumulated later in the decade the emphasis shifted more and more decidedly to the fallacies of those who resisted reform. This makes it the more important to notice that to Bentham at this stage of his thinking the attack on 'anarchical fallacies'—he coined the phrase about this time—formed a natural part of his now broadening critique of political absurdity in general. The *Book of Fallacies* as originally planned would have included the destructive analysis of what Bentham was now calling the 'Anarchy-preacher's fallacy'—a sub-species of the fallacy associated with 'Logical Highfliers'. As late as 1811 this was still part of the plan; and when the first published version of Bentham's work on fallacies —Etienne Dumont's redaction appended to the *Tactique des assemblées législatives*—appeared in 1816, the attack on *Sophismes anarchiques* was included. Three years later, it is true, when the subject was being reopened by Bentham himself—a process issuing in Peregrine Bingham's English edition of 1824—the situation had changed. Bentham was now puzzled as to what he should do with the attack on the rights of man—omit it, or perhaps 'print it as it stands conveying as it does the sentiments entertained A° 1811: and then subjoin the change produced A° 1819 by regarding the same subject in a different point of view'.[11]

In the event, omission was preferred. So far as I can discover, no papers survive to show how Bentham would have described and explained this 'change' in his view of natural rights. It is hard to believe that he could or would have receded from his rejection of the theory. But he may have sensed the awkwardness of incorporating in what was now intended as a contribution on the radical side to the debate with the conservatives an attack, however just, on so widely accepted a doctrine of political radicalism. The mislaying of the relevant papers, referred to by Bingham in his 1824 preface, sounds very much like the equivalent of a diplomatic illness; and the suggestion in the same place that the discussion of 'anarchical fallacies' would not have been strictly relevant in an examination of fallacies employed in debate is somewhat lame. It is true that there are differences between the fallacies Bentham found in the Declaration of Rights and most of those he found in anti-reform speeches and pamphlets twenty or thirty years later. But it would seem idle to pretend that the rhetoric of natural rights could not be and was not in fact widely misused in political debate.

The conclusion of the argument thus far is that Bentham's earliest preoccupation with fallacious reasoning in matters strictly political was concentrated upon the doctrine of natural rights; and that for forty years, from the American Revolution to the end of the Napoleonic Wars, he consistently and repeatedly attacked this kind of fallacy. But during the last ten years or so of that period and during the ten years that followed, his attention in this field was diverted more and more from the fallacies of the left to the fallacies of the right. Without formally abandoning his position in regard to 'anarchical fallacies' he came to see more immediately formidable obstacles to rational improvement in the fallacies of conservatism and reaction. In a sense this was merely to recognize in politics what he had from the very beginning recognized in the special field of legal reform; and there is at least some evidence of earlier awareness of this kind of political absurdity. But the shift in emphasis remains, and it has still to be considered whether and to what extent Bentham in fact brought the same kind of analysis to bear upon the two main types of political fallacy with which he was concerned.

This part of the discussion may perhaps best be opened by emphasizing the practical import of Bentham's concern. His interest in fallacy is never a merely theoretical interest, seeking to distinguish and classify various forms of error in a spirit of detached analytical curiosity. What concerns him is the use—the baleful use—of fallacious reasoning, whether to prevent good effects or to bring about bad ones in matters of policy and legislation. This accounts for the striking extent to which his attack concentrates upon the motives behind the use of fallacies—a concentration particularly obvious in *The Book of Fallacies*. The point is one of those which emerge more clearly from Bentham's own plan for arranging the contents of the book than from the arrangement adopted by Bingham, following Dumont, in the 1824 edition. In Bentham's arrangement, reproduced by Bowring in his *Memoirs*, and set out in a manuscript of 1821,[12] nearly every individual fallacy is attributed to some specific type of person with his own motives for employing it—the hobgoblin-crier, the official-malefactor, the practical-man, the self-trumpeter, and so on. This evidently fits the immediate polemical purpose of the book, which, like so much of Bentham's work in the last twenty years of his life, was directed as much against the sinister character of the interests ranged against reform as against the weakness of their case when judged by the test of utility. At first sight the preoccupation with motives is less evident in the attack on 'anarchical fallacies'. But it is there all the same:

What, then, was their object in declaring the existence of inprescriptible rights . . . ? This and no other—to excite and keep up a spirit of resistance to all laws—a spirit of insurrection against all governments . . .[13]

And again—

To engage others to join with him in applying force, for the purpose of putting things into a state in which he would actually be in possession of the right of which he thus pretends to be in possession, is at bottom the real object and purpose of the confusion thus endeavoured to be introduced into men's ideas, by employing a word in a sense different from what it had wont to be employed, and from this causing men to accede in words to positions from which they dissent in judgment.[14]

To treat fallacious arguments consistently as part of a political process, and a process conceived essentially as a struggle or contest, is a virtue of Bentham's analysis. This again is more sharply evident in Bentham's own plan for *The Book of Fallacies*, already referred to. Here the fallacies are deliberately grouped in relation to a party struggle between the 'Ins' and the 'Outs', and other classifications are subordinated to this. Accordingly, Bentham sees the party in power resisting reform by playing fallaciously on the fears, the self-diffidence, the superstitions, the indolence, and the antipathies of those whom they address; nor is it surprising to find as many as thirty-one out of fifty-two chapters devoted to these topics. But Bentham is also aware that other fallacies are available to and used by both sides in the struggle—these 'either side fallacies' work upon men's sympathies by misdirected puffing ('trumpeting' as Bentham calls it) or else distort men's judgment by false distinctions, question-begging, and the like. Finally, there is a small but not insignificant group of fallacies peculiar to the 'Outs', the opposition party. The political aim of that party is of course to replace the 'Ins' in possession of the benefits of office at the expense of the public interest. To this end they must lower the political reputation of their opponents; and Bentham argues that this makes their need to oppose any genuinely good measure proposed by government (by which government's reputation would be enhanced) still more urgent than their need to oppose bad measures. To illustrate the fallacious arguments

employed for this purpose Bentham had envisaged in his original
plan two 'cries': the 'Blind-place-abhorrer's cry. What? More
places?' and the 'Blind-job-denouncer's cry. What? More jobs?'
The essential appeal of these fallacies of the 'Outs' is 'to men's
jealousies and *envyings*'.[15]

This last part of the analysis is somewhat obscured in the published text of *The Book of Fallacies*, where no special discussion is
devoted to opposition arguments of this kind. Yet it is surely not the
least shrewd of Bentham's achievements to have seen that the pursuit
of political power by the 'Outs' can, no less than the defence of an
established order and its vested interests, corrupt political discourse.
There may even be a sense in which Bentham regarded this kind of
fallacy as more pervasive and incurable than the rest. In the last part
of *The Book of Fallacies* he makes some interesting comparisons
between the place and function of fallacy in the working of the
British and American political systems. The upshot is that whereas
'on the side of the *Outs*, the demand for fallacies stands without any
difference worth noting' on a similar footing in both countries, this
is not true of the 'Ins'. Here 'the demand for fallacies depends upon
the aggregate mass of abuse'; and since this mass is, in the American
case, negligible in comparison with what it is in Britain, the need for
fallacious reasoning by the party in power is correspondingly small.
Bentham naturally takes care to emphasize that where the 'Ins' do,
as in Britain, need fallacious support, the harvest of absurdity will
far surpass anything the 'Outs' in any system can ever require. But
if the demand of the 'Ins' is thus, where it exists at all, more extensive, that of the 'Outs' seems to be more persistent.[16]

When, towards the end of *The Book of Fallacies*, Bentham sums
up the common characteristics of all the false arguments he has
examined, he gives first place to the fact that 'Whatever be the
measure in hand, they are, with relation to it, irrelevant.'[17] The presumption is, he goes on, that they are employed because there are
few, if any, relevant arguments of substance to take their place. Now
it is true that the kind of argument Bentham is mainly concerned
with can be shown to be, whether deliberately or not, off the point.
One or two instances will make this clear.

In the 'Chinese argument', which, Bentham says,

consists in stating a supposed repugnance between the proposed measure
and the opinions of men by whom the country of those who are discussing
the measure was inhabited in former times—[18]

the 'ancestor-worshipper's argument' as he calls it elsewhere[19]—the
fallacy is precisely to divert attention from the relevant evidence of
experience to principles or institutions devised in the past on the

basis of far more limited and imperfect experience. Again, the various fallacies dealing in 'vituperative personalities'—attacking a measure by imputing to its proposers bad designs, characters, or motives, inconsistency, suspicious connections, and so on—are nothing to the purpose:

Among 658[20] or any such large number of persons taken at random, there will be persons of all characters: if the measure is a good one, will it become bad because supported by a bad man? If it is bad, will it become good because supported by a good man? If the measure be really inexpedient, why not show at once that it is not so? Your producing these irrelevant and inconclusive arguments in lieu of direct ones, though not sufficient to prove that the measure you thus oppose is a good one, *contributes* to prove that you yourselves regard it as a good one.[21]

Finally, the Procrastinator's Argument: 'Wait a little, this is not the time.' Here Bentham's argument is that the contention is a kind of Pharisaism, concealing behind the advocacy of delay a hostility to the measure which really knows no limit of time.[22]

Enough has perhaps been said to bring out at least one point. *The Book of Fallacies* is at least as much a piece of political satire as it is of political analysis. Arguments such as those just examined have an evident affinity with another handbook for politicians—F. M. Cornford's *Microcosmographia Academica*. That tragi-comical 'Guide for the Young Academic Politician' is indeed one of the few successors Bentham's book has had; and the affinity, the near-identity of some of the positions satirized by the two authors is striking. Cornford's Principle of Unripe Time is precisely the Procrastinator's Argument of *The Book of Fallacies*:

people should not do at the present moment what they think right at that moment, because the moment at which they think it right has not yet arrived.[23]

The ancestor-worshipper's fallacy appears in Cornford as the argument 'that you remember exactly the same proposal being rejected in 1867'.[24] And Cornford's 'method of *Prevarication* ... which comes out in the common remark, "I was in favour of the propsal until I heard Mr – – –'s argument in support of it"' is an interesting variant, in the gentlemanly tones appropriate to an ancient University, of the appeal to 'vituperative personalities'.[25]

This comparison suggests a further comment. Satire has its risks and limitations as well as its uses. The effectiveness of some of Bentham's satirical demonstrations of irrelevancy should not mask the defects of other parts of his case. These are indeed well illustrated by his account of the Procrastinator's Argument, mentioned above. He does not show that the argument is in itself necessarily irrelevant. What he does is to claim that the argument is never in fact used save by those whose real motive is to delay reform indefinitely. This is suspiciously similar to what Bentham himself condemns as the fallacy of imputing bad motives, and in fact brings our attention back to the preoccupation with motives already described. If this preoccupation gives Bentham's analysis most of its force and impact, it also imports certain weaknesses into the argument. In the present instance, for example, it seems perfectly reasonable to maintain that the circumstances prevailing at a given time may well be and perhaps must be a relevant consideration in matters of policy. An extreme illustration would be this: to say 'Wait a little, this is not the time' in respect of implementing the Beveridge Report on social security at the end of 1943 is an argument with no element of fallacy in it. And what is true in an extreme degree in such a case is obviously true in smaller measure elsewhere.

Similar doubts may be raised at other points in Bentham's analysis. The 'Snail's-pace Argument—One thing at a time! Not too fast! Slow and sure!', which is to Bentham

neither more nor less than a contrivance for making out of a mere word an excuse for leaving undone an indefinite multitude of things which, the arguer is convinced, and cannot forbear acknowledging, ought to be done.[26]

may indeed be this and nothing more; but there seem to be no grounds in experience for holding that it can never be anything else. Again, it seems by no means obvious that Bentham's 'Fallacy of Distrust, or, What's at the bottom?' is always as absurd as he claims and as it sometimes doubtless is. Bentham's argument is the apparently unexceptionable one that each proposed measure should be judged simply on its merits and if found beneficial endorsed without any irrelevant reflection as to what measures of another character may be associated with it or follow it.[27] But there is perhaps a more complex and subtle inter-connection between measures of government than this rather *simpliste* view allows. It is not always mere wrongheaded distrust to judge a measure as part of an overall policy with implications beyond itself and its immediate consequences. And this in turn may suggest that even in the discussion of 'vituperative personalities' a politically significant baby may have been thrown out with the bath-water of irrelevance. After all, in assessing the policy of nationalizing large-scale industry as advocated in the Twenty-Five Points of February 1920 it would surely not have been irrelevant to consider the personal character and associations of the leaders of the National Socialist German Workers' Party.

This is not to deny that Bentham does in *The Book of Fallacies* expose and effectively dispose of a substantial number of political absurdities. It is worth noting, however, that a large proportion of the book—as the sub-titles of its parts as published make clear—is directed against fallacies which are not so much erroneous forms of argument as attempts to prevent rational argument altogether. These fallacies are pseudo-logical or a-logical, and (to reiterate) Bentham is as much concerned with the psychological and political origins of their employment as he is with their irrelevance to any properly logical discussion of political issues. It is in the fourth part of the book, devoted to 'Fallacies of Confusion, the Object of which is to perplex, when Discussion can no longer be avoided,' that Bentham deals more directly with political fallacies of a strictly logical kind. He is concerned here with question-begging; with sham distinctions (such as that between liberty and licence); with 'allegorical idols' like the use of the terms 'the Law' and 'the Church' when lawyers and churchmen are the real subjects; with the use of 'imposter terms' to defend things 'which under their proper name are manifestly indefensible.'[29] The polemical purpose is as strong as ever, and an urgent, even strident, note is still to be heard; but it is still true that Bentham here is more of a political logician, less of a satirist. As the comparison with Cornford illustrated one aspect, so this facet of the book suggests comparisons with what Susan Stebbing tried to do in *Thinking to Some Purpose*, with instances of fallacious reasoning drawn from the speeches of Stanley Baldwin, yet writing as a logician, not a pamphleteer.

One effect of this modified context is important. In the satirical attack on the merely irrelevant absurdities of 'anti-innovationists', Bentham had little need to be specific about his own conception of what political reasoning should be. He had only to indicate that by these fallacies attention was diverted from the application of the only proper test of the merits of a proposed measure of government —its tendency to promote the greatest happiness of the greatest number. Ready reference to the principle of utility, taken for granted as the standard of political right and wrong, was sufficient. But to develop an adequate critique of fallacies where more than irrelevance was involved meant a more thorough and explicit account of the nature of correct reasoning. There is not, perhaps, a great deal of this even in the part of *The Book of Fallacies* where it would be most appropriate. But in dealing with the 'anarchical fallacies' which might have found, though they did not in fact find, a place in the more general treatise, Bentham had at an earlier period given a very clear and striking indication of what correct reasoning in political discourse meant for him. It was by this kind of reasoning that Bentham in the 1790's developed his attack on the doctrine of natural rights.

The base from which Bentham attacks may be indicated by quoting first this sentence:

The more *abstract*—that is, the more *extensive* the proposition is, the more liable is it to involve a fallacy.[29]

It is the abstract and general character of the principles enunciated in the Declaration of Rights that attracts much of Bentham's hostility. He sees it as involving a radically vicious approach to the problems of legislation. This mistakes the logical order of demonstration—from principles to consequences—for the order 'of conception, of investigation, of invention.' In fact,

The proper order is—first to digest the laws of detail, and when they are settled and found to be fit for use, then, and not till then, to select and frame *in terminis*, by abstraction, such principles as may be capable of being given without self-contradiction as fundamental laws.[30]

The reference in the passage just cited to 'self-contradiction' is crucial; for it is in the 'insuperable incongruities' inherent in propositions about natural rights that Bentham sees the clearest evidence of their logical and social viciousness. Just as in 1776 he had pointed to the inconsistency of arguing that the 'inalienable' rights of man should be protected by governments whose very existence depended on the alienation of some of those very rights, so twenty years later he argues, for instance, that to assert a natural right to property cannot in the nature of the case define any specific proprietary right with a determinate subject: it can therefore mean only 'that every man has a right to do every thing':

Unfortunately, in most matters of property, what is every man's right is no man's right; so that the effect of this part of the oracle, if observed, would be, not to establish property, but to extinguish it . . .[31]

So the argument runs throughout: nothing is added to the security of actual, legally guaranteed rights by the attempt to deduce them from general principles which are in fact incompatible with the existence of such rights. Nothing is gained, while on the debit side there is an actual weakening of the security for rights by encouraging 'the selfish and dissocial passions.'[32]

Bentham is convinced that one radical vice of the natural rights theory is its persistent abuse of language—notably the recurrent tendency to represent as statements of fact or principle what are really no more than expressions of emotion. In this connection he seizes particularly upon statements to the effect that laws 'cannot' derogate in this or that way from allegedly natural rights. These statements are intended, he argues, to give an unjust weight and force to the will of those who enunciate or embrace them:

I make the absurd choice of a term expressive in its original and proper import of a physical impossibility, in order to represent as impossible the very event of the occurrence of which I am apprehensive ... I raise my voice to the people—tell them the thing is impossible; and they are to have the goodness to believe me, and act in consequence.[33]

In fact—the point is familiar enough since the work of Ogden and Baumgardt—Bentham, here and elsewhere, anticipated much later philosophical criticism tending to the conclusion that the language of moral, social, and political evaluation is commonly emotive language concealed in assertive forms. In place of this Bentham would put 'the question of utility':

Now the question is put, as every political and moral question ought to be, upon the issue of fact; and mankind are directed into the only true track of investigation which can afford instruction or hope of rational argument, the track of experiment and observation.[34]

Politics for Bentham is a matter for rational discourse, purged of the accretions and impurities of fallacy; and this is possible because politics is capable of being made an experimental science. The logic of the laboratory can be substituted for the rhetoric of the senate and the hustings.

It is clear that much of what may be called the more purely logical part of Bentham's critique of political fallacies has found a sequel in recent and contemporary thinking. His insights have been followed up, his analyses refined, though one may question whether a much better attack on metaphysical politics than *Anarchical Fallacies* has been or need be developed. But it is worth noting that where Bentham criticized the emotive use of moral terms in propositions which, being emotive, could not be verified, later analyses have often tended to conclude that the propositions of moral discourses have in any case no verifiable content—a view which undermines Bentham's own position, where moral questions are to be settled 'upon the issue of fact'.

At the same time Bentham's approach to political propositions by way of the motives inspiring their use and determining their efficacy has also had its sequel and development. Here, obviously, we have access to much more extensive knowledge of the mechanics of motivation than Bentham could have. New dimensions have transformed this particular universe of discourse and have gone far towards transforming our conception of politics as a field of human behaviour. Bentham saw how politicians played upon the fears and hopes, the sympathies and antipathies of men; how psychological tensions and conflicts opened the door to logical absurdity and irrelevance. We can now see the same kind of phenomena far more generally diffused in the social universe and in the perspective of a very different range of psychological knowledge. But in fact we do not see what Bentham saw at all.

Bentham regarded the world of fallacy as a distortion of the true nature of politics. Properly understood and conducted, the political process was a process of rational discourse: not a discourse leading to absolute and universally agreed propositions—'for certainty belongs not to human affairs',[35] but at least a discourse governed by generally accepted critical principles. He believed that human societies, beginning with force, were for long periods sustained by habit and tradition; and he saw that when there first emerged societies where persuasion was replacing force and inertia, the persuasion was frequently irrational. But he looked forward to 'an epoch in the history of civilization' (the closing words of *The Book of Fallacies*)[36] when rational argument should have replaced the shams of rhetoric. He carried into his theory of democratic government the great principles of the Enlightenment.

These principles can hardly help appearing somewhat illusory now. We have come to see politics as a matter of evoking appropriate responses, projecting effective images, playing upon impulses and appetites. Sometimes this can and will be done by employing the appearance of rational argument—by using fallacies of the kind Bentham condemns, and not infrequently the same old fallacies. Sometimes it will be done by means of genuinely logical argument, argument which can bear the most rigorous analysis. Many of us— most professional academic persons, no doubt—have a deeply ingrained prejudice in favour of this method. We feel that a political conviction arrived at by this means is somehow better than, preferable to, one which is no more than habitual prejudice or a response to 'propaganda'. But in what sense, if any, could we maintain, as Bentham could, that this is the way in which politics should be conducted? We still believe in the possibility of a rational science of politics. We do not believe any longer, as Bentham did, that the process of politics is itself, when properly conducted, a rational science. And this seems to me to leave us with a final question prompted by the subject of this paper. Are there for us, can there be, any 'political fallacies' at all?

NOTES

1. Harold A. Larrabee (ed.), *Bentham's Handbook of Political Fallacies*, Baltimore, 1952.
2. Ed. C. W. Everett, Oxford 1928: a revised and augmented edition, ed. J. H.

Burns and H. L. A. Hart, will be published, with *A Fragment on Government* in *The Collected Works of Jeremy Bentham*, London, 1968.

3. Cf. J. H. Burns, 'Bentham and the French Revolution' in *Transactions of the Royal Historical Society*, 5th series, vol. 16, 1964, 95–114.
4. Bowring, x, 62–63 and n.
5. *The Correspondence of Jeremy Bentham* (in *Collected Works*), vol. 1, ed. T. L. S. Sprigge, 1968, 341–343. This incomplete letter from Bentham to Lind, written in September 1776, comprises part of Bentham's draft for what was printed later in the autumn on pp. 120–122 of Lind's pamphlet.
6. Bentham MSS, University College London [hereafter U.C.], lxix, 161.
7. U.C., lxix, 62 (undated: probably mid-1770's).
8. U.C., cvii. 34; quoted in J. H. Burns, *Jeremy Bentham and University College*, London, 1962, 26.
9. U.C., cxlvi, 238–40 (1801).
10. U.C., cv, 7 (8 June 1804).
11. U.C., cv, 17 (note dated August 1819 on MS. originally written in June 1810 and revised in May 1811). For Bentham's views in 1810–11 cf. also U.C., cv, 16, 18–20 (June 1810) and civ, 49 (August 1811).
12. Bowring, x, 519–521; and cf. U.C., cv, 120 (18 March 1821).
13. Bowring, ii, 501 (*Anarchical Fallacies*).
14. Bowring, iii, 218 (*Pannomial Fragments*); also C. K. Ogden (ed.), *Bentham's Theory of Fictions*, London, 1932, 120. The manuscript (British Museum, Additional MS. 33550, f. 87) shows that the passage was written on 30 December 1823: it is thus an interestingly late reassertion of Bentham's hostility to natural rights.
15. Bowring, x, 521. For a general discussion of the position and aims of the 'Outs' see Bowring, ii, 481ff. (*The Book of Fallacies*.)
16. Bowring, ii, 481–482.
17. Ibid., 474.
18. Ibid., 398.
19. Bowring, x, 519.
20. The membership of the House of Commons when Bentham was writing.
21. Bowring, ii, 414.
22. Ibid., 434ff.
23. F. M. Cornford, op. cit., Cambridge, 1949 [1st ed. 1908], 16.
24. Ibid., 19.
25. Ibid., 18.
26. Bowring, ii, 433.
27. Ibid., 421.
28. Ibid., 436ff.
29. Ibid., 496 (*Anarchical Fallacies*).
30. Ibid., 493–494.
31. Ibid., 503.
32. Ibid., 497.
33. Ibid., 494.
34. Ibid., 495.
35. Ibid., 495.
36. Ibid., 487.

Chapter 9

Bentham's Felicific Calculus*

Wesley C. Mitchell

Jeremy Bentham has one service yet to perform for students of the social sciences. He can help them to work free from that misconception of human nature which he helped their predecessors to formulate. This rôle of emancipator he plays in the following paper.

In the social sciences we are suffering from a curious mental derangement. We have become aware that the orthodox doctrines of economics, politics and law rest upon a tacit assumption that man's behaviour is dominated by rational calculation. We have learned further that this is an assumption contrary to fact. But we find it hard to avoid the old mistake, not to speak of using the new knowledge. In our prefaces and introductory chapters some of us repudiate hedonism and profess volitional psychology or behaviourism. Others among us assert that economics at least can have no legitimate relations with psychology in any of its warring forms. In the body of our books, however, we relapse into reasonings about behaviour that apply only to creatures essentially reasonable.

Bentham cannot help toward making the social sciences valid accounts of social behaviour. But better than any one else he can help us to see the absurdity of the intellectualist fallacy we abjure and practise. For Bentham has no rival as an exponent of the delusions that haunt the backs of our heads, and gain control over our speculations when we are not thinking of psychology. The way to free ourselves from these delusions is to drag them into the light of full consciousness and make them face our other thoughts about behaviour. We can perform this psycho-analytic operation upon our own minds best by assembling in orderly sequence the pertinent passages scattered through Bentham's writings.

I

Bentham dealt not only with many branches of jurisprudence—criminal law, evidence, procedure, codification, international law, constitutional law—but also with economics, psychology, penology, pedagogy, ethics, religion, logic and metaphysics. Yet all his books read as one. They work out a single idea in diverse materials. They

* Reprinted from *Political Science Quarterly*, vol. XXXIII, June 1918 (Ed.).

apply the sacred principle of utility whether the subject matter be colonies or Christianity, usury or the classification of the sciences, the crimes of judges or the reformation of criminals.

But utilitarianism as such is not the differentiating characteristic of Bentham. A line of English philosophers running back at least to Richard Cumberland in 1672 had expounded that doctrine before him. About these predecessors Bentham knew little; but 'Utilitarianism had been so distinctly in the air for more than a generation before he published his *Principles of Morals and Legislation* that he could not possibly have failed very substantially to profit by the fact.'[1] Indeed, Bentham was conscious of doctrinal indebtedness to Hume, Hartley and Priestley in England, Helvetius in France, and Beccaria in Italy.[2] Among his own contemporaries Utilitarianism prevailed widely outside the circle of professed philosophers. The regnant theologian of the day, William Paley, was as grim an exponent of the sacred principle as Bentham himself.[3] In the English controversy about the French Revolution all parties agreed tacitly or explicitly in accepting utility as the final test of political institutions—Burke as well as Godwin, the respectable Whig Mackintosh as well as the agitator Tom Paine. And when Malthus, a clergyman, answered Godwin on the population issue he showed himself as good a utilitarian as his atheistical opponent.[4] No one has studied currents of English thinking in these times so thoroughly as Elie Halévy, and he remarks: 'Towards the end of the eighteenth century, it is not only the thinkers, it is all the English who are speaking the language of utility.'[5] 'It was plain,' he adds in another volume, 'that the doctrine of utility was becoming the universal philosophy in England, and that the reformers must speak the language of utility if they wished their opinions to be understood—let alone accepted—by the public they were addressing.'[6] This view certainly accords with Bentham's own impression as recorded in his commonplace book: 'The opinion of the world (I am speaking of the people in this country) is commonly in favour of the principle of utility. . . .'[7]

What did distinguish Bentham from other utilitarians, what made him the leader of a school, what keeps his work instructive to this day, was his effort to introduce exact method into all discussions of utility. He sought to make legislation, economics, ethics into genuine sciences. His contemporaries were content to talk about utility at large; Bentham insisted upon measuring particular utilities—or rather, the net pleasures on which utilities rest.

The ideal of science which men then held was represented by celestial mechanics; its hero was Newton, whose system had been popularized by Voltaire; its living exemplars were the great mathematicians of the French Academy. Bentham hoped to become 'the

Newton of the Moral World.' Among the mass of his papers left to University College Halévy has found this passage:

The present work as well as any other work of mine that has been or will be published on the subject of legislation or any other branch of moral science is an attempt to extend the experimental method of reasoning from the physical branch to the moral. What Bacon was to the physical world, Helvetius was to the moral. The moral world has therefore had its Bacon, but its Newton is yet to come.[8]

II

Bentham's way of becoming the Newton of the moral world was to develop the 'felicific calculus.' There are several expositions of this calculus in his *Works*; but the first and most famous version remains the best to quote.[9]

Nature has placed mankind under the governance of two sovereign masters, *pain* and *pleasure*. It is for them alone to point out what we ought to do, as well as to determine what we shall do. On the one hand the standard of right and wrong, on the other the chain of causes and effects, are fastened to their throne.

Hence to know what men will do, to tell what they should do, or to value what they have done, one must be able to measure varying 'lots' of pleasure or pain. How are such measurements to be made?

To a person considered *by himself*, the value of a pleasure or pain considered *by itself*, will be greater or less, according to the four following circumstances: 1 Its *intensity*. 2 Its *duration*. 3 Its *certainty* . . . 4 Its *propinquity* . . . But when the value of any pleasure or pain is considered for the purpose of estimating the tendency of any *act* by which it is produced, there are two other circumstances to be taken into the account; these are, 5 Its *fecundity* . . . 6 Its *purity* . . . [When a community is considered, it is also necessary to take account of] 7 Its *extent*; that is, the number of persons to whom it *extends*. . . .

The unit of intensity is the faintest sensation that can be distinguished to be pleasure or pain; the unit of duration is a moment of time. Degrees of intensity and duration are to be counted in whole numbers, as multiples of these units. Certainty and propinquity are reckoned as fractions whose limit is immediate actual sensation; from this limit the fractions fall away. In applying the calculus, one begins with the first distinguishable pleasure or pain which appears to be produced by an act, multiplies the number of its intensity units by the number of duration units, and then multiplies this product by the two fractions expressing certainty and proximity. To bring in fecundity one computes by the preceding method the value of each pleasure or each pain which appears to be produced after the first one; the resulting values are to be added to the value previously obtained. To bring in purity one computes the values of all pains that attend a given series of pleasures, or of pleasures that attend a given series of pains; these values are to be subtracted from the preceding sums. That is, pleasure is a positive, pain a negative quantity. Since the unit of extent is an individual, one completes the computation by multiplying the net resultant pain or pleasure ascertained as above by the number of individuals affected. Usually however this last step is more complicated: not all the people affected are affected in the same way. In that case one does not multiply by the number of individuals, but makes a separate computation for each individual and then strikes the algebraic sum of the resultants.[10]

III

If these technical directions for measuring 'lots' of pleasure and pain be taken seriously, the felicific calculus is a complicated affair at best. In addition it is beset by subtler and graver difficulties, some that Bentham saw clearly, others that he barely glimpsed. Unfortunately the disciples who pieced his manuscripts together into books did not think fit to publish his sharpest bits of insight into the haze, so that later writers had to rediscover much that their master had descried. The type of social science on which Bentham worked might have been completed and superseded much sooner than it was had his difficulties been made known in his own lifetime.

(1) That all comparisons of the feelings of different men are questionable Bentham was perfectly aware. In his *Principles of Morals and Legislation*, indeed, he enlarged upon this topic by discussing thirty-two 'circumstances influencing sensibility' to pleasure and pain.[11] Since these thirty-two circumstances exist in an indefinite number of combinations, it would seem that the felicific calculus can scarcely be applied except individual by individual—a serious limitation. So long as he was thinking only of the problem of punishments Bentham accepted this conclusion. The legislator and the judge ought each to have before him a list of the several circumstances by which sensibility may be influenced: the legislator ought to consider those circumstances which apply uniformly to whole classes, for example, insanity, sex, rank, climate and religious profession; the judge ought to consider the circumstances which apply in varying degrees to each individual, for example, health, strength, habitual occupation, pecuniary circumstances etc.[12]

But as Bentham's problems widened he concluded that his calculus must apply to men at large, if it was to yield scientific generalizations, although he still thought that this application rested upon an assumption contrary to fact. One manuscript found by Halévy runs:

'Tis in vain to talk of adding quantities which after the addition will continue distinct as they were before, one man's happiness will never be another man's happiness: a gain to one man is no gain to another: you might as well pretend to add 20 apples to 20 pears . . . This addibility of the happiness of different subjects, however when considered rigorously it may appear fictitious, is a postulatum without the allowance of which all political reasoning is at a stand: nor is it more fictitious than that of the equality of chances to reality, on which that whole branch of the Mathematics which is called the doctrine of chances is established.[13]

(2) Of course, this postulate of the 'addibility' of the happiness of different men tacitly assumes that numerical values can be set on the feelings of each individual. But is that really true? Indeed, can any individual put a definite figure upon his own pleasures and pains, let alone compare them with the pleasures and pains of other men? The more Bentham dwelt upon this aspect of his calculus, the more difficulties he developed and the more assumptions he found necessary to his type of social science.

One fundamental doubt he sometimes overlooked, and sometimes admitted. Intensity is the first 'element' in which feelings differ. Can any man count the intensity units in any one of his pleasures or pains, as he counts the duration units? Bentham usually assumes that he can, without telling how.

. . . the degree of intensity possessed by that pleasure which is the faintest of any that can be distinguished to be pleasure, may be represented by unity. Such a degree of intensity is in every day's experience: according as any pleasures are perceived to be more and more intense, they may be represented by higher and higher numbers. . . .[14]

In his *Codification Proposal*, however, Bentham frankly grants that intensity is not 'susceptible of measurement.'[15]

(3) With a closely-related problem, Bentham wrestled frequently: can a man make quantitative comparisons among his qualitatively-unlike pleasures or pains?

The difficulty here was aggravated by one of Bentham's favourite ideas. He held that most of our feelings are complexes made up of simple elements. One of the tasks which he essayed was to enumerate exhaustively the 'simple' pleasures and the 'simple' pains, which like the elements in chemistry cannot be decomposed themselves, but which can combine with each other in the most diverse ways. In his *Principles of Morals and Legislation* he listed fourteen simple pleasures (counting nine alleged pleasures of the senses as one) and twelve simple pains.[16] In his *Table of the Springs of Action* he, or his editor,

James Mill, modified the lists somewhat, but kept the general idea that in the last analysis our pleasures and pains are compounded of qualitatively unlike elements.[17] Now, if that be literally true, how can one apply the felicific calculus even in the case of a single individual? Some common denominator seems needed for the two dozen or more elements; but if there exists a common denominator, are not the elements themselves homogeneous?

When he wrote his *Principles of Morals and Legislation* Bentham did not discuss, perhaps did not think of these questions. Despite all the trouble he took to describe 'the several sorts of pains and pleasures,' he referred to pain and pleasure as 'names of homogeneous real entities.'[18] Throughout the book he assumed tacitly not only that different pains and different pleasures, but also that pains and pleasures are commensurable. Yet the one passage most to the present purpose shows that his method of comparing quantities was strictly limited. He says:

The only certain and universal means of making two lots of punishment perfectly commensurable, is by making the lesser an ingredient in the composition of the greater. This may be done in either of two ways. 1. By adding to the lesser punishment another quantity of punishment of the same kind. 2. By adding to it another quantity of a different kind.[19]

Indeed in this whole treatise Bentham relies upon classification, and not upon calculation.[20] He splits everything he discusses—pleasures, pains, motives, dispositions, offences, 'cases unmeet for punishment' etc. into kinds, limits his quantitative comparisons to relations of greater and less, and makes even these comparisons chiefly among phenomena belonging to the same kind. He does indeed bid the authorities do things which imply bolder comparisons, as when he rules that 'the value of the punishment must not be less in any case than . . . the profit of the offence;'[21] but he does not make such comparisons himself.

And yet Bentham did find a way of reducing qualitatively unlike pleasures and pains to a common denominator, and so of putting figures on felicity. There are traces of this method in his published works,[22] but much the best exposition remained in manuscript until Halévy's day. The following passages have peculiar interest as anticipations of Edgeworth's use of 'indifference' and more definitely of Marshall's 'money measures.'

If of two pleasures a man, knowing what they are, would as lief enjoy the one as the other, they must be reputed equal. . . . If of two pains a man had as lief escape the one as the other, such two pains must be reputed equal. If of two sensations, a pain and a pleasure, a man had as lief enjoy the pleasure and suffer the pain, as not enjoy the first and not suffer the latter, such pleasure and pain must be reputed *equal*, or, as we may say in this case, *equivalent*.

If then between two pleasures the one produced by the possession of money, the other not, a man had as lief enjoy the one as the other, such pleasures are to be reputed equal. But the pleasure produced by the possession of money, is *as* the quantity of money that produces it: money is therefore the measure of this pleasure. But the other pleasure is equal to this; the other pleasure therefore is as the money that produces this; therefore money is also the measure of that other pleasure. It is the same between pain and pain; as also between pain and pleasure.

. . .If then, speaking of the respective quantities of various pains and pleasures and agreeing in the same propositions concerning them, we would annex the same ideas to those propositions, that is, if we would understand one another, we must make use of some common measure. The only common measure the nature of things affords is money. . . .

I beg a truce here of our man of sentiment and feeling while from necessity, and it is only from necessity, I speak and prompt mankind to speak a mercenary language. . . . Money is the instrument for measuring the quantity of pain or pleasure. Those who are not satisfied with the accuracy of this instrument must find out some other that shall be more accurate, or bid adieu to Politics and Morals.[23]

(4) That Bentham did not follow up this promising lead was due to a further difficulty. Every time he began thinking about money measures of feeling he was checked by the diminishing utility of wealth. The 'quantity of happiness produced by a particle of wealth (each particle being of the same magnitude) will be less and less at every particle; the second will produce less than the first, the third than the second, and so on.'[24] '. . . for by high dozes of the exciting matter applied to the organ, its sensibility is in a manner worn out.'[25] Consider the monarch with a million a year and the labourer with twenty pounds:

The quantity of pleasure in the breast of the monarch will naturally be greater than the quantity in the breast of the labourer: . . . But . . . by how many times greater? Fifty thousand times? This is assuredly more than any man would take upon himself to say. A thousand times, then?—a hundred?—ten times?—five times?—twice?—which of all these shall be the number? . . . For the monarch's, taking all purposes together, *five times* the labourer's seems a very large, not to say an excessive allowance: even *twice*, a liberal one.[26]

Quite apart from differences in the sensibility of different men to pleasure, then, equal sums of money can by no means be supposed to represent equal quantities of feeling.

Once, at least, Bentham thought he had found a solution of this difficulty. In the manuscript last quoted he argues:

... money being the current instrument of pleasure, it is plain by uncontrovertible experience that the quantity of actual pleasure follows in every instance in some proportion or other the quantity of money. As to the law of that proportion nothing can be more indeterminate. ... For all this it is true enough for practice with respect to such proportions as ordinarily occur (var.: small quantities), that *cæteris paribus* the proportion between pleasure and pleasure is the same as that between sum and sum. So much is strictly true that the ratios between the two pairs of quantities are nearer to that of equality than to any other ratio that can be assigned. Men will therefore stand a better chance of being right by supposing them equal than by supposing them to be any otherwise than equal. ...

Speaking then in general, we may therefore truly say, that in small quantities the pleasures produced by two sums are *as* the sums producing them.[27]

This passage lies on the frontier of Bentham's realm of thought. It shows that the idea of dealing with small increments of feeling occurred to him, as a method of avoiding the embarrassment caused by diminishing utility and still using money as a common denominator. But all this was rather dim; the idea did not develop vigorously in his mind. He missed, indeed, two notions that his disciples were to exploit later on: Bernoulli's suggestion that, after bare subsistence is provided, a man's pleasure increases by equal amounts with each equal successive percentage added to his income; and the plan of concentrating attention upon the increments of pleasure or pain at the margin.

The net resultant of all these reflections upon the felicific calculus collected from Bentham's books and papers might be put thus: (1) The intensity of feelings cannot be measured at all; (2) even in the case of a single subject, qualitatively unlike feelings cannot be compared except indirectly through their pecuniary equivalents; (3) the assumption that equal sums of money represent equal sums of pleasure is unsafe except in the case of small quantities; (4) all attempts to compare the feelings of different men involve an assumption contrary to fact. That is a critic's version of admissions wrung from Bentham's text; a disciple's version of his master's triumphs might run: (1) The felicific calculus attains a tolerable degree of precision since all the dimensions of feeling save one can be measured;[28] (2) the calculus can handle the most dissimilar feelings by expressing them in terms of their monetary equivalents; (3) in the cases which are important by virtue of their frequency, the pleasures produced by two sums of money are as the sums producing them; (4) taken by and large for scientific purposes men are comparable in feeling as in other respects. ... Heat these two versions in the fire of controversy and one has the substantial content of much polemic since Bentham's day.

IV

The quintessence of Bentham's social science is the double rôle played by the felicific calculus. On the one hand this calculus shows how the legislator, judge and moralist ought to proceed in valuing conduct; on the other hand it shows how all men do proceed in guiding conduct. That is, Bentham blends utilitarian ethics with a definite theory of functional psychology. The ethical system has been more discussed, but the psychological notions are more important to students of the social sciences.

1. Human nature is hedonistic. It is for pain and pleasure alone 'to determine what we shall do . . . They govern us in all we do, in all we say, in all we think: . . .' These words from the first paragraph of *Principles of Morals and Legislation* put simply the leading idea. 'Nothing'—Bentham remarks in *A Table of the Springs of Action*, 'nothing but the expectation of the eventual enjoyment of pleasure in some shape, or of exemption from pain in some shape, can operate in the character of a *motive*. . . .'[29]

The psychological processes by which pleasure incites to action are more fully described in later passages. 'Every operation of the mind, and thence every operation of the body,' says the *Essay on Logic*, 'is the result of an exercise of the will, or volitional faculty.'[30] The relations between will and intellect are explained by the *Table of the Springs of Action*:

To the *will* it is that the idea of a pleasure or an exemption [from pain] applies itself in the *first* instance; in *that* stage its effect, if not conclusive, is *velleity*: by velleity, reference is made to the *understanding*, viz. 1. For striking a *balance* between the *value* of this *good*, and that of the *pain* or *loss*, if any, which present themselves as eventually about to stand associated with it: 2. Then, if the balance appear to be in its favour for the choice of *means*: thereupon, if *action* be the result, *velleity* is perfected into *volition*, of which the correspondent *action* is the immediate consequence. For the process that has place, this description may serve alike in *all* cases: *time* occupied by it may be of any length; from a minute fraction of *a second*, as in ordinary cases, to any number of years.[31]

2. Human nature is rational. There is nothing in the felicific calculus 'but what the practice of mankind, wheresoever they have a clear view of their own interest, is perfectly conformable to.' This passage from Chapter IV of the *Principles*[32] is supported in Chapter XVI by an answer to the objection that 'passion does not calculate.' But, says Bentham:

When matters of such importance as pain and pleasure are at stake, and these in the highest degree (the only matters, in short, that can be of importance) who is there that does not calculate? Men calculate, some

with less exactness, indeed, some with more: but all men calculate. I would
not say, that even a madman does not calculate. Passion calculates, more
or less, in every man: in different men, according to the warmth or coolness
of their dispositions: according to the firmness or irritability of their
minds: according to the nature of the motives by which they are acted
upon. Happily, of all passions, that is the most given to calculation, from
the excesses of which, by reason of its strength, constancy, and universality,
society has most to apprehend: I mean that which corresponds to the
motive of pecuniary interest: ...[33]

3. Human nature is essentially passive. Men do not have propen-
sities to act, but are pushed and pulled about by the pleasure-pain
forces of their environments.

... on every occasion, *conduct*—the *course* taken by a man's conduct—is
at the absolute command of—is the never failing result of—the *motives*,
and thence, in so far as the corresponding interests are perceived and
understood, of the corresponding *interests*, to the action of which, his
mind—his will—has, on that same occasion, stood exposed.[34]

Of course, this view of human nature as a passive element in the
situation greatly simplifies the task of social science. Whenever one
can make out what it is to men's interest to do, one can deduce what
they will do. The only uncertainty arises from the actor's imperfect
comprehension of his interest, of which more in a moment.

Human nature is also passive in the sense that men are averse to
work. In his *Table of the Springs of Action*, Bentham includes both
pleasures and pains of the palate, of sex, of wealth, of amity, of
reputation, and so on through eleven heads until he comes to labour—
under that head he recognizes nothing but pains. If any pleasure in
activity is to be found in this table we must read it into the pleasures
of power or of curiosity.[35] Enlarging upon this point, Bentham says
'*Aversion*—not *desire*—is the emotion—the only emotion—which
labour, taken by itself, is qualified to produce: of any such emotion as
love or *desire*, *ease*, which is the *negative* or *absence* of labour—*ease*,
not *labour*—is the object.'[36]

4. Since men ought to follow the course which will secure them the
greatest balance of pleasure, and since they do follow that course so
far as they understand their own interests, the only defects in human
nature must be defects of understanding.

Indigenous intellectual weakness—*adoptive* intellectual weakness—or, in
one word, *prejudice*—*sinister interest* (understand self-conscious sinister
interest)—lastly, *interest-begotten* (though not self-conscious) *prejudice*—
by one or other of these denominations, may be designated (it is believed)
the cause of whatever is on any occasion amiss, in the opinions or conduct
of mankind.[37]

There is no such thing as a bad motive—or a disinterested action—but men may blunder.

Similarly, whatever lack of uniformity in human nature we find must be due to differences in men's intellectual machinery for calculating pleasures and pains. Such is the sole reason for the gulf that separates civilized men from savages. In 'the variety and extent of the ideas with which they have been impressed . . . may be seen the only cause of whatsoever difference there is between the mind of a well educated youth under the existing systems of education, and the mind of the Esquimaux, or the New Zealand savage at the same age.'[38] Men do vary in sensibility, as we have seen; but the thirty-two 'circumstances influencing sensibility'[39] act by associating the motor ideas of pleasure and pain with the ideas of different objects or actions. So Bentham asserts, 'Legislators who, having freed themselves from the shackles of authority, have learnt to soar above the mists of prejudice, know as well how to make laws for one country as for another.' They must master the peculiar local circumstances affecting sensibility—that is all.[40] In the *Condification Proposal addressed by Jeremy Bentham to all Nations professing Liberal Opinions* he even argues that a foreigner is in a better position to draft a general code of laws than a native.[41]

The understanding, it will be noted, is conceived as a matter of associations among ideas. As hedonism explains the functioning of mind, so the 'association principle' explains the structure of mind. Bentham derived this principle from Hartley, and left its working-out to James Mill.[42]

5. Since whatever is amiss in the opinions or conduct of mankind is due to 'intellectual weakness, indigenous or adoptive,' education must be the one great agency of reform. And since the understanding is made up of associations among ideas, the forming and strengthening of proper associations must be the great aim of education.

In the possibility of establishing almost any desired associations in a child's mind, and even in the possibility of dissolving old and forming new associations in an adult mind Bentham had considerable faith. 'As respects pleasures, the mind of man possesses a happy flexibility. One source of amusement being cut off, it endeavours to open up another, and always succeeds: a new habit is easily formed. . . .'[43] Hence Bentham's interest in the educational experiments of the day, hence the time he spent in planning a 'chresto-mathic school . . . for the use of the middling and higher ranks in life,' hence his financial support of Robert Owen's scheme of industrial education at New Lanark, hence his claims for the Panopticon Penitentiary as 'a mill for grinding rogues honest, and idle men industrious.'[44]

In a larger sense, Bentham conceived all his work on law as part of an educational program. 'The influence of government,' says one of Dumont's treatises, 'touches almost everything, or rather includes everything, except temperament, race, and climate. ... The manner of directing education, of arranging employments, rewards, and punishments determines the physical and moral qualities of a people.'[45] A sharper point and a graver meaning were given to this task by Bentham's slow discovery that men do not all spontaneously desire 'the greatest happiness of the greatest number.'[46] Thereafter the 'self-preference principle' was a regular component of human nature as Bentham saw it, and the great task of statecraft was to contrive cunning devices by which necessarily selfish individuals must serve the pleasure of others to get pleasure for themselves. While Adam Smith and his disciples assumed that a natural identity of interests bound men together in economic affairs, Bentham thought it necessary to establish an artificial identity of interests in law and politics.[47] The ruler himself was to be kept in tutelage his whole life long.

But robust as was Bentham's faith in the potency of schools and government to improve man's character and lot, it was modest in comparison with the expectations cherished by certain among his masters and his contemporaries. Helvetius and Priestley, Condorcet, William Godwin and Robert Owen believed in the 'perfectability' of man. Bentham put his views in opposition to Priestley's:

Perfect happiness belongs to the imaginary regions of philosophy, and must be classed with the universal elixir and the philosopher's stone. In the age of greatest perfection, fire will burn, tempests will rage, man will be subject to infirmity, to accidents, and to death. It may be possible to diminish the influence of, but not to destroy, the sad and mischievous passions. The unequal gifts of nature and of fortune will always create jealousies: there will always be opposition of interests; and, consequently, rivalries and hatred. Pleasures will be purchased by pains; enjoyments by privations. Painful labour, daily subjection, a condition nearly allied to indigence, will always be the lot of numbers. Among the higher as well as the lower classes, there will be desires which cannot be satisfied; inclinations which must be subdued: reciprocal security can only be established by the forcible renunciation by each one, of every thing which might wound the legitimate rights of others.[48]

V

Social science nowadays aims to give an intelligible account of social processes, to promote the understanding of social facts. While we may value such 'science' mainly for its practical serviceability, we profess to distinguish sharply between our explanations of what is and our schemes of what ought to be.

In Bentham's world, on the contrary, the felicific calculus yields a social science that is both an account of what is and an account of what ought to be. For on the one hand 'the chain of causes and effects' and on the other hand 'the standard of right and wrong' are fastened to the throne of our two sovereign masters—whose books the felicific calculus keeps.[49] Indeed, of the two aspects of the science the more reliable, and therefore the more scientific, is the account of what ought to be. The account of what is holds only in so far as men understand their own interests—that is, associate the ideas of pleasure and pain with the ideas of the proper objects and acts. Really to account for what is, on Bentham's basis, one would have either to observe with elaborate care what men do, or to work out their defects of understanding and deduce the consequences for conduct. Needless to say Bentham spent little time on such procedures.

Bentham plumed himself, indeed, upon assigning priority to normative science—in strict accordance with his philosophy. He writes:

When I came out with the principle of utility, it was in the *Fragment*, I took it from Hume's *Essays*, Hume was in all his glory, the phrase was consequently familiar to every body. The difference between Hume and me is this: the use he made of it, was—to account for that which *is*, I to show what *ought to be*.[50]

Practical conclusions regarding what ought to be done, then, were the chief product of Bentham's science. That, indeed, was what made Bentham the leader of the Utilitarians or philosophical radicals, who were first and foremost reformers. But it must be admitted that Bentham's attitude upon the crucial problem of reform was not derived strictly from his science. The felicific calculus turned out to be a singularly versatile instrument. Men could make it prove what they liked by choosing certain assumptions concerning the relative importance of various imponderable factors, or concerning the relative sensitiveness to pleasure of different classes of people. Some assumptions have to be made on these heads before the argument can proceed far, and the assumptions which seem natural to the utility theorist are those which yield the conclusions in which he happens to believe on other than scientific grounds. 'All history proves' anything that a writer has at heart. The felicific calculus is equally obliging.

Now Bentham and his school believed firmly in the institution of private property. They might have proved that property, despite its resulting inequalities of wealth, is necessary to produce the greatest amount of happiness if they had been willing to assume that the propertied classes are more sensitive to pleasure than the poor. For, if some men are better pleasure machines than others, then to maximize happiness more wealth—the most important raw material of pleasure—should be fed to the better machines than to the poorer ones. Such is the course Professor Edgeworth was to take many years later.[51] Bentham did not like that course: to make social science possible he felt obliged to assume that men are substantially alike in their capacity for turning commodities into pleasure. But he had another shift, just as effective, just as little needing proof to those who agreed with him, and just as unconvincing to a doubter.

Every code of laws that is to promote the greatest happiness, he argues, must do so by promoting 'the four most comprehensive particular and subordinate *ends*, viz. *subsistence*, *abundance*, *security*, and *equality*.'[52] 'Equality is not itself, as security, subsistence, and abundance are, an immediate instrument of felicity.'[53] It gets its claim upon us from the diminishing utility of wealth—other things being the same, a given quantity of wealth will produce more pleasure if distributed equally among a given population than if distributed unequally. But other things are not the same. Unless people had security in the possession of their wealth, they would not produce it, and so there would be nothing to distribute—equally or otherwise. Thus from the viewpoint of maximum happiness security is more important than equality. And granted security in enjoying the fruits of labour a certain inequality results. The conclusion is 'that, so far as is consistent with security, the nearer to equality the distribution is, which the law makes of the matter of property among the members of the community, the greater is the happiness of the greatest number.'[54]

Equality . . . finds . . . in security and subsistence, rivals and antagonists, of which the claims are of a superior order, and to which, on pain of universal destruction, in which itself will be involved, it must be obliged to yield. In a word, it is not equality itself, but only a tendency towards equality, after all the others are provided for, that, on the part of the ruling and other members of the community, is the proper object of endeavour.[55]

VI

We have seen that Bentham relied upon the felicific calculus to make himself the Newton of the moral world—the felicific calculus which was to treat the forces pain and pleasure as Newton's laws treated gravitation. But he did not really frame a quantitative science of the Newtonian type. His calculus, indeed, bore little resemblance to the mathematical conceptions by which in his own day chemistry and crystallography were being placed upon a secure foundation. No man could apply Bentham's calculus in sober earnest, because no man could tell how many intensity units were included in any one of his pleasures—to go no further. And indeed Bentham did not use the calculus as an instrument of calculation; he used it as a basis of classification. It pointed out to him what elements should be considered in a given situation, and among these elements *seriatim* he was often able to make comparisons in terms of greater and less—comparisons that few men would challenge, though Bentham might not be able to prove them against a sceptic. So his science as he elaborated it turned out to be much more like the systematic botany than like the celestial mechanics of his day. Bentham himself was a classifier rather than a calculator; he came nearer being the Linnæus than the Newton of the moral world.[56]

Far as he fell short of his dream, Bentham's line of attack upon social problems represented a marked advance upon the type of discussion common in his day—or in ours. Though he could not literally work out the value of any 'lot' of pain or pleasure, he had a systematic plan for canvassing the probable effects of rival institutions upon the happiness of populations. By pinning debates conducted in 'vague generalities' down to fairly definite issues he was often able to find a convincing solution for practical problems. The defects of the rival method if not the merits of his own stand sharply outlined in what Bentham says about the dispute between England and her American colonies:

I . . . placed the question . . . on the ground of the greatest happiness of the greatest number, meaning always in both countries taken together. With me it was a matter of calculation: pains and pleasures, the elements of it. . . . No party had any stomach for calculation: none, perhaps, would have known very well how to go about it, if they had. The battle was fought by assertion. *Right* was the weapon employed on both sides. 'We have a *right* to be as we now choose to be,' said people on the American side. 'We have a right to continue to make you what we choose you should be,' said rulers on the English side. 'We have a right to legislate over them, but we have no *right* to tax them,' said Lord Camden, by way of settling the matter. . . .[57]

What he claimed for his results in his *Codification Proposal* may well be granted:

How far short soever this degree of precision may be, of the conceivable point of perfection . . . at any rate, in every rational and candid eye, unspeakable will be the advantage it will have, over every form of argumentation, in which every idea is afloat, no degree of precision being ever attained, because none is ever so much as aimed at.[58]

Probably every reader of this article will share the impression that Bentham's conception of human behaviour is artificial to an extreme degree. That impression is not due, I think, to any trick in my exposition. Nor is it due to any quirk in Bentham's mind. He can hardly be charged with doing violence to the commonsense notions of his day, unless it be violence to develop and accept their full consequences. The real reason why we find the conception artificial is that we have another stock of ideas about behaviour with which Bentham's ideas are incompatible. Our business is to be consistent as he was, and to use the set of ideas in which we believe as fully as he used the set in which he believed. Then if our ideas prove wrong, as is not unlikely, we may at least give later comers the same kind of help that Bentham now gives us.

NOTES

1. Ernest Albee, *A History of English Utilitarianism*, 1902, 167.
2. For Bentham's numerous references to these writers see the index of *The Works of Jeremy Bentham*, published under the superintendence of his executor, John Bowring, 11 volumes, Edinburgh, 1843.
3. Compare Paley's famous definition of virtue: 'the doing good to mankind, in obedience to the will of God, and for the sake of everlasting happiness.' *Principles of Moral and Political Philosophy*, bk. I, chap. vii (21st edition 1818, vol. i, 42). Further see Paley's remarks upon population in bk. vi, chap. xi. 'The final view of all rational politics is, to produce the greatest quantity of happiness in a given tract of country . . . the quantity of happiness in a given district, although it is possible it may be increased, the number of inhabitants remaining the same, is chiefly and most naturally affected by alteration of the numbers: . . . consequently, the decay of population is the greatest evil that a state can suffer; and the improvement of it the object which ought, in all countries, to be aimed at in preference to every other political purpose whatsoever.' Vol. ii, 345–347.
4. See particularly bk. iv, chap. iii, of the second and later editions of the *Essay on the Principle of Population*. For example, 'I do not see how it is possible for any person, who acknowledges the principle of utility as the great foundation of morals, to escape the conclusion that moral restraint, till we are in a condition to support a family, is the strict line of duty. . . .' 2d. ed., 1803, 504.
5. *La Formation du Radicalisme Philosophique*, 1901, vol. i, 231.
6. Ibid., vol. ii, ii-iii.
7. *Works*, vol. x, 141. Written sometime between Bentham's thirty-third and thirty-seventh years.
8. Halévy, *Radicalisme Philosophique*, vol. i, 289, 290.
9. 'Introduction to the Principles of Morals and Legislation,' *Works*, vol. i, 1, 16. The exposition in 'Logical Arrangements, or Instruments of Discovery and Invention employed by Jeremy Bentham,' *Works*, vol. iii, 286, 287 is a convenient summary. Another brief statement is given in 'A Table of the Springs of Action,' *Works*, vol. i, 206. The value of the calculus is best stated in the curious 'Codification Proposal,' *Works*, vol. iv, 540–542. A

more discursive version appears in chap. iv, of *Deontology*, vol. i (not in-cluded in the *Works*). As will appear below, several of the most important points are best explained in passages which remained unpublished until Halévy's day—see the notes and appendices of his first and third volume.

10. 'Principles of Morals and Legislation,' *Works*, vol. i, 16, and extracts from Bentham's MSS. published by Halévy in *Radicalisme Philosophique*, vol. i, 398 *et seq.*
11. Chap. vi. The list includes health, strength, firmness of mind, habitual occupations, pecuniary circumstances, sex, age, rank, education, climate, lineage, government, religious profession etc.
12. *Works*, vol. i, 31, 32. Compare the discussion of this theme in Bentham's essay 'Of the Influence of Time and Place in Matters of Legislation,' *Works*, vol. i, 172, 173, 180, 181.
13. Halévy, *Radicalisme Philosophique*, vol. iii, 481.
14. Ibid., vol. i, 398.
15. *Works*, vol. iv, 542.
16. *Works*, vol. i, 17–21.
17. Ibid., 195–219.
18. Ibid., 22, footnote.
19. *Works*, vol. i, 92.
20. Compare Halévy, vol. i, 47, 48.
21. *Works*, vol. i, 87.
22. For example, 'Codification Proposal,' *Works*, vol. iv, 540–542; *Deontology*, vol. i, 76, 131, 192.
23. Halévy, vol. i, 410, 412, 414.
24. 'Pannomial Fragments,' *Works*, vol. iii, 229.
25. 'Constitutional Code,' *Works*, vol. ix, 15.
26. 'Codification Proposal,' *Works*, vol. iv, 541.
27. Halévy, vol. i, 406, 408, 410.
28. This is substantially Bentham's own language. 'Codification Proposal,' *Works*, vol. iv, 542.
29. *Works*, vol. i, 215.
30. Ibid., vol. viii, 279.
31. Ibid., vol. i, 209.
32. Ibid., vol. i, 17.
33. *Works*, vol. i, 90, 91. Compare the similar passage in Principles of Penal Law, vol. i, 402.
34. 'A Table of the Springs of Action,' *Works*, vol. i, 218.
35. This omission of pleasure in labour is clearly no oversight; indeed it must represent a deliberate change of opinion; for in his Introduction to the Principles of Morals and Legislation Bentham had included 'The pleasures of skill, as exercised upon particular objects. . . .' *Works*, vol. i, 18.
36. *Works*, vol. i, 214. In 'Chrestomathia' Bentham discusses the 'pain of ennui.' 'Ennui is the state of uneasiness, felt by him whose mind unoccupied, but without reproach, is on the look out for pleasure . . . and beholds at the time no source which promises to afford it . . . the pain of ennui soon succeeds to the pleasure of repose.' *Works*, vol. viii, 8.
37. 'Springs of Action,' *Works*, vol. i, 217.
38. 'Chrestomathia,' *Works*, vol. viii, 11.
39. 'Introduction to the Principles of Morals and Legislation,' *Works*, vol. i, 22.
40. 'Influence of Time and Place in Matters of Legislation,' *Works*, vol. i, 180, 181.
41. *Works*, vol. iv, 561–563.

42. *Works*, vol. x, 561; Mill's *Analysis of the Phenomena of the Human Mind* appeared in 1829, three years before Bentham's death.
43. 'Principles of Penal Law,' *Works*, vol. i, 436.
44. See 'Chrestomathia,' *Works*, vol. viii, and the following passages in Bowring's life of Bentham—*Works*, vol. x, 476, 477, 226.

Bentham once suggested—not more than half in jest—that 'metaphysics' might be made an experimental science by applying his 'inspection-house principle' to the training of children. That plan would enable the instructor to determine what sensible objects, conversation, books should have part in forming the child's mind. Then, 'The geneology of each observable idea might be traced through all its degrees with the utmost nicety: the parent stocks being all known and numbered.' 'Panopticon,' *Works*, vol. iv, 65.

Mr. C. E. Ayers has just propounded a modern version of this suggestion. Epistemology, he argues, is becoming a science, 'whence comes the mental content of every man's mind, what are the limitations that are imposed upon that content by its sources? The solution of this problem lies along the path of the investigation of the social sources of all mental content and of the limitations which are imposed upon the human mind by the fact that it is always the product of some particular environment and so must always receive an environmental bias. This investigation is the business of social psychology.' *Journal of Philosophy, Psychology and Scientific Methods*, January 17, 1918; vol. xv, 43.

45. Quoted by Halévy, vol. i, 139.
46. In his earlier period Bentham had tacitly assumed that the authorities would spontaneously adopt any plan that promised to increase social happiness. It took him sixty years to learn that the authorities were seeking their own happiness, not that of the nation. See his own account of how his eyes were opened, *Works*, vol. x, 79, 80 and vol. i, 240–259.
47. The contrast between these two views of the relations between society and the individual is one of the chief points developed fully by Halévy in the course of his three volumes. See particularly his first and last chapters.
48. 'Of the Influence of Time and Place on Matters of Legislation,' *Works*, vol. i, 193, 194.
49. 'Principles of Morals and Legislation,' *Works*, vol. i, 1.
50. From a manuscript found by Halévy, *Radicalisme Philosophique*, vol. i, 282. Compare the 'History of the Greatest-happiness Principle' given in *Deontology*, vol. i, 293–294.

Like many a modern, Bentham held that the value of science consists in its subserviency to art—though he admits that in so far as science pleases it is an end in itself ('Chrestomathia,' *Works*, vol. viii, 27; 'Manual of Political Economy,' *Works*, vol. iii, 33). That is as true of his science of what ought to be as of his science of what is. The peculiarity of his position from the modern viewpoint is in conceiving his account of what ought to be as itself a science—not in making a pragmatic view of science.

51. See his *Mathematical Psychics*, 1881, especially 77–82.
52. 'Codification Proposal,' *Works*, vol. iv, 561.
53. 'Constitutional Code,' *Works*, vol. ix, 14.
54. Ibid., 18.
55. *Logical Arrangements, Works*, vol. iii, 294. For still other expositions than the three cited above, see *Pannomial Fragments*, vol. iii, 228–230; *Leading Principles of a Constitutional Code for Any State*, vol. ii, 271–272.
56. Compare Bentham's own reference to Linnæus in *Deontology*, vol. i, 202; his discussion of his own 'natural method' of classification by bi-partition—including the reference to botany in a footnote in *Principles of Morals and*

Legislation, Works, vol. i, 139; and certain other references to the merits of classification in botany, *Works*, vol. vi, 442; vol. viii, 121–126 and 254, 255.

57. Historical Preface to the Second Edition of A Fragment on Government, *Works*, vol. i, 248.

58. *Works*, vol. iv, 542.

Chapter 10

Jeremy Bentham and the Victorian Administrative State

David Roberts

[The nature and extent of Bentham's influence on nineteenth century legislative, administrative and political reform have been a subject of considerable controversy in recent years. A. V. Dicey in his *Lectures upon the relation between Law and Public Opinion in England during the Nineteenth Century* saw Bentham as providing a philosophical rationale of both individualism and collectivism and regarded him as one of the most powerful influences in moulding public opinion in the nineteenth century. Dicey's view was widely accepted until Oliver MacDonagh questioned it in his influential article, 'The Nineteenth Century Revolution in Government: A Reappraisal', in *Historical Journal*, I, 1958. MacDonagh contended that Benthamism was in many ways 'an obstacle . . . to the development of modern government' and that its genuine contribution consisted not so much in creating a new climate of public opinion as in inspiring particular individuals to propose and pursue particular policies. Professor Roberts in his article, reprinted here from *Victorian Studies*, March, 1959 shares MacDonagh's scepticism but suggests that, although Bentham can by no stretch of imagination be said to have fathered the nineteenth century 'revolution in government', he did offer a forceful justification of reform and some interesting concrete proposals. Dicey on the one hand and MacDonagh and Roberts on the other thus provide two opposing views on Bentham's influence. Other writers take positions somewhere in between. An interested reader will find the following articles of particular interest: Henry Parris, The Nineteenth Century Revolution in Government: A Reappraisal Reappraised, *Historical Journal*, III, 1960; Jennifer Hart, Nineteenth Century Social Reform: A Tory Interpretation of History, *Past and Present*, XXXI, 1965; Valerie Cromwell, Interpretations of Nineteenth Century Administration: An Analysis, *Victorian Studies*, March, 1966; L. J. Hume, Jeremy Bentham and the Nineteenth Century Revolution in Government, *Historical Journal*, X, 1967; and William Aydelotte, The Conservative and Radical Interpretations of Early Victorian Social Legislation, *Victorian Studies*, December, 1967—Editor.]

In 1830 Jeremy Bentham published the first volume of his *Constitutional Code*. Two years later, with the monumental *Code* nearly completed, he died. In 1841 his friend John Bowring, using in places the author's rough notes, published it in its entirety. The world thus received from a philosopher already famous for his radical attacks on institutions a complete constitution suitable for any country and for all time. Its massive detail, dealing with every facet of government, was exactingly subordinated to universally valid, rational, and efficient principles. Manhood suffrage, the secret ballot, and a single chamber legislature would insure a true democracy; trained judges, simple rules of evidence, and a codified law would guarantee justice; and thirteen ministries supervising locally elected authorities would secure clean towns, free public education, effective police, good roads and efficient poor relief. The government would so regulate society that man's own self-interest would promote the greatest happiness.

The *Code*, for its time, was radical and impertinent. It asked the aristocracy to forego power; it recommended the reconstruction of England's sacred legal system; and, in an age when local government formed the palladium of English liberties and the small central government consisted mainly of customs officials and excise men chosen by favouritism, it asked for a large central administration staffed by paid and trained experts chosen by examination. Thirteen ministers were to preside over an extensive central bureaucracy. There were to be ministers of Education, Health, and Indigence, all at the time unknown to England's constitution. And stranger yet were the Ministries of Preventive Service, Elections, and Legislation. The other Ministries listed, those of Trade, Interior, Domain, Foreign Affairs, Finance, Army, and Navy, already had their counterparts in the English government; but the Ministries under the *Code* were to enjoy considerably more power than the traditional departments which constituted the English government. The Minister of Interior, for example, was to regulate all modes of transportation and the Minister of Trade was to collect and publish statistics on every aspect of the economy. The *Code* gave all thirteen Ministers ample powers. They could inspect, advise, and dismiss local officials, they could issue rules and regulations, hold inquiries, and publish reports, and they could formulate policies. At the apex of a uniform and symmetrical bureaucracy, they were to supervise the district-elected 'headmen' and the district schools and health authorities; and they were to require that mines and factories be kept healthy.[1]

Bentham wished this administrative state to be active and useful, but not despotic. He had the radical's fear of government, which he said was 'taken in itself one vast evil,' yet he saw at every turn its usefulness in ordering social affairs (*Works*, IX, 24). To square the circle, to reconcile individual liberty and collective welfare, he contrived a system of checks and balances. He hoped that an elected sovereign legislature would keep check on ambitious ministers, that a Public Opinion Tribunal would publicize their misgovernment, and that a just appreciation of the virtues of *laissez-faire* capitalism would prevent any undue meddling in the economy. A balance between local and central government and a belief in *laissez faire* were two major themes of this administrative state, while the main technique for reconciling freedom with an efficient and active government was the principle of inspection. By inspection of school boards, poor law authorities, prisons, and asylums, central bureaux could insure local efficiency without destroying local autonomy. The problem which filled de Tocqueville with forebodings and bothered John Stuart Mill, the encroachments of a centralized state, was for Bentham dispelled by the principle of central inspection.[2] The great end for which this administrative structure was fashioned was of course the greatest happiness to the greatest number, a condition which Bentham hoped to achieve by the government's insuring the rights of property and the liberty of the individual while at the same time it guaranteed to all equal rights and promoted for all an abundance of wealth—all noble aims, though not without serious contradictions (*Works*, IX, 11–22). In the *Constitutional Code*, however, Bentham felt that he had resolved these contradictions, and had offered the English people a neat and comprehensive blueprint for an administrative state that was both efficient and benevolent.

Nothing differed more from that blueprint than England's public administration in 1833. It was not orderly, it was not planned, it was not centralized, it was not efficient, and it did little for the well-being of the citizens. The Home Office employed only thirty persons and the Board of Trade but twenty.[3] The central government did nothing about education, health, and poor relief. In the countryside 15,000 parishes administered in a haphazard fashion poor relief, highways, and police; and in the growing towns a medley of magistrates, councils, and statutory authorities ruled as they wished, tolerating filthy streets and wretched prisons. Neither local nor central government concerned themselves with the widespread ignorance of urban workers, nor with the exploitation of child labour in textile mills.

By the 1850's the scene had altered. A series of momentous social reforms had brought about an administrative revolution. In 1834 Parliament established the Poor Law Commission, in 1839 the Education Committee of the Privy Council, and in 1848 a Board of Health, each with a staff of professional servants who were to inspect local authorities. Here were Bentham's Ministries of Indigence, Education, and Health. In 1833, 1835, and 1842 Parliament attached to the Home Office inspectors of factories, prisons, and mines. In 1841 it set up a Railway Board and in 1845 it made the Metropolitan Lunacy Commissioners a national agency. In 1850 it created a Merchant Marine Department and in 1853 a Charity Commission and a Department of Science and Art. Each of these twelve new central departments had inspectors with powers to carry out the increased functions recommended in the *Constitutional Code*. Bentham's blueprint for an administrative state had been translated, albeit very roughly, into the reality of the mid-Victorian administrative state.

The obvious similarities between Bentham's *Code* and the mid-Victorian administrative state suggests a possible causal relation. That some of the leading architects of that state were disciples of Bentham makes the suggestion even more appealing, and raises at once an interesting problem in intellectual and administrative history. How important were the ideas of Bentham in fashioning the Victorian administrative state? What influence did this retiring, eccentric philosopher have upon the history of his time? A. V. Dicey, Sidney and Beatrice Webb, B. L. Hutchins, Elie Halévy, and Samuel Finer, with varying emphasis, consider his influence on the growth of English government to have been of profound importance.[4] The distinguished economic historian, Sir John Clapham, wrote that the nineteenth-century inspectorates rested 'on foundations laid for them by Jeremy Bentham,' and the late J. Bartlett Brebner, in his revisionist article, 'Laissez Faire and State Intervention in Nineteenth Century Britain,' argued that the Victorian administrative state conformed to the *Constitutional Code*, that Bentham's secretary, Edwin Chadwick, was 'the architect of most of [that] state intervention,' and that even the aristocracy in imposing 'intervention on nearly every economic activity . . . practically always [kept] as close as possible to Bentham's model of artificial identification of interests by central authority and local inspection.' The belief that Bentham's ideas have had a striking effect on nineteenth-century governmental changes is one of wide currency. Even G. M. Trevelyan gives it his blessing. 'It would be difficult to find,' he writes, 'a better instance of that favourite maxim of our grandfathers' that the pen is mightier than the sword than the effect upon British Institutions of the uneventful life of Jeremy Bentham.[5]

His life at Queen Square was indeed uneventful, but the disciples who visited there were men of energy and action. Edwin Chadwick, his private secretary in his last years, and Southwood Smith, one of his most intimate friends, both sat on the Factory Commission of 1833, and both, along with their friend Dr. James Kay (the future Sir James Kay Shuttleworth), were destined for bureaucratic positions of great influence.[6] James Mill, Bentham's closest friend, gathered around himself and his son a group of young intellectuals who called themselves Utilitarians. The most important of these were John and Edward Romilly, George Grote, Charles Buller, Arthur Roebuck, and Sir William Molesworth, all of whom sat in the reformed House of Commons. Other friends of Bentham in the Commons were Joseph Hume, Henry Warburton, and Edward Strutt. Albany Fonblanque, John Black, and John Bowring, all admirers of Bentham edited, respectively, the *Examiner*, the *Morning Chronical*, and the

Westminster Review, and many of the writers for the *Edinburgh Review*, the *Globe*, and the *Scotsman*, looked favourably on the ideas of England's celebrated philosopher.[7]

His influence even penetrated into the House of Lords, Oxford, and Cambridge, and into the salons of Whig peers. Lord Brougham argued the cause of public education in the House of Lords and Nassau Senior and Charles Austin lectured to young Oxonians and Cantabrigians on political economy and law reform. Charles Austin took the same ideas to Bowood in rural Wiltshire, where the first Marquis of Lansdowne had entertained Bentham and where his son, the third Marquis, once heard Austin and Lord Macaulay engaged in an eight-hour intellectual joust.[8] Holland House, too, occasionally heard Philosophical Radicals declaim with a Benthamite vigor against Tory institutions. A Whig might be offended by such arid expressions as the 'aptitude maximization principle,' or the 'elicitive, statistic, inspective, melioration suggestive, and locative functions' of central ministers, but he could applaud the noble and reasonable rules for politics and ethics laid down in Bentham's *Introduction to the Principles of Morals and Legislation* and could readily comprehend the principle of the greatest happiness to the greatest number. Even the witty Canon of St. Paul's, Sydney Smith, confessed he had read all of Bentham, and the Irish radical Daniel O'Connell boasted he was a disciple (*Works*, X, 560, 597). The Chadwicks and Austins, the Sydney Smiths and Lord Broughams, constituted, to be sure, only a small minority of English society. The great bulk of the governing class thought Bentham's ideas crotchety and subversive. But the Benthamites possessed ability, purpose, and a creed. Through them Bentham had his greatest influence. They alone could be expected to read the laborious, detailed, rigorous schemes of the *Constitutional Code*. 'He acted upon the destinies of his race,' claimed Bulwer-Lytton in 1832, 'by influencing the thoughts of the minute fraction who think.'[9] Bulwer-Lytton, as did Trevelyan a century later, estimated highly the power of ideas in shaping history.

Such generalizations, seductively attractive to intellectual historians and political philosophers, are illuminating but dangerous, and always difficult to prove. Connections between the ideas of one man and political action inevitably are involved and elusive; yet they must be closely examined if the history of an age is to be understood. Did Bentham's ideas define the Victorian administrative state?

The answer to that question can best be found by looking at Bentham's particular influence on Parliamentary legislation in the 1830's and 1840's. Did his idea of central inspection, for example, define, as B. L. Hutchins asserts, the Factory Act of 1833? There is some evidence to suggest that it did. Both Edwin Chadwick and Southwood Smith (along with Thomas Tooke) sat on the government's Factory Commission of 1833. They wrote the Commission's report and helped prepare the bill which would exclude from textile factories all children below nine years of age, and would limit to eight hours the labour of those between nine and thirteen.[10] Central inspectors were to enforce the act and factory owners were to provide the children with two hours of schooling. The clauses which provided for central inspection and factory schools gave the act a Benthamite stamp. But the Benthamites on the Commission did not initiate the reforms nor did they give them their final form. These reforms had their origin in the agitation of Evangelicals and Tories like Lord Ashley and Richard Oastler, to whom Benthamism was an anathema. And it was the unphilosophical Whig, Lord Althorp, who insisted that the bill prohibit young people and women from working over twelve hours,[11] a provision which Chadwick called pernicious. He considered any regulation of adult women an un-called-for interference with capital. Because the Whigs included this pernicious clause and because they dropped the effective education clause, Chadwick disclaimed any responsibility for the act.[12]

Nor, for that matter, is there any suggestion found anywhere in the *Constitutional Code* that the government should regulate hours of labour. Bentham's faith in *laissez faire* ran deep. He wished the government to regulate many things, but the economy was not one of them; he wished inspectors to guarantee that factories were sanitary, but not that working hours be limited. Though inclining towards collectivism on social questions, in economic matters he remained an individualist. In the bulky reports of the assistant factory commissioners in 1833 there is no reference to his *Code*. What these records do show is that the idea of central inspection was a commonplace and that the larger manufacturers favoured it in order to prevent isolated mills from working longer hours.[13] Inspection of manufacturers was no new device in a country where hundreds of excise men had long supervised the making of spirits, glass, and paper.[14]

The Poor Law Amendment Act of 1834 appears at first glance to have been more completely coloured by Benthamism than the Factory Act. Chadwick's influence was again apparent to everyone. Along with Nassau Senior, the head of the Commission to inquire into the poor laws, he wrote the famous report calling for a central-ized poor law administration. Following these recommendations Parliament passed an act establishing a central board of three com-missioners to formulate policy, and nine assistant commissioners to inspect and supervise locally elected boards of guardians. The inspectors were to insure, through a strict policy, that relief to the poor was much less attractive than the lot of the common labourer.[15] Some of the principal features of this act, such as those providing for central control, inspection, and local paid officials, can be found in the *Code*, while Bentham in his *Pauper Management Scheme* urged that workhouses be established and relief strictly apportioned (*Works*, IX, 441; XVIII, 361ff.). Out of mere default the refashioning of England's poor law had fallen to Benthamites. Tory and Whig leaders had despaired of any solution to the chaos of badly administered parish relief.[16] They feared that revolutionary measure of centralization which alone could bring order out of chaos, yet they had no alternative suggestion. In a spirit of resignation they turned the problem over to Nassau Senior's Commission. Senior himself, in 1831, had hoped that the county J.P.'s could solve the problem, and Bentham much earlier had placed his hopes in a private joint stock company.[17] It was Edwin Chadwick who had the audacity to make a complete break with the past and who called for an effective centralization of poor relief. He was the one person able to grapple with the welter of inefficient local authorities and construct an efficient measure of control over them. He collected more evidence than any other Commissioner, wrote more reports, and recommended more reforms. He helped the Cabinet draw up the Poor Law Amendment Bill, briefed M.P.'s on its merits, and wrote in the *Globe* defending it.[18] When Tories and Whigs proved unable to construct a workable solution, his industry and genius brought England its first revolutionary measure of administrative centralization.

Chadwick's influence was profound on the growth of the central government. But were his reforms inspired by Bentham? This is a question that raises one of the most difficult problems facing anyone who attempts to assess the role of ideas in determining political action. What influence arises from personal relations, relations that appear so intangible to the historian? Chadwick himself, after admitting that in fields which he had not investigated he owed a great debt to Bentham, wrote quite explicitly, 'My own responsible measures have invariably been the result of my own independent labour.' John Stuart Mill was so impressed by that 'independent labour' that he called Chadwick 'one of the organizing and contriving minds of the age.'[19] Chadwick, before he was Bentham's secretary, had written articles on life insurance, police, and French charities that demonstrated a zeal for social investigation, an empirical cast of mind, and a talent for administrative criticism.[20] He applied these talents to the New Poor Law, a law which departs from several of Bentham's most insistent strictures. A board of three commissioners and not one minister administered the law, though

Bentham called all such boards screens for hiding waste and in-efficiency. The new law had no sign of Bentham's beloved 'duty and interest junction principle,' whereby pauper labour would pay the costs of poor relief, and no sign of the panopticon, Bentham's hexagonal structure suitable for prisons, asylums, or workhouses.[21] Furthermore, the chief principle of the Poor Law Report, the urging of a strict workhouse relief, was a common notion, stemming not so much from Bentham as from the severe doctrines of the economists. In October 1832 even the Tory *Quarterly Review* argued for work-houses, and later astonished the editor of the *Law Magazine* by boasting that they had suggested the idea of a central authority supervising poor relief.[22] The plea for some central control (usually quite limited) and for larger units of administration was in fact more than a century old. William Hay had suggested it in 1735, and other poor law reformers had written of its need.[23] The New Poor Law reflected many commonly accepted notions just as it reflected some Benthamite suggestions; but its main themes and its general con-struction came from the mind of Edwin Chadwick.

Parliament passed the bill by an overwhelming majority. It did not need the votes of the few Benthamites in the Commons. Nor were the country gentlemen and magistrates persuaded by Benthamite logic. There was no need for that. They were already prepared to support the bill from a desire to rid themselves of burdensome duties and rates. In order to secure lower poor rates they would accept that measure of centralization designed for them by Edwin Chadwick. The Poor Law Amendment Act thus had its origin in the conjunc-tion of 'one of the organizing and contriving minds of the age' with the economic interests and administrative necessities of the time.

The Privy Council's order of 1839 to establish a Committee on Education with inspectors of schools, was also penned by friends of Jeremy Bentham. The President of the Privy Council, the nominal author of the order, was the third Marquis of Lansdowne, and its real author was James Kay. Lansdowne's father had been for many years Bentham's patron. Bentham spent many enjoyable months at Bowood, and on his advice the future third Marquis was sent to Edinburgh rather than Oxford. In the 1830's Benthamites still visited Bowood, and Lansdowne counted them among his friends. James Kay was also a friend of the Benthamites, especially of Edwin Chadwick, with whom he had much in common.[24] Both came from Nonconformist manufacturing cities; both were energetic, dedicated, and sturdily independent; both reflected their middle-class origins. From their experience in Manchester and London they became aware of the need for the government to end both the profound ignorance of the working class and the unsanitary state of the industrial towns. Both men were attracted to Benthamism, but brought to their reading of Bentham social attitudes already formed. The education order which Kay helped Lansdowne draw up was quite simple: the government would establish a normal school and would aid and inspect church schools of all denominations. As simple and modest as this proposal seemed to the Whigs, to the Tories and Churchmen it was blasphemy. Their hostility forced the abandonment of the normal school, and threatened the whole measure itself. Lansdowne told Russell to hold firm even if beaten, because, he added, 'we are so decidedly right.' The appropriation of £30,000 to carry out the order passed the Commons by two votes.[25] It would not have passed but for the Benthamites in Parliament—for Grote, Buller, Hume, Molesworth, and Roebuck.

According to the same sort of calculation, however, it would not have passed except for the Irish members. Outraged Tory journals even ascribed the origins of the measure to 'that junto of papists, infidels and radicals which forms the Irish Board of Education,' and blamed most of all John Wyse, the Irish M.P. who headed the Central Society for Education. Wyse could and did retort that the Tory Lord Stanley, the most hostile opponent of the new order and no Benthamite, had strengthened in 1831 the control of the Irish Board of Education over Irish schools.[26] Wyse could also have added that it was the Tories in 1824 who established that central Board, and gave it power to inspect schools. Central inspection of schools was in fact a commonplace notion; education reformers of all parties knew of its effectiveness on the Continent, in Ireland, and in America; the British Society and the Church of England's National Society had inspectors, and in arguing for school inspection Lansdowne cited their experiences. Not once did he cite Bentham's *Code*.[27] What persuaded the Commons to support the education order were the dangers of a badly educated working class addicted to drink and crime. This problem, particularly acute in the new industrial towns, had to be answered. Yet the religious jealousies made its solution difficult. These prevented the creation of secular, local, rate-supported schools, while the poverty of church schools made purely voluntary schools inadequate. The only workable answer was to aid these voluntary schools and to inspect them in order to see that the aid was not misspent. In 1839 Parliament grudgingly accepted that compromise. It was a far cry from the local rate-supported schools of Bentham's *Code*.

Conditions in the manufacturing towns demanded sanitary improvements as insistently as they did educational reform. Open sewers, stagnant cesspools, impure water, refuse-littered streets, overcrowded, squalid tenements: all these brought disease and misery to the working classes, and a mortality rate in towns that was twice as great as in the countryside. To Edwin Chadwick, Southwood Smith, and James Kay, all employees of the Poor Law Commission and all Benthamites, these evils were intolerable and unnecessary. In their reports to the Poor Law Commission in 1838 and 1839 they exposed the unhealthy conditions of these towns and urged reforms. Chadwick's graphic report of 1842 made a deep impression on the governing class. The Bishop of London demanded reform, and many a member of Commons agreed.[28] Sir Robert Peel, faced with these demands, postponed any drastic reform by appointing the Health of Towns Commission to investigate that which had already been investigated. The Commission included engineers and politicians, but no Benthamites. They corroborated Chadwick's report and recommended both central and local boards of health. These recommendations were incorporated into Lord Morpeth's Public Health Act of 1848.[29] Chadwick was a close friend of Lord Morpeth and the acknowledged leader of the sanitary movement. He was close to government leaders and later became a member of the General Board of Health. The Hammonds in their *Lord Shaftesbury* thus concluded that the Public Health Act was Chadwick's act. But this was not Chadwick's view of the situation. He met once with those who drew up the Bill. Thereafter he merely wrote notes expressing his vexation at being ignored. 'I have never been able,' he told Lord Campbell, 'to take any part in the framework or details of the bill since the first meeting at Lord Morpeth's.' A timid Cabinet and a Parliament fearful of centralization curtailed the Bill's power so decisively that an exasperated Chadwick finally wrote, 'the health bill which passed is a mere wreck of what was intended,' and he disclaimed, as he had on the Factory Act, any responsibility for the measure.[30] The Act was not Chadwick's, nor was it particularly Benthamite; rather it was a compromise between the demands of powerful local interests to be let alone and the insistence of Parliament that the intolerable conditions of the towns be remedied, even if it meant the creation of a central department. The idea of a central department was also no innovation. Charles Greville, no Benthamite, had headed a temporary Central Board in 1830, and had sent medical inspectors to visit local authorities.[31] By 1848 the idea of central inspection was certainly no longer a novelty.

The same response to pressing social evils led to other minor reforms—of prisons, insane asylums, private charities, railways, and merchant marine service—all of which added more central agencies to the growing administrative state. The Prison Act of 1835, which provided for the central inspection of prisons, arose not from the ratiocinations of Benthamites, but from the persuasions of the Evangelicals. They fought for and drew up the Prison Act of 1835. The Evangelicals were supported by some interested peers, such as the Duke of Richmond, who personally investigated some of the grimmest of London prisons. The peers found that central inspection was a necessity. Many county magistrates, probably none of whom were learned in the *Code*, confessed to the Lords' Select Committee on Prisons that only inspection could establish a uniform discipline and end gross abuse. The Act which established such inspection owed its origins to a few peers and to the hard-working Evangelicals of the Prison Discipline Society.[32] There was no trace in the Act of Bentham's panopticon scheme. Its chief feature, a great faith in separate confinement (which Bentham opposed), was copied from Philadelphia prisons. Chadwick, a severe critic of *ad hoc* reform, condemned the Act as the improvisation of 'a mere voluntary society.'[33] He would have had no better estimation of Lord Ashley's Lunacy Act of 1845, for it too owed its origins to the humanitarian work of Evangelicals. The Lunacy Act, with its twenty-six Commissioners performing different functions, was a cumbersome agency. Furthermore there was nothing symmetrical or uniform in the chaos of local asylums, private hospitals, and workhouses which that Commission supervised.[34] No Benthamite helped Ashley in fashioning this Lunacy Commission, and the *Code* says little about such problems, yet it was of such bricks that the Victorian administrative state was built.

The *Code* did call for the inspection of all modes of transportation, though it failed to mention the railway (*Works*, IX, 441). Neither Lord Seymour, the Whig author of the Railway Act of 1840 which established the Railway Board, nor Gladstone, the Tory author of the Act of 1842 extending the powers of the Board, frequented Utilitarian circles. And Henry Labouchere, who drew up and carried through Parliament an Act establishing a Merchant Marine Board, did not count himself an admirer of Bentham.[35] The *Code* in fact specifically exempted merchant shipping from the regulations of the Ministry of Interior. It is of course very doubtful if Labouchere ever read the *Code*, or ever attended upon the sage of Queen Square. Like Lord Ashley, Lord Seymour, and Gladstone, Labouchere planned these reforms to meet the urgent problems of an industrial age, not to fulfil the ideals of a philosopher. Local government could not handle these new problems, and their neglect had permitted abuses to arise which the conscience of the Victorian governing class could not endure. The only means to remedy these abuses was to empower the central government to intervene. In this *ad hoc* manner, and not from reading the *Constitutional Code*, did Parliament lay the basis for the early Victorian administrative state.

The above sketch of the connections between the ideas of Jeremy Bentham and the creation of a more centralized administration in England raises doubts about the all-pervasive influence of his political philosophy. At first glance there appear many immediate and close ties between Bentham and administrative reform. Disciples of Bentham planned great measures of reform, his admirers defended them in the Commons, and Utilitarian journals espoused them in learned articles. Did not Bentham's friend John Austin, in an article in the *Edinburgh Reviews* (Jan. 1847) entitled 'Centralization', argue frankly for a centralized administration? Did not the Utilitarian *Westminster Review* argue frequently and at length for social, governmental, and legal reforms?[36] And in the Commons did not his followers, like Lord Brougham, Charles Buller, and John Roebuck, champion law reform, factory regulations, and state aid to, and inspection of, schools. Was there not, as Bentham's old friend Joseph Hume confessed, a new spirit of improvement which pervaded society?[37] Was it not a spirit at once rational, questioning, innovating, a Benthamite spirit, dedicated to the greatest good of the greatest number? The historian is indeed sorely tempted to see in that spirit the inspiration of Bentham's ideas and thus to agree with Trevelyan that 'his principles were beginning to invade the seats of power,' or with J. Bartlett Brebner, that the growth of state intervention was 'Benthamite, Benthamite in the sense of conforming to that forbidding, detailed blueprint for a collective state, the *Constitutional Code*.'[38]

Yet when each particular reform is closely scrutinized Bentham's ideas seem less and less to have been the decisive factor. Austin's article on centralization appeared in January of 1847, which was after, not before, the major reforms had set the pattern of the new administrative state. In like manner the articles in the *Westminster Review* on education, railways, and prisons, came after Parliament had passed its measure of reform. Furthermore most of the other articles neither outlined nor argued for any scheme of administrative improvement, but merely described conditions in mines, asylums, and factories. And none of them cited the *Code*.

It is also dangerous to assume that these articles, or the speeches of Brougham, Buller, and Roebuck, were invariably inspired by Bentham. Brougham was so often at variance with true Utilitarian doctrine that Bentham despaired of the wayward efforts of this unpredictable Scotsman. As for the kindly, reasonable, liberal-minded

Buller, who can say whence arose his compassion for the working classes and zeal for reform? Did he learn it from Bentham's writings or from the stern lectures given him by his tutor, Thomas Carlyle? He was twenty-one when he joined John Stuart Mill's Utilitarian circle in London. His friend George Grote was twenty-four when he joined that circle and Chadwick and Roebuck were twenty-five when they first met the Benthamites.[39] It is quite possible that their passion for reform, their critical intelligence, their radical sentiments were by then deeply ingrained. In Bentham they found the same rationalism and the same zeal for improvement, only bolder, more systematic, and more brilliantly expressed.

What indeed was remarkable about Bentham was not so much his influence over numerous men, but the foresight, the clarity, and the logic with which he expressed those truths which other forces, far stronger than his own ideas, would bring to pass. He saw more comprehensively than his contemporaries the necessity of an expanded administrative state. He saw the anachronisms and inefficiences in English law and administration, and the need to reform both. He saw the importance of government by paid, professional civil servants. He saw the failures of local government and the need of a stronger central administration. And since, like so many Englishmen, he feared an overbearing centralization, he realized that the necessary central controls could be best applied through central inspection. None of the truths which he saw were wholly new, certainly not the key idea of central inspection. The reformers of English prisons and schools not only knew of American and Continental schemes for inspection, but of British inspectors of excise surveyors, and sanitary reformers knew of the Central Board of Health of 1831.[40] Bentham did not introduce the principle of central inspection to England, he only called for its systematic application.

Neither did he introduce, *de novo*, those Utilitarian principles that were so fundamental to the reforming spirit of the age and to the legislation which led to the Victorian administrative state. He candidly admitted that he learned of the greatest happiness principle from reading Joseph Priestley.[41] The idea that happiness defines the good is at least as old as Aristotle. Bentham gave it a clear and logical application and embodied it in a succinct and dogmatic principle that was appealing to an age increasingly doubtful of theological and metaphysical systems of ethics. His exaggerated application of that principle won him sharp criticism. He made it a formula too neat, too simplified, too all embracing to serve as an explanation of the complexities and passions of human nature. John Stuart Mill in his *Autobiography* recognizes its shallowness and its limits. Still, on matters of legislation it was and is a widely approved and useful guide.

The simple calculation of doing the greatest good to the greatest number, and not God's will or natural law, offered Victorian social reformers a strong justification for the establishment of a larger and more active state, one guaranteeing the well-being of the factory worker, the railway passenger, and the tenement dweller. Even the jaunty and unphilosophical Palmerston openly confessed it in arguing for the repeal of the Corn Laws. We must follow, he said, 'the fundamental maxim which bids us legislate for the good of the many and not the few.' *The Times*, the declared enemy of Benthamites, also confessed in 1845, 'It is a settled principle of very constitution however liberal that the legislature is not merely empowered, but obliged to interfere at all times . . . where the general advantage of the community requires it.'[42] It is unlikely that either Palmerston or John Delane, editor of *The Times* in 1845, reach much of Bentham. Palmerston's teacher was the Scottish moral philosopher Dugald Stewart of Glasgow University; and Delane was educated first at Kings College, London, a college founded in protest against the Benthamite University College, and secondly at Magdalen College, Oxford, hardly a set of Benthamism.[43] It is much more likely that Palmerston and Delane, both pre-eminently sensitive to public opinion, realized that in a representative government legislation must bring the greatest good to the greatest number (or at least appear to do so). Like the principle of central inspection, the idea that the aim of legislation is to promote the general good is almost a commonplace notion, an implicit axiom of human affairs, and one bound to become more explicit in a more rational and democratic age. Bentham had the forthrightness to give a logical formulation to what others, from Palmerston to Delane, felt to be quite true. His cogent expression of this principle won the admiration of men already eager for improvements; but it was not necessarily his statement of it which made these men determined reformers, nor did his writings define the events which impelled them to pass effective legislation.

Had Bentham never written his epochal works, Victorian reformers would probably have contrived their poor laws, factory acts, and educational schemes, all fitted out with central inspectors.[44] Such social legislation was in fact a necessity, the necessity of the factory, the jerry-built town, the discontented and ignorant proletariat. Not Bentham's *Code*, but the reports on Sunderland's cholera epidemic, deeply moved Greville, the Whigs' gossiping clerk of the Privy Council. He had never heard, he wrote in 1831, of such misery and human degradation. It filled him with forebodings of revolution and persuaded him that these wretched conditions must be ameliorated. Macaulay felt the same. 'Civilization is threatened,' he said in referring to urban conditions, 'by a barbarism it has engendered.' In 1848 *The Times* put it more bluntly: 'A great town is a great evil.'[45] In the towns came the exploitation of children, a concentrated and dangerous ignorance, and foul sewerage, bad water, and cholera; in the towns crime mounted, while poverty, aggravated by industrial depressions, was quick to strike. The conditions of the towns overwhelmed James Kay and Edwin Chadwick, and impressed members of Parliament more vividly than the dull detail of Bentham's *Code*; and they demanded more insistently those reforms which brought into existence, as a sheer necessity, the Victorian administrative state. The urban problems were simply too great for antiquated local authorities. Town councils failed to lay good drains and voluntary societies failed to build good schools. As a result the central government had to aid and supervise these local authorities in the promotion of health and education and the administration of prisons, the poor law, and asylums for the insane. And for similar reasons it had to regulate privately owned mines, factories, and merchant shipping. The political power and the entrenched interests of local authorities and private property rule out complete central management, so in most cases the compromise reached was that of central inspection, and hence the development of those inspectorates which Clapham rightly saw as the basis of the Victorian administrative state, but too enthusiastically attributed to the ideas of Bentham.

The ideas of Bentham had, to be sure, an influence on the growth of the central administration. His perceptive and telling attacks on old institutions pleased men anxious for reform, and the coherence and completeness of the *Code* excited those few of similar ideas who laboriously waded through its formidable detail. Above all it excited those able to see the needs of the future. But to foresee future developments, to inspire veneration, and to lay down principles that justify change, is not always to cause those developments nor to govern the actions of those men. The Victorian administrative state was a practical contrivance shaped by men of various persuasions, all of whom were disturbed at the existence of ignorance, disease, and misery in their changing society. It was a very confused and disjointed state, and in all probability Bentham himself, the passionate lover of logic and efficiency, would have vigorously disclaimed its authorship.

NOTES

1. John Bowring, ed., *The Complete Works of Jeremy Bentham* (London, 1843), IX, 98–118, 303, 428–454, 512–525, 612–614; hereafter referred to as *Works*.

2. John Stuart Mill, *Autobiography* (New York, 1924), 134–136. See also Mill's essay on Bentham, in *Mill on Bentham and Coleridge*, ed. F. R. Leavis (London, 1950).
3. *Parliamentary Papers of Great Britain*, 1833, XXIII, 'Finance and Accounts,' 439 and 465.
4. A. V. Dicey, *Law and Public Opinion in England* (London, 1905), 305–309; Sidney and Beatrice Webb, *English Poor Law History*, Part II (London, 1929), I, 26–32; B. L. Hutchins, *The Public Health Agitation* (London, 1929), 140; Elie Halévy, *The History of the English People in the Nineteenth Century* (London, 1950), III, 98–129; Samuel Finer, *The Life and Times of Edwin Chadwick* (London, 1952), 12–37 and 74–75.
5. Sir John Clapham, 'Work and Wages,' *Early Victorian England* (G. M. Young, ed., London, 1934), I, 46–47; J. Bartlett Brebner, 'Laissez Faire and State Intervention in Nineteenth Century Britain,' *Journal of Economic History*, VIII (1948), Supplement, 59–73; G. M. Trevelyan, *Britain in the Nineteenth Century* (London, 1937), 181.
6. Mrs. C. L. Lewes, *Dr. Southwood Smith, A Retrospect* (London, 1889), 20–47; Frank Smith, *Life of Sir James Kay Shuttleworth* (London, 1923), 26–27.
7. Leslie Stephen, *Utilitarianism* (London, 1950), II, 28–32, III, 26–30; Mill, *Autobiography*, 136.
8. Sir G. O. Trevelyan, *Life and Letters of Lord Macaulay* (London, 1901), 56–57.
9. Bulwer-Lytton, *England and the English* (London, 1833), II, 108.
10. Edwin Chadwick Manuscripts, University College, London, Chadwick to Normanby, 12 May 1841.
11. Cecil Driver, *Richard Oastler, Tory Radical* (New York, 1946), 100–177 and 245–246.
12. Chadwick MSS., memo on central administration, c. 1841, and Chadwick to Russell, 10 July 1838.
13. *Parliamentary Papers*, 1833, XX, 'Factory Report,' 68.
14. *Parliamentary Papers*, 1834, XXIV, 'Seventh Excise Report,' 110–113.
15. Finer, *Chadwick*, 39–50.
16. Add. MSS., 40447, Peel Papers (British Museum), Graham to Peel, 9 Jan. 1840; T. C. Hansard, ed., *The Parliamentary Debates of Great Britain* (henceforth cited as Hansard), 1828, XVIII, 1544, and 1830, XXIII, 534.
17. Chadwick MSS., Senior's memo to Lord Brougham, Jan. 1833; Bentham, *Works*, VIII, 361.
18. Chadwick MSS., letters of Chadwick to Lord Althorp in April 1838.
19. Bentham MSS., University College, London, Box 155, 110, Chadwick to the President of the Law Amendment Society; Finer, *Chadwick*, 2.
20. Edwin Chadwick, 'On the Means of Insurance,' *Westminster Review*, IX (1828), 384–421; 'On Preventive Police' and 'Medical Charities in Review,' *London Review*, I (1830), 252–308 and 536–565.
21. *Works*, VIII, 361ff.; IV, 39–59, 6–7, and 214–219.
22. Stephen, *Utilitarianism*, II, 223; *Quarterly Review*, Oct. 1832, 332–334, and Aug. 1834, 233; *Law Magazine*, May 1835, 438.
23. William Hay, 'Remarks on the Laws Relating to the Poor,' *Works* (London, 1794), I, 78–91, 155, and 191; Patrick Colquhoun, *The State of Indigence and the Situation of the Casual Poor* (London, 1799).
24. *DNB*; Thomas Adkins, *History of St. John College, Battersea* (London, 1901), 27; Public Record Office, Russell MSS., 22/30/4, Lansdowne to Russell, 1839.
25. Hansard, 1839, XLVIII, 793; Odo Russell, *The Early Correspondence of*

Lord John Russell (London, 1913), II, 269; the *Standard*, 21 May 1839, citing the *Morning Herald*.

26. Hansard, 1839, XLVII, 530–531.
27. Victor Cousin, *Education in Holland* (London, 1838); 'The Education Bill,' *Edinburgh Review*, Jan. 1838, 439–449; Rev. Thaddeus O'Malley, *A Brief Sketch of the State of Popular Education in Holland, Prussia, Belgium and France* (London, 1838); Henry Dunn, *National Education* (London, 1838), 10–21; Hansard, 1839, XLVIII, 1270.
28. R. A. Lewis, *Edwin Chadwick and the Public Health Movement* (London, 1952), 29–60; *Parliamentary Papers*, 1839, XX, appendices, and 1842, XXVI, 'Sanitary Conditions of the Labouring Classes.'
29. Parliamentary Papers, 1844, XXIV, 'First Report,' 1; and 1845, XXVI, 'Second Report,' 269; Chadwick MSS., Chadwick to C. May, 20 July 1852: 'the Public Health Act is mainly founded on the report signed by Sir W. Cubitt and drawn up by Robert Stephenson.'
30. Chadwick MSS., Chadwick to Lord Campbell, 26 July 1848; John and Barbara Hammond, *Lord Shaftesbury* (London, 1923), 163.
31. Public Record Office, P.R.O./P.C., I, 105.
32. *Parliamentary Papers*, 1835, XI, 'Select Committee on Prisons,' 1–5, 16, 67, 129, 177, and 290; T. F. Buxton, *Memoirs* (London, 1848), 64–80; Rev. W. Clay, *Memoirs of John Clay* (London, 1861), 80–170.
33. *Law Magazine*, Aug. 1835, 31–46; Chadwick MSS., memo on central administration, c. 1841.
34. Kathleen Jones, *Lunacy, Law and Conscience* (London, 1945), 170–195.
35. DNB; Hansard, 1842, LXI, 165–170; Russell MSS., P.R.O. 30/22/7, Labouchere to Russell, Jan. 1848; Hansard, 1850, CXII, 111; Oliver MacDonagh, in 'Delegated Legislation and Administrative Discretion in the 1850's' in *Victorian Studies*, II (1958), 29–44 shows in detail how the establishment and growth of the Emigration Commissioners occurred and how it reflected practical concerns. He makes no mention of Bentham's ideas at work.
36. *Westminster Review*, on factories, Apr. 1833; poor law, Apr. 1834; law reform, Oct. 1834; prisons, Oct. 1835; education, June 1840; lunacy, Apr. 1842; law reform, Feb. 1843; railways, Sept. 1844; lunacy, Mar. 1846; mining, July 1842.
37. Hansard, 1838, XVIII, 127–255; 1833, XX, 139–160; 1836, XXV, 51; 1844, LXXIV, 958; 1853, CXXIV, 1249.
38. Trevelyan, *Britain in the Nineteenth Century*, 181; Brebner, *JEH*, 63.
39. *DNB*; Bentham, *Works*, X, 588–597; Mill, *Autobiography*, 89; R. E. Leader, ed., *Life and Letters of J. A. Roebuck* (London, 1897), 25–28; Finer, *Chadwick*, 11; Mrs. Grote, *The Personal Life of George Grote* (London, 1873), 22.
40. *Index to Parliamentary Papers* (London, 1938), 420 and 480. By 1835 the inspectors of Irish prisons had made twelve annual reports and by 1839 the Irish Education Commissioners had made fifteen annual reports.
41. Elie Halévy, *The Growth of Philosophic Radicalism* (London, 1955), 22.
42. Hansard, 1846, LXXXV, 256; *The Times*, 26 Dec. 1845.
43. Arthur I. Dasent, *John T. Delane, Editor of the Times* (London, 1908), I, 1–22; H. C. F. Bell, *Lord Palmerston* (London, 1936), I, 7. There is no mention of Bentham in any of the four biographies of Palmerston nor in either of the two biographies of Delane.
44. Oliver MacDonagh in 'The Nineteenth Century Revolution in Government: A Reappraisal,' *Historical Journal*, I (1958), 52–67, considers the correlation between the pressure for social reform and the resulting administrative growth 'up to a point true,' but cautions that the correlation is not exact. In

this brilliant study of the processes of administrative growth, MacDonagh warns of ascribing too great an influence to the ideas of Bentham.

45. Lytton Strachey, ed., *The Memoirs of Charles Greville* (London, 1938), II, 219; R. H. Mottram, 'Town Life' *Early Victorian England*, I, 68; *The Times*, 10 May 1848.